# APPRECIATIVE INQUIRY

The Instructor's Manual for the second edition of *Appreciative Inquiry: Change at the Speed of Imagination* is available free online to qualified college and university instructors. If you would like to download and print out a copy of the guide, please visit: **www.wiley.com/college/ watkins**.

# About Pfeiffer

Pfeiffer serves the professional development and hands-on resource needs of training and human resource practitioners and gives them products to do their jobs better. We deliver proven ideas and solutions from experts in HR development and HR management, and we offer effective and customizable tools to improve workplace performance. From novice to seasoned professional, Pfeiffer is the source you can trust to make yourself and your organization more successful.

**Essential Knowledge** Pfeiffer produces insightful, practical, and comprehensive materials on topics that matter the most to training and HR professionals. Our Essential Knowledge resources translate the expertise of seasoned professionals into practical, how-to guidance on critical workplace issues and problems. These resources are supported by case studies, worksheets, and job aids and are frequently supplemented with CD-ROMs, websites, and other means of making the content easier to read, understand, and use.

**Essential Tools** Pfeiffer's Essential Tools resources save time and expense by offering proven, ready-to-use materials—including exercises, activities, games, instruments, and assessments—for use during a training or team-learning event. These resources are frequently offered in looseleaf or CD-ROM format to facilitate copying and customization of the material.

Pfeiffer also recognizes the remarkable power of new technologies in expanding the reach and effectiveness of training. While e-hype has often created whizbang solutions in search of a problem, we are dedicated to bringing convenience and enhancements to proven training solutions. All our e-tools comply with rigorous functionality standards. The most appropriate technology wrapped around essential content yields the perfect solution for today's on-the-go trainers and human resource professionals.

*Essential resources for training and HR professionals*

This book is dedicated to David Cooperrider, friend and mentor, who embodies the appreciative life, and to friends and colleagues, known and unknown, who are working together toward a positive future for the world.

We also dedicate this book to all our clients and students who have taught us so much.

# APPRECIATIVE INQUIRY

## Change at the Speed of Imagination

### SECOND EDITION

JANE MAGRUDER WATKINS
BERNARD MOHR
RALPH KELLY

**Pfeiffer**
A Wiley Imprint
www.pfeiffer.com

Published by Pfeiffer
An Imprint of Wiley
989 Market Street, San Francisco, CA 94103-1741
www.pfeiffer.com

For additional copies/bulk purchases of this book in the U.S. please contact 800-274-4434.

Pfeiffer books and products are available through most bookstores. To contact Pfeiffer directly call our Customer Care Department within the U.S. at 800-274-4434, outside the U.S. at 317-572-3985, fax 317-572-4002, or visit www.pfeiffer.com.

Pfeiffer also publishes its books in a variety of electronic formats. Some content that appears in print may not be available in electronic books.

**Library of Congress Cataloging-in-Publication Data**

Watkins, Jane Magruder.
  Appreciative inquiry : change at the speed of imagination / Jane Magruder Watkins, Bernard J. Mohr, Ralph Kelly. – 2nd ed.
      p. cm. – (Practicing organization development series ; 35)
  Includes bibliographical references and index.
  ISBN 978-0-470-52797-9 (pbk.); ISBN 978-1-118-01510-0 (ebk); ISBN 978-1-118-01511-7 (ebk); ISBN 978-1-118-01512-4 (ebk)
  1. Organizational change.  2. Appreciative inquiry.  I. Mohr, Bernard J.  II. Kelly, Ralph, 1938-  III. Title.
  HD58.8.W388 2011
  658.4'06–dc22

Acquiring Editor: Matthew Davis
Marketing Manager: Brian Grimm
Editorial Assistants: Michael Zelenko, Halley Sutton
Production Editor: Michael Kay
Editor: Rebecca Taff
Manufacturing Supervisor: Becky Morgan

Printed in the United States of America
Printing   10   9   8   7   6   5   4   3   2   1

# CONTENTS

CHAPTER 5

# Inquire into Stories of What Gives Life in the System (Discover) 145

CHAPTER 6

# Locate Themes That Appear in the Stories (Discover) 191

# Chart of Case Stories

| Chapter | Organization Name | Intervention Focus | Author and Affiliation |
|---|---|---|---|
| 2 | National Health Service, East Midlands Development Centre | Living Well with Dementia: Creating a Regional Strategy for the East Midlands | Julie Barnes, Julie Barnes Organization Development Services, and Jill Guild, NHS East Midlands Development Centre |
| 3 | Aerospace Alliant International | Using the SOAR Framework at Aerospace Alliant International | Jacqueline M. Stavros, Lawrence Technological University |
| 3 | Jefferson Wells Great Lakes Region | The Results of Appreciative Management by a Corporate Manager | Daniel Saint, Daniel K. Saint Consulting |
| 4 | The College of William and Mary Training and Technical Assistance Center | AI Stories from a Training and Technical Assistance Center (T/TAC): New Possibilities for Improving Outcomes for Students with Disabilities | Denyse Doerries, Donni Davis-Perry, and Lori Korinek, The College of William and Mary: T/TAC System, and Ralph Kelly and Jane Magruder Watkins, Appreciative Inquiry Unlimited |
| 4 | Almond Insight | From Deficits to Strengths: Six Sigma from the AI Perspective | David Shaked, Almond Insight |

| Chapter | Organization Name | Intervention Focus | Author and Affiliation |
|---|---|---|---|
| 5 | Appreciative Living | Appreciative Living: Using AI in Daily Life | Jacqueline Kelm, Appreciative Living |
| 5 | LifeTrek Coaching | Appreciative Life Coaching | Bob Tschannen-Moran, LifeTrek Coaching |
| 6 | LAUP | Appreciative Inquiry at Los Angeles Universal Preschool (LAUP): The LAUM/UDEM Dream Team | Terri Egan, Pepperdine University, Nancy Westrup Villarreal, University of Monterrey, and Daphne Deporres, Los Angeles Universal Preschool |
| 7 | Newark-Beth Israel Medical Center | Advancing the Safety and Quality of Care in the Emergency Department Over Time: A Story with Three Acts | Nancy Shendell-Falik, Tufts Medical Center, Amy Doran, Emergency Department, Beth Israel Medical Center, and Bernard Mohr, Innovation Partners International |
| 7 | St. Andrew's Episcopal Cathedral | Appreciative Inquiry with a Search Committee | Liz Workman, Interact |
| 8 | Toronto District School Board | Building Momentum for Sustainable Changes in Education | Maureen McKenna and Sue Derby, The Sumo Experience, Karen Leckie and Nancy Nightingale |

| Chapter | Organization Name | Intervention Focus | Author and Affiliation |
|---|---|---|---|
| 8 | Liverpool Culture Company | Introducing Appreciative Inquiry into a Community Network Project in Liverpool | Tim Slack and Phil Taylor, Appreciating People |
| 9 | Zambia Police Services–Victim Support Unit | Valuation of the Effectiveness of AI for the Zambia Police Services Victim Support Unit | Mette Jacobsgaard, Appreciative Inquiry Unlimited |

# CHAPTER 1

# The Case for a New Approach to Change

"Change is not what it used to be. The status quo will no longer be the best way forward … we are entering an Age of Unreason, when the future, in so many areas, is there to be shaped, by us and for us; a time when the only prediction that will hold true is that no predictions will hold true; a time, therefore, for bold imaginings in private life as well as public, for thinking the unlikely and doing the unreasonable."

Charles Handy, *The Age of Unreason*

**AS WE ENTER THE SECOND DECADE OF THE 21ST CENTURY,** we see and experience a world in constant and relentless change. In the decade since the first edition of this book was published, the shifts and emerging versions of reality have approached change at the speed of imagination. We live in a time unimaginable even by our parents' generation—a time of rapid and continuous shifts in how human beings experience, describe, and interact with the world around us. This macro shift calls for new levels of knowledge and a higher capacity to understand and live in an environment that is no longer experienced as stable, predictable, or even comprehensible.

In this chapter, we will describe some of these changes that are observable in both the natural and social sciences and look at the impact of those changes on organizations and on the theories and practices in the field of organization development and change. Finally, we will look at Appreciative Inquiry (AI) as a theory that can be a perspective and approach for any model or method in the practice for organization change and transformation, that is, any process traditionally used in the field of organization development. We will provide information and examples of ways in which the intentionally positive and strength-based theory of Appreciative Inquiry can be applied to traditional OD models and methods in ways that enable human systems to develop the capacity and flexibility to live in a world that is created by the interactions of those who inhabit it.

We used Charles Handy's quote (above) in the first edition of this book published in 2000. As we write this second edition a decade later, we find ourselves in the midst of the kind of world that Handy predicted! The change was, indeed, "unimaginable!"

One of the most articulate of the writers struggling to describe the magnitude and speed of change in the last decade is Thomas Friedman in *The World Is Flat*. We add his comments here to share with you what seems to us to be a remarkable explanation for the phenomenal changes we are experiencing. Friedman writes of "a tale of technology and geo-economics that is fundamentally reshaping our lives—much, much more quickly than many people realize." He tells the story of a visit to India and a conversation that woke him up to the realization that globalization is already here. He writes: "I wish I could say I saw it all coming.... The longer I was there, the more upset I became—upset at the realization that globalization had entered a whole new phase, and I had missed it."

His Indian colleague explained to him: "What happened over the last years is that there was a massive investment in technology when hundreds of millions of dollars were invested in putting broadband connectivity around the world, undersea cables, all those things. At the same time, computers became cheaper and dispersed all over the world, and there was an explosion of e-mail software, search engines like Google, and proprietary software that can chop up any piece of work and send one part to Boston, one part to Bangalore, and one part to Beijing, making it easy for anyone to do remote development. When all of these things suddenly came together around 2000, they created a platform where intellectual work, intellectual capital, could be delivered from anywhere. It could be disaggregated, delivered, distributed, produced, and put back together again—and this gave a whole new degree of freedom to the way we do work, especially work of an intellectual nature."

Friedman describes the evolution over time: "This has been building for a long time. Globalization 1.0 (1492 to 1800) shrank the world from a size large to a size medium, and the dynamic force in that era was countries globalizing for resources and imperial conquest. Globalization 2.0 (1800 to 2000) shrank the world from a size medium to a size small, and it was spearheaded by companies globalizing for markets and labor. Globalization 3.0 (which started around 2000) is shrinking the world from a size small to a size tiny and flattening the playing field at the same time. And while the dynamic force in Globalization 1.0 was *countries* globalizing and the dynamic force in Globalization 2.0 was *companies* globalizing, the dynamic force in Globalization 3.0—the thing that gives it its unique character—is *individuals and small groups globalizing*. Individuals must, and can, now ask: Where do I fit into the global competition and opportunities of the day, and how can I, on my own, collaborate with others globally? But Globalization 3.0 not only differs from the previous eras in how it is shrinking and flattening the world and in how it is empowering individuals. It is also different in that Globalization 1.0 and 2.0 were driven primarily by European and American companies and countries. But going forward, this will be less and less true. Globalization 3.0 is not only going to be driven more by individuals but also by a much more diverse—non-Western, non-white—group of individuals. *In Globalization 3.0, you are going to see every color of the human rainbow take part.*"

Friedman continues: "Today, a fourteen-year-old in Romania or Bangalore or the Soviet Union or Vietnam has all the information, all the tools, all the software easily available to apply knowledge however they want.... As bioscience becomes more computational and less about wet labs and as all the genomic data becomes easily available on the Internet, at some point you will be able to design vaccines on your laptop.... The upside is that by connecting all these knowledge pools we are on the cusp of an incredible new era of innovation, an era that will be driven from left field and right field, from West and East and from North and South. Today, anyone with smarts, access to Google, and a cheap wireless laptop can join the innovation fray."

(It is not hyperbole to note that collaborative, innovative, and strength-based processes emerge when people dialogue in an appreciative mode. The process itself enables them to co-create a future that is "owned" by all involved in the dialogue; and this mutual "ownership" results in collaborative processes for co-creation. Once individual members of a group or organization internalize the power of focusing on the positive aspects of a situation, the more facile the group or organization gets at managing the reality of constant and relentless change.)

Unlike the world of 2000, Appreciative Inquiry as well as other innovative and strength based approaches to the field of organization development (OD) and change are recognized and sought after by those who live and work in "human systems." We are seeing methods and practices that deal with whole systems. Traditional practices are being revised and adapted in order to take into account the speed of change, the complexity of the environment, and the unpredictability of human behavior. The concept of "social construction," so problematic for many years, is more and more understood to be causal. We do, indeed, create what we imagine together!

In a major paper titled "Organization Discourse and New Organization Development Practices," written by David Grant and Robert J. Marshak and published in 2008 in the *British Journal of Management* (eight years after the publication of the first edition of this book and nearly twenty years after the emergence of AI in the work of David Cooperrider and colleagues at Case Western Reserve University) the authors write:

> "A new ensemble of organization development (OD) practices have emerged that are based more on constructionist, post modern and new sciences premises than on the assumptions of the early founders (of OD). These include practices associated with Appreciative Inquiry, large group interventions, changing mindsets and consciousness, addressing diversity and multicultural realities, and advancing new and different models of change....In particular, studies of organizational discourse based upon social constructionist and critical perspectives offer compelling ideas and practices associated with the establishment of change concepts, the role of power and context in relation to organizational change, and specific discursive interventions designed to foster organizational change.... Recently, organizational change research has undergone a 'metamorphosis,' one that encompasses a pluralism of approaches and a strengthening of the links between organizational studies and the social sciences (Pettigrew, Woodman, & Cameron, 2001, p. 697). We contend that one possible outcome of this metamorphosis is that there may now be an emerging set of new organization development (OD) practices—what we refer to collectively here as 'New OD.' Taken together, these practices emphasize a number of philosophical assumptions and associated methodologies that differ in varying degrees from key assumptions of those who founded the OD movement in the 1950s and 1960s."

## Table 1.1. Classical vs. New OD

| Classical OD (1950s Onward) | New OD (1980s Onward) |
| --- | --- |
| Based in classical science and modern thought and philosophy | Influenced by the new sciences and post-modern thought and philosophy |
| Truth is transcendent and discoverable; there is a single, objective reality | Truth is immanent and emerges from the situation; there are multiple, socially constructed realities |
| Reality can be discovered using rational and analytic processes | Reality is socially negotiated and may involve power and political processes |
| Collecting and applying valid data using objective problem solving methods leads to change | Creating new mindsets or social agreements, sometimes through explicit or implicit negotiation, leads to change |
| Change is episodic and can be created, planned, and managed | Change is continuous and can be self-organizing |
| Emphasis on changing behavior and what one does | Emphasis on changing mindsets and how one thinks |

R. J. Marshak and D. Grant (2008). Organizational Discourse and New Organization Development Practices. *British Journal of Management, 19,* S7–S19.

These shifts are described by Marshak and Grant in Table 1.1 above:

In another paper, Gervase Bushe and Bob Marshak compare diagnostic and dialogic forms of OD, as shown in Table 1.2.

After reading the Marshak and Grant's work, the late Udai Pareek (an "elder" in introducing organization development in India and founder of the Indian Society for Applied Behavioral Science, added the following interesting information about the impact of this shift on young people growing up in this rapidly changing world. (This generation is often called the "Millennials." In Table 1.3 below, Pareek describes the older generation as "geezers" and the "Millennials as "geeks" and describes the shift from one generation to another in these turbulent times.)

### Table 1.2. Contrasting Diagnostic and Dialogic OD

| Topics | Diagnostic OD | Dialogic OD |
|---|---|---|
| Influenced by | Classical science, positivism, and modernist philosophy. | Interpretive approaches, social constructionism, critical and post-modern philosophy. |
| Dominant organizational construct | Organizations are like living systems. | Organizations are meaning-making systems. |
| Ontology and epistemology | Reality is an objective fact. There is a single reality. Truth is transcendent and discoverable. Reality can be discovered using rational and analytic processes | Reality is socially constructed. There are multiple realities. Truth is immanent and emerges from the situation. Reality is negotiated and may involve power and political processes. |
| Constructs of change | Usually teleological. Collecting and applying valid data using objective problem-solving methods leads to change. Change can be creative, planned, and managed. Change is episodic, linear, and goal oriented | Often dialogical or dialectical. Creating containers and processes leads to change. Change can be encouraged but is mainly self-organizing. Change may be continuous and/or cyclical. |
| Focus of change | Emphasis on changing behavior and what people do. | Emphasis on changing mindsets and what people think. |

Pareek also writes that technological advancement seems to have had the following impact on the new generation:

1. Impact of technological advancement:

   - The new generation has never experienced life without computers

   - There is reverse accumulation of knowledge—the younger you are, the more you know

   - All information is a click away; so is the competition

   - The world is a click away

2. Further, he notes that Millennials have been characterized at work as follows:

- Work well with friends and on teams

- Collaborative, resourceful, innovative thinkers

- Love a challenge

- Seek to make a difference

- Want to produce something worthwhile

- Desire to be heroes

- Impatient

- Comfortable with speed and change

- Thrive on flexibility and space to explore

- Partner well with mentors

- Value guidance

- Expect respect

## Table 1.3. The Shift from Geezers to Geeks

| Shifts in | Geezers | Geeks |
|---|---|---|
| World View | Analogue world | Digital world |
| Perception of World | Newtonian, mechanical | Living organisms and biological systems |
| Thinking | Linear narratives and thinking | Nonlinear thinking |
| Preference of Structure | Organizational hierarchy and chain of command | Flat organizations |
| Mode of Understanding | A map that can help only in known worlds | A compass that is helpful in unsure territory and can give only a general sense of direction |
| Main Concern | Making a living | Aspiring to change the world |
| Value | Work | Balance in work, family, and personal lives |
| | Has heroes | Far less likely to have heroes |

Pareek writes: "It seems that the eras influence the ways in which OD is both conceptualized and practiced." He suggests that the two contrasting forms might better be called "research versus search," with research being investigation of a known field, whereas for search more exploration is required. He sums it up with a quote from Bennis and Thomas: "Maps, by definition, can help only in known worlds—worlds that have been charted before. Compasses are helpful when you are not sure where you are and can get only a general sense of direction."

Appreciative Inquiry is all about being a "compass." It provides a process for exploration, rapid prototyping, and constant exploration through continuous dialogue that focuses on what one is learning and how that is a precursor for the next exploration.

## The Emerging Paradigm

We previously wrote that we are living in a time of unprecedented and unpredictable change. And we noted that the impact of such a rapid pace of change on all of our human systems—families, schools, organizations, communities, governments—had become the focus of great interest and concern. Now, a decade later, we are beginning to comprehend that our task is not necessarily to *adjust* to rapid change. Rather, we face the reality of the necessity to shift the very ground of our previous beliefs that human behavior, like inanimate objects such as computers, could be programmed and made predictable. We recognize that we live in a world that is continuously unpredictable and emerging. Our task now is to recognize that "change" is the water we swim in and, more importantly, it is what makes life possible. Our task is to learn how to embrace this "reality" and to free ourselves from the idea that change is an object that can be managed. This reality requires a major shift in how we define and relate to "change;" which leads us to recognize the need for new ways of working within human systems as they cope with the reality of the idea that change is continuous, relentless, and accelerating!

"We've reached a Breakpoint!" George Land and Beth Jarman wrote in 1992 in their book, *Breakpoint and Beyond.* "Breakpoint change abruptly and powerfully breaks the critical links that connect anyone or anything with the past. What we are experiencing today is absolutely unprecedented in all of humanity's recorded history. We have run into change so different from anything preceding it that it totally demolishes normal standards. It has swept us into a massive transformation that will completely reorder all we know about living in this world."

We are also learning that, even though some ideas are surely transferable from one group to another, by far the strongest and most effective way to imagine our own future is to engage in continuous dialogue and exploration from an open and curious mindset. We are living in a time when our attachment to a process that was created in another time and place by people no longer present is obsolete and, often, destructive. Time and energy spent in convincing people that someone else's "construction" is the best or most desired is giving way to the work of the future, which is to create environments that encourage individuals to engage with others to continuously create the "reality" needed for each circumstance as it emerges.

Will human beings continue to debate and even fight over what is right and wrong in any given situation? Or will the 21st Century be the beginning of our realization that with every breath we take and every conversation we have, we are creating a new reality! As Margaret Wheatley wrote prophetically in her book, *Leadership and the New Science* (1994): "There is no objective reality out there; there is only what we create through our engagements with others and with events. Nothing really transfers; everything is always new and different and unique to each of us."

In 1970, Alvin Toffler wrote a mind-bending book called *Future Shock* in which he talked not just of change, but of the changing rate of change. Those born early in the 20th Century (our parents' generation) have experienced change in both speed and kind unimaginable in all of human history. Toffler and others scanning and predicting the future were like modern prophets, seeing the waves of an emerging paradigm that would call all of what we "know" and "believe" into question.

*Classical (Newtonian) mechanics* is the science of how bodies move in our universe. The assumption is that the universe is a vast machine with interacting parts much like a clock. Each part has only a few properties and movements, determined by its mass and the forces acting on it. This view was articulated by the philosophers Descartes and Locke, during the time when philosophy and science were the same discipline, and scientifically by Galileo. The key concepts are space, time, mass, forces, and particles. Anything else, such as consciousness, has remained outside the realm of physics altogether.

Newton's work and that of his predecessors led to the scientific paradigm that has dominated our view of what is real for several centuries. Frederick Taylor's early theories of "scientific management" came out of that paradigm, applying the image of a machine to a human system. When studies of the importance of human behavior in organizations began to be developed by social scientists in the 1940s (most notably by Kurt Lewin and his colleagues, Ken Benne, Leland Bradford, and Ron Lippitt, who in 1947 founded the National Training Laboratory, now known as the NTL Institute for Applied Behavioral Science), it was often assumed that one could measure human behavior using the methods of the natural sciences. It was assumed that human behavior was governed by the same principles as the material world: cause and effect, natural hierarchy, force exerted to cause movement, and individuals as separate and isolated "parts."

Wheatley (1994) describes the impact of this thinking on our behavior and on our organizations.

> "Each of us lives and works in organizations designed from Newtonian images of the universe. We manage by separating things into parts; we believe that influence occurs as a direct result of force exerted from one person to another; we engage in complex planning for a world that we keep expecting to be

predictable; and we search continually for better methods of objectively perceiving the world. These assumptions come to us from 17th-Century physics, from Newtonian mechanics. They are the base from which we design and manage organizations and from which we do research in all of the social sciences. Intentionally or not, we work from a worldview that has been derived from the natural sciences.

"Scientists in many different disciplines are questioning whether we can adequately explain how the world works by using the machine imagery created in the 17th Century.... In the machine model, one must understand parts. Things can be taken apart, dissected literally or representationally (as we have done with business functions and academic disciplines), and then put back together without any significant loss. The assumption is that by comprehending the workings of each piece, the whole can be understood. The Newtonian model of the world is characterized by materialism and reductionism—focus on things rather than relationships and a search, in physics, for the basic building blocks of matter." (p. 8)

## The New Sciences

In 1927, a group of scientists met in Denmark to discuss revolutionary new discoveries in physics. As technology and new methods of experimentation made possible new discoveries in the realm of sub-atomic particles, all of the orthodoxy of classical physics was being called into question. Albert Einstein and Danish physicist Niels Bohr had been embroiled in a difference of opinion often referred to as the Copenhagen Debates. Bohr had discovered that two particles separated by a vast distance were able to behave coherently as if they were communicating instantaneously. Einstein argued that it wasn't possible because the information between the two would have to travel faster than the speed of light. Bohr argued that such speed would be required only if one assumed that the two particles were separate and independent units. And the paradigm began to shift! What if all things are connected? From the conference in Copenhagen came public statements about these new discoveries that were so confounding the physicists. Since that time, terms such as quantum physics, chaos theory, self-organizing systems, and complexity theory have become common in our vocabulary.

While classical physics focuses on parts, the common denominator of the new sciences is the search for a theory of wholeness. The language of these new sciences has a major impact on how we think about human systems. Certainly the language of quantum physics challenges our most sacred assumptions about the concepts of organization development.

Here are a few of the dilemmas:

While classical physics speaks of waves and particles as separate, quantum theory suggests that there is a wave/particle duality (a wavicle) and that these basic building blocks of the universe have the potential to behave as a wave or as a particle, depending on their surroundings. This means that we can never know the momentum (wave) and the position (particle) of these quantum entities at the same time. This turns Newtonian determinism on its head, as the predictability that B will always follow A, as Newton proved, gives way to Heisenberg's uncertainty principle: B *may* follow A and there is a probability that it will do so, but there is no certainty (Marshall & Zohar, 1998).

Classical physics describes complex things as reducible to a few simple absolute and unchanging components. This is "What is." Quantum physics describes the phenomena of the new properties that come from the combination or relationships of simple things. Possibility is the key. Every quantum in the universe has the potential to be here *and* there, now *and* then. In classical physics things happen as part of a chain of events, of cause and effect. In quantum reality, all things move in harmony as some part of a larger, invisible whole. We might describe this as a quantum shift! From understanding the world as parts, each alone in space and time linked only through force, quantum physics presents us with a universe in which every part is linked to every other part.

This view of the way the world works challenges any assumption about being able to isolate one thing from another, and it goes further to suggest that the observer cannot be separated from that which is observed. It challenges us to re-examine our assumptions about how organizations function as well.

*Chaos theory* presents another challenge to Newton's clockwork universe with its predictable tides and planetary motion. In chaos theory, very simple patterns become complex and unpredictable, as demonstrated by fractals, weather patterns, and the stock market. No level of accuracy is exact enough for long-term predictions. Such an idea rocks the very foundation of such organizational sacred cows as long-range planning, which in its most linear application requires a belief in a reasonable amount of predictability in the future.

*Self-organizing systems* behave in the reverse way. A complex and unpredictable situation develops into a larger, more ordered pattern like a whirlpool or a living organism. Although most organizations have, no doubt, experienced the sudden clarity that can come out of seeming chaotic situations, few have learned to embrace chaos, often short-circuiting times and situations that hold the potential for high levels of innovation and creativity.

*Complexity theory*, the focus of study at the Sante Fe Institute, is most often described as "order at the edge of chaos." It is also the study of complex systems that cannot be reduced to simple parts. Along with quantum and chaos theory, complexity theory focuses on the emergent whole that cannot be reduced to the sum of its parts. It involves unpredictability, nonlinear and discontinuous change—the phenomena that lead to surprising new forms (Marshall & Zohar, 1997).

Wheatley (1994) writes:

> "In New Science, the underlying currents are a movement toward holism, toward understanding the system as a system and giving primary value to the relationships that exist among seemingly

discrete parts.... When we view systems from this perspective we enter an entirely new landscape of connections, of phenomena that cannot be reduced to simple cause and effect, and of the constant flux of dynamic processes." (p. 8)

Applying these theories to human systems, Peter Senge (Senge, Scharmer, Jaworski, & Flowers, 2005) writes: "The solvent we propose is a new way of thinking, feeling and being; a culture of systems. Fragmentary thinking becomes systemic when we recover "the memory of the whole," the awareness that wholes precede parts." Table 1.1 illustrates the kinds of shifts that are occurring in response to our broader vision of science. In this post-modern era, the marvel is that all of these things are present and in good order.

These "new sciences" give us radically different ways of making sense of our world. The most exciting ramification for the field of organization change/transformation is the realization that organizations as living systems do not have to look continually for which part is causing a problem or which project is not living up to some set of criteria. The "new" science embraces the magnificent complexity of our world while assuring us that built into the very fabric of the universe are processes and potentials enough to help us and all of our organizations move toward our highest and most desired visions.

For past generations the Newtonian paradigm fit nicely into the comfort zone for most people. It is still hard for most of us to wrap our brains around such questions as: "Is order essential to the structure of the universe or is it simply a product of human perception?" The challenge is to step out of our dichotomous, simple, and orderly version of the universe and embrace those "wavicles" until we engage with them. Whether we experience wave or particle will depend on what we seek. Stephen Hawking, the noted Cambridge physicist, puts it this way: "Quantum physics is the nether world of physical law. It is a realm beyond comprehension, where logic is replaced by chance; where matter is ruled by mere probability; and scientists must resort to summing up the rolls of the dice." This, perhaps, is a vivid description of our work in human systems once we give up the idea that anything about human behavior and relationships is predictable!

And so we come again to "social constructionism" and Appreciative Inquiry. In Chapter 2 we will look at the theoretical basis for AI from a social science point of view, asking: "How is it that we know what we know?" Suffice it to say that in its simplest form, social constructionism suggests that we create the world by the language we use to describe it and we experience the world in line with the images we hold about it. The Appreciative Inquiry process provides human systems with a way of inquiring into the past and present, seeking out those things that are life-giving and affirming as a basis for creating images of a generative and creative future.

## Thinking About Problems Using the New Paradigm

So what about all those problems caused by this changing rate of change? Does AI just ignore those? Are we engaging in denial? Doesn't organization development as a method promote the identification and resolution of problems? Indeed, the practice of OD has traditionally highlighted deficits in the belief that the organization can be returned to a healthy state. Appreciative Inquiry suggests that, by *focusing* on the deficit, we simply *create more* images of deficit and potentially overwhelm the system with images of what is "wrong." All too often, the process of assessing deficits includes a search for *who* is to blame. This leads to people being resistant to the change effort and to a large amount of literature in the field describing ways to deal with that resistance.

In Appreciative Inquiry, we take a different perspective. When we define a situation as a "problem," it means that we have an image of how that situation ought to be—how we'd like it to be. Appreciative Inquiry suggests that, by focusing on an image of health and wholeness, the organization's energy moves to make the image real. Indeed, the seeds of the solution are in the images, and therefore it is not unusual to see a system shift directions "at the speed of imagination!"

In the early days of working with Appreciative Inquiry, we compared problem solving and Appreciative Inquiry as if the two were parallel processes, with one being superior to the other. If AI is seen as just one more organization development methodology, it might usefully be compared to traditional problem solving. If, however, we shift into new paradigm thinking, AI becomes not a methodology, but *a way of seeing and being* in the world. In other words, when we are using the AI frame, we do not see problems and solutions as separate, but rather as a coherent whole made up of our wishes for the future and our path toward that future. (See Figure 1.1.)

## Figure 1.1. Two Different Processes for Organizing Change

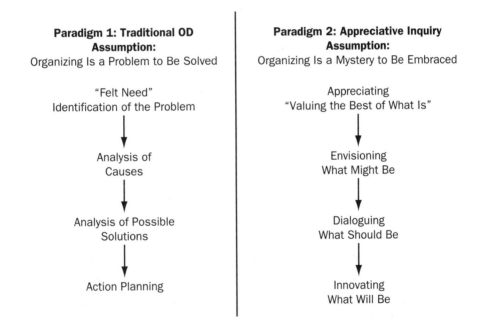

**Paradigm 1: Traditional OD Assumption:**
Organizing Is a Problem to Be Solved

"Felt Need"
Identification of the Problem

↓

Analysis of
Causes

↓

Analysis of Possible
Solutions

↓

Action Planning

**Paradigm 2: Appreciative Inquiry Assumption:**
Organizing Is a Mystery to Be Embraced

Appreciating
"Valuing the Best of What Is"

↓

Envisioning
What Might Be

↓

Dialoguing
What Should Be

↓

Innovating
What Will Be

The commitment to our current deficit-based paradigm, particularly in our Euro-Centric "Western" culture, is our "default setting," as it were. That paradigm places high value on the machine metaphor (that we can take things apart, fix what is broken, and return to some ideal state). It takes a great deal of "re-training" of our thought processes to shift our metaphor, our view of the world, to a more organic and holistic image. Margaret Wheatley (1994) writes:

> "For months, I have been studying process structures—things that maintain form over time yet have no rigidity of structure. This stream that swirls around my feet is the most beautiful one I've encountered.... What is it that streams can teach me about organizations? I am attracted to the diversity I see, to these swirling combinations of mud, silt, grass, water, rocks. This stream has an impressive ability to adapt, to shift the configurations, to let the power balance move, to create new structures. But driving this adaptability, making it all happen, I think, is the water's need to flow. Water answers to gravity, to downhill, to the call of the ocean. The forms change, but the mission remains clear. Structures emerge, but only as temporary solutions that facilitate rather than interfere. There is none of the rigid reliance on single forms, on true answers, on past practices that I have learned in business. Streams have more than one response to rocks; otherwise, there'd be no Grand Canyon. Or else Grand Canyons everywhere. The Colorado [River] realized that there were ways to get ahead other then by staying broad and expansive." (pp. 15–16)

If we follow the organic metaphor, we begin to value and embrace the unlimited diversity of nature. In such a frame of mind, it becomes easy to believe that finding one truth—or one right way to do anything—is not the goal. Rather, the goal is to engage the organization in dialogue that creates multiple positive possibilities and moves the organization in the direction of the most desired future. It becomes important to create the most generative and effective way to move forward.

Appreciative Inquiry is rooted in the values of the emerging paradigm. In this mode, organizations create and move toward their vision of the desired future in harmony with a world view that sees the interconnection of all parts of a system; that accepts the complexity and subjectivity of the world; that knows planning to be a continuous and iterative process; that embraces the concept of many truths and multiple ways to reach a goal; that understands the relational nature of the world; that believes information to be a primal creative force; and that knows language to be the creator of "reality." In other words, the Newtonian paradigm process of dividing things into parts, believing that there is one best way of doing any action and assuming that language describes some ultimate truth for which we all search, creates a way of solving problems that looks backward to what went "wrong" and tries to "fix" it. Appreciative Inquiry, on the other hand, looks for what is going "right" and moves toward it, understanding that in the forward movement toward the ideal the greatest value comes from embracing what works. As Charles Handy (1989) noted in his book *The Age of Unreason*: "Change is not what it used to be. The status quo will no longer be the best way forward…we are entering an Age of Unreason, when the future, in so many areas, is there to be shaped, by us and for us; a time when the only prediction that will hold true is that no predictions will hold true; a time, therefore, for bold imaginings in private life as well as public, for thinking the unlikely and doing the unreasonable."

This being said, Chapter 2 provides a definition of Appreciative Inquiry in the context of an approach to organization change that enables OD practitioners to shift not the tools of their practice (team building, strategic planning, organization redesign), but rather to shift the perspective from which they approach these processes.

# Appreciative Inquiry: History, Theory, and Practice

"As I considered the importance of language and how human beings interact with the world, it struck me that in many ways the development of language was like the discovery of fire—it was such an incredible primordial force. I had always thought that we used language to describe the world—now I was seeing that this is not the case. To the contrary, it is through language that we create the world, because it's nothing until we describe it. And when we describe it, we create distinctions that govern our actions. To put it another way, we do not describe the world we see, but we see the world we describe."

Joseph Jaworski, *Synchronicity*

SUSTAINABLE TRANSFORMATIVE CHANGE IN HUMAN SYSTEMS is the Holy Grail of organization development and the focus of this book. Appreciative Inquiry represents a radical shift in how human systems, particularly complex organizations, can pursue this goal. This chapter will provide an operational definition of Appreciative Inquiry and an overview of the theory and research base that underlie AI, that is, social constructionism and the power of image. This chapter also describes what we mean by transformative change in complex organizations and outlines the challenges of such change.

Subsequent chapters describe in more detail the phases and processes that are core to an AI-based change process, as well as the "mechanics" of the early steps.

## Defining Appreciative Inquiry

Appreciative Inquiry is, essentially, a collaborative and highly participative, system wide approach to seeking, identifying and enhancing the "life-giving forces" that are present when a system is performing optimally in human, economic and organizational terms. It is a journey during which profound knowledge of a human system at its moments of wonder is uncovered and used to co-construct the best and highest future of that system.

Our use of the term "appreciative" emphasizes the idea that when something increases in value, it "appreciates." Therefore, "appreciative inquiry" is inquiry that focuses on the generative and life-giving forces in the system that are the things we want to increase. By "inquiry" we mean the process of seeking to understand through asking questions.

As David Cooperrider writes in *Appreciative Inquiry: A Positive Revolution in Change:*

> "AI involves, in a central way, the art and practice of asking questions that strengthen a system's capacity to apprehend, anticipate and heighten positive potential. It centrally involves the mobilization of inquiry through the crafting of the "unconditional positive question" often involving hundreds and sometimes thousands of people.

"In AI the arduous task of intervention gives way to the speed of imagination and innovation. Instead of negation, criticism, and spiraling diagnosis, there is discovery, dream and design. AI seeks fundamentally to build a constructive union between a whole people and the massive entirety of what people talk about as past and present capacities: achievements, assets, unexplored potentials, innovations, strengths, elevated thoughts, opportunities, benchmarks, high point moments, lived values, traditions, strategic competencies, stories, expressions of wisdom, insights into the deeper corporate spirit or soul – and visions of valued and possible futures." (Cooperrider & Whitney, 2005)

To give the reader a more informed context in which to consider Appreciative Inquiry, we devote this chapter to the history, theory, and research related to AI.

## A History of Appreciative Inquiry

The history of Appreciative Inquiry is the history of a major shift in the practice of organization development and transformation. In fact, it is also the history of an unplanned, even unintended, process with no particular intent at all to use it for changing organizations or other human systems. At its inception, the idea that someday Appreciative Inquiry would become a major approach to change in human systems, with associated processes, methods, and theories, was far from the conscious minds of its two most central "parents," David Cooperrider and Suresh Srivastva of Case Western Reserve University.

But Appreciative Inquiry did, of course, evolve. It developed from a theory-building process used primarily by academics to an organization change process that enables organizations to build their own generative theory as an integral part of a new approach for enabling transformational shifts.

Since 1980, David Cooperrider and others, experimenting with Appreciative Inquiry in organizational settings, discovered that AI is a powerfully effective way to enable organizations to learn about their systems in ways that result in transformative change, often literally at the speed of imagination. Exhibit 2.1 outlines some of the key developments in the evolution of AI.

## Exhibit 2.1. A Brief History of the Development of Appreciative Inquiry

| Date | Event |
|------|-------|
| 1980 | *Cleveland Clinic Project is initiated.* As a young doctoral student, David Cooperrider, is asked to do an organizational analysis of "What's wrong with the human side of the organization?" In gathering his data, he becomes overwhelmed by the level of cooperation, innovation, and general social effectiveness he sees in the organization. Having been influenced by earlier writings by Schweitzer and Rader, he obtains permission from the clinic's board of directors to focus totally on an analysis of the factors contributing to the highly effective functioning of the clinic. The Cleveland Clinic become the first large site where a conscious decision to use an inquiry focusing on life-giving factors forms the basis for an organizational analysis. |
| 1982 | *Ken Gergen publishes* Toward Transformation of Social Knowledge, a powerful critique of conventional scientific meta-theory, pointing to a whole new way of thinking about theory. He calls this new method "generative theory," described by Cooperrider as "anticipatory theory that has the capacity to challenge the guiding assumptions of the culture, to raise fundamental questions regarding contemporary life, to foster reconsideration of that which is taken for granted, and thereby furnish new alternatives for social action." (AI listserv, 1999) |
| 1984 | *NTL Institute for Applied Behavioral Science holds international conference in Tampa, Florida,* with a focus on applied behavioral science. John Carter makes a presentation on Appreciative Inquiry for OD practitioners. |

| Date | Event |
|------|-------|
| 1984 | *Cooperrider makes the first public presentation of his still evolving ideas about AI to the Academy of Management* where, he reports, his ideas are treated with snickering and derision. |
| 1986 | *Cooperrider completes his doctoral dissertation "Appreciative Inquiry: Toward a Methodology for Understanding and Enhancing Organizational Innovation"* at Case Western Reserve University in Cleveland, Ohio. What began as a study of the development of generative theory had evolved into a strategy for organization change. |
| 1986 | *Suresh Srivastva and Cooperrider publish "The Emergence of the Egalitarian Organization,"* a case history of work at the Cleveland Clinic (from 1980 to 1985) that started out as an organizational diagnosis of pathologies and problems, and became instead the first major large-scale AI project. |
| 1987 | *Cooperrider and Srivastva publish "Appreciative Inquiry in Organizational Life."* This marks the first time that the term Appreciative Inquiry appears in a professional publication. The article is noteworthy not only because it makes public the term Appreciative Inquiry but because it represents the beginning of the transition from thinking of AI as just a theory-building approach to seeing its potential as a full-blown intervention framework. |
| 1987 | *The first public workshop on AI,* promoted by two MBA students, is held in San Francisco with David Cooperrider as the key presenter. |
| 1987 | *The Roundtable Project* at a Canadian accounting firm (with John Carter as the external lead) becomes the first large-scale change effort in which AI is conceived of as a comprehensive intervention framework from data gathering to implementation. After four years of collaboratively searching for the right organization-wide intervention, John Carter offers his client Appreciative Inquiry as a possible framework for change. Within less than three months and without any coaching from Carter, the client selects AI as the way to ensure the future of the firm. Over a one-year period, Carter and his client system plan and implement a twelve-step process that starts with the establishment of a philosophically congruent project |

Continued

**Date**   **Event**

structure, incorporates the systematic design of a customized AI protocol, and includes widespread interviews followed by the development of provocative propositions (PPs), followed in turn by widespread consensual validation of the PPs and an organic, rather than mechanistic, implementation process. A major innovation in the use of AI—having members of the organization interview each other—was piloted by Carter and has become a major part of AI methods for organization intervention. Note, however, that although this project was highly collaborative, the data analysis (the meaning making) was still in the hands of the external consultants.

1988   *The Appreciative Research Carnival*, an innovation that resulted from Tojo Joseph Thatchenkery's dissertation research, marked the first incidence in which clients took over the "meaning making" (analysis) with the data. As part of his dissertation research at Case, Thatchenkery begins a major three-year AI-based data gathering process with the Institute for Cultural Affairs (ICA) in the United States. Much to his surprise, members of the client system wrest from his control the data analysis and the process of developing future plans based on the data. Thatchenkery calls the process, which had been initially designed to gather data to build more grounded theory, "The Appreciative Research Carnival." The following year Thatchenkery experienced the same phenomenon again. ICA inadvertently becomes the most "fully blown" collaborative use of Appreciative Inquiry for organizational change to date.

1989   *SIGMA Center for Global Change* is founded by The Weatherhead School of Management at Case as a center for research and education dedicated to the study and development of worldwide organizations and leaders capable of addressing the most complex and pressing global issues of our time. Committed to the premise that there are no limits to cooperation, the center mandate asserts that virtually every item on the global agenda for change can be dealt with given the appropriate forms of effective management and organization. SIGMA focuses its attention on innovative

| Date | Event |
|------|-------|

organizations that are pioneers in building a healthy and vibrant world future. Highlighted are organizations from across sectors (public, private, non-profit, cross-sector partnerships) that take a lead role in advancing positive global change. Issues of focus include (1) intelligent environmental policy and practice, (2) people-centered approaches to sustainable economic development, (3) the growth and support of local and global civil society, and (4) the emergence of a global ethic or set of higher values that inspire human action in service of the widest possible good.

1989  *Social Innovations in Global Management Conference*, held at Case Western in November of 1989 highlighted studies of five global social change organizations, one of which was ICA. Articles from these studies, along with papers on the subject of social innovations in management in the global arena were subsequently published in *Research in Organizational Change and Development* (Vol. 5; Pasmore & Woodman, 1989) from JAI Press Inc. This marked the first major activity of SIGMA and laid the groundwork for what in 1990 developed into a role for SIGMA in the Global Excellence in Management initiative for management of international development agencies.

1990  *Srivastva, Fry, and Cooperrider publish* Appreciative Management and Leadership: The Power of Positive Thought and Action in Organizations. This book contains Cooperrider's much quoted research on the power of the positive image, an article entitled "Positive Image; Positive Action."

1990  *The Organizational Excellence Program (OEP)*, a pilot project to create ways for the U.S. Agency for International Development (USAID) to offer innovative management and leadership training to U.S. Private Voluntary Organizations (PVOs), was founded under the leadership of Ada Jo Mann. Case Western Reserve was chosen as the university partner for the pilot because of the work of David Cooperrider and his colleagues with global social change organizations. At the end of the pilot phase, the OEP became the

Continued

**Date**    **Event**

Global Excellence in Management Initiative (GEM) operating under a USAID grant given to SIGMA/Case Western Reserve University. GEM's goals are to (1) promote organizational excellence in development organizations in the US and abroad; (2) create new forms of global cooperation; and, (3) sustain excellence, develop capacity to continually learn, adjust and innovate over time. AI provides the foundational operating principles. The OEP and the GEM Initiatives have fostered major innovative ways to use AI in the global arena, creating approaches and models that are being used in all organizations today.

1992    *Imagine Chicago* is created. This is a major community development effort based heavily on AI principles and practice.

1993    *NTL Institute for Applied Behavioral Science* initiates an internal Appreciative Inquiry based diversity project to discover and promulgate the innovative and effective lessons that NTL learned from nearly twenty years of work with organizations on ways to value diversity. Cathy Royal is the lead consultant for the project. In preparation for the year-long diversity study project, Jane Watkins, Cathy Royal, David Cooperrider, and John Carter offer a three-day AI lab for NTL members.

1994    *NTL's Professional Development Workshop in Appreciative Inquiry* is offered for the first time, trained by Jane Watkins and Cathy Royal. Subsequently, the team of Watkins, Royal, Bernard Mohr, and Barbara Sloan staff yearly workshops in basic AI and an AI practicum workshop.

1995    *Cooperrider is elected president of National Academy of Management* (OD Division).

1996    *The Organization Development Practitioner publishes an issue devoted completely to AI.*

1996    The Thin Book of Appreciative Inquiry *is published* by Sue Annis Hammond, providing the first widely available, basic introduction to AI as a philosophy and methodology of change.

| Date | Event |
|------|-------|
| 1997 | *AI listserv is established* by Jack Brittain at University of Texas, Dallas. It serves as a forum for practitioners at all levels to share and learn from each other. (The listserv continues to operate from the University of Utah.) |
| 1998 | Lessons from the Field, edited by Sue Hammond and Cathy Royal, is published. It is the first widely available book of case histories of organization development projects done from an appreciative perspective. |
| 1998 | *The electronic* AI Newsletter is established by Anne Radford in London. |
| 1999 | Locating the Energy for Change: An Introduction To Appreciative Inquiry, written by Dr. Charles Elliott, Dean of Trinity Hall, Cambridge, is published. |
| 2001 | Appreciative Inquiry: Change at the Speed of Imagination, *the first edition of this book* written by Jane Magruder Watkins and Bernard Mohr for OD practitioners and consultants who want to use AI as the perspective for their work, is published by Jossey-Bass/Pfeiffer and becomes, over the following decade, a top seller around the globe. Over the ensuing years, dozens of articles and books have been added to the wide network of resources available on the subjects of AI as theory and AI as a perspective for OD practice. |
| 2001 to 2010 | *Global Appreciative Inquiry Conferences.* During the past decade, four major Appreciative Inquiry conferences have been held around the world, with the 2009 Global Conference held in Katmandu, Nepal, attracting more than four hundred people in person and online from forty-three countries around the globe. |
| 2001 to 2010 | The Power of the Positive. Toward the end of the 20th Century, a young research psychologist, Barbara Fredrickson, began studying the impact of positive emotions on human behavior. This seminal work has become a major reference for those who want to understand the power of searching for the generative and positive in human systems. Appreciative Inquiry has the capacity to give people an experience of learning from positive experiences in the |

Continued

| Date | Event |
| --- | --- |

past as a way to focus on creating a desirable future. Fredrickson's work describes the impact that a focus on the positive has on people's sense of well being.

| 2001 to 2010 | *European AI Network.* In 2006 countries in Europe began to organize what has now become a widespread network of AI and strength-based change practitioners across the continent. Gatherings take place several times a year with countries volunteering to host meetings. A website (www.Networkplace.eu) created and managed by Leif Josefsson of Norway, is open to people across the globe. |

| 2001 to 2010 | *Major Events and Activities.* Over the past decade AI has spread to every corner of the globe and has impacted every form of human organization—corporations, governments, international groups, schools, churches, and more. AI books and materials exist in nearly every major language on the planet. David Cooperrider created for the United Nations a "Global Compact" meeting among leaders of major global corporations; local community projects such as "Imagine Cleveland" and "Imagine Capetown" are spreading across the globe; AI works well for family interventions and personal growth work; schools at every level are using AI for planning and in the classrooms; in fact, Appreciative Inquiry has been adapted and found to be generative and creative in any and all gatherings of human being. At the Global AI Conference in Nepal, Jane Magruder Watkins was awarded the first "Lifetime Achievement Award" for spreading AI around the globe. |

*A "Certificate Track" in Appreciative Inquiry* was established by the NTL Institute of Applied Behavioral Science and Case Western Reserve University's School of Organizational Behavior to train people who want to use AI in their workplace and consulting practices.

*On "The AI Commons"* and other websites around the globe, the history and spread of AI is documented with examples and stories of the myriad of uses and successes that the positive perspective coupled with models and processes in the field of OD have brought to the world.

## AI and the Field of Organization Development

Describing Appreciative Inquiry as yet another OD tool, technique, or intervention is, at best, only partially accurate, and, at worst, a disservice to those who seek to facilitate the co-creation of quantum shifts in the capability of an organization to meet the needs of its customers, members, and other key stakeholders. Rather, *we invite the reader to think of Appreciative Inquiry as a philosophy and orientation to change that can fundamentally reshape the practice of organization learning, design, and development in much the same way that the philosophy of "process consultation" reshaped the field of management consulting fifty years ago.*

In the early days of management consulting, the consultant was the outside expert who came to study an organization, decide what needed to be done to fix it, and propose a course of action. Long reports were written and, more often than not, sat on shelves gathering dust. Consultants became discouraged, employees resisted, and clients became cynical.

With the advent of organization development as a discipline in the 1950s, the behavioral scientists, who were experts not in the work of the organization but in the behavior of people, introduced the idea that the people of an organization were the ones best equipped to identify what needed to be changed and to formulate ways to make those changes. Instead of prescribing solutions, consultants began to facilitate members of the organization in formulating their own solutions to problems that they had identified.

Called "process consultation," this new orientation—new philosophy of consulting—was indeed used sometimes in the form of a tool, technique, or method. For example, a consultant might sit with a team and comment on their interpersonal and group-level processes. But it was "process consultation" in the macro sense—for example, providing a client system with processes for co-creation of its future—that the value of process consultation as a philosophy, an orientation to all that a management consultant does, really emerged. The paradigmatic shift was from consultants bringing in solutions to the problem, to consultants providing models and processes to help organizations study themselves and formulate their own unique solutions.

What is happening with Appreciative Inquiry is very similar. Like process consultation, AI can be and is sometimes applied effectively as a micro tool. For example, in team building a team could engage in a process of inquiry to strengthen its capability to function effectively. We often hear people say, "We did AI in our team and it really energized us." (A team-building session in an AI frame would generally use positive questions, follow-up visioning, and some form of planning.) But as with process consultation, the real power and impact of AI is seen when it is used as a comprehensive orientation to change in complex systems. By comprehensive change we mean change in an orientation to discerning strategic shifts in the relationship of the enterprise with its environment, changes in the way the work of the organization is done, and/or changes in how the organization approaches problems of leadership, performance, conflict, power, and equity. AI is a philosophy and perspective that provides an approach to strategic planning, organization design, diversity, evaluation, and so on, rather than an alternative to these interventions.

Appreciative Inquiry as a theory of practice and a methodologically fluid process continues to expand, develop, and change as we learn about the power of its perspective and how to integrate that perspective into all the work done under the umbrella of organization change. In the year 2000 when the first edition of this book was written, AI had already evolved substantially since David Cooperrider first introduced the term in 1986. In 2000 when the organization called AI Consulting was created, the list of those practicing OD from an AI perspective included forty-three names. In 2009, less than a decade later, a global AI Conference in Nepal included participants from forty-three countries. AI's growth and impact is spreading exponentially as it becomes global. If those of us using AI remain true to its principles and theoretical base, it will continue to look different in every setting and in subsequent years.

Any attempt at a simple, static definition is challenged by both the rapidly evolving nature of AI theory and practice as well as by the subtle and dramatic implications of the paradigmatic shift embedded in its application to human and organization change.

The evolution of Appreciative Inquiry from an academic interest in grounded theory building to AI as a new orientation and philosophical base for organization development is documented in the history of AI. Our continuing argument that AI is far more than just another OD methodology comes from our conviction that the practice of AI as an organization change process is deeply rooted in the theory of social constructionism and the research base on the power of image in determining what human beings consider to be "reality."

We think of Appreciative Inquiry as three interconnected concepts:

1. AI is a philosophy of knowledge—a way of coming to understand the world.

2. AI is a principle-based intervention theory that emphasizes the role of language, dialogue, and story with a particular focus on the power of inquiry in the social construction of reality.

3. AI, embedded in its own philosophy and intervention theory, can be applied to any process and methodology for working in organizations.

We will describe each of these three in more detail in this chapter. To begin, we will set a context for the practice of Appreciative Inquiry in today's world.

## The Relevance of AI to Complex, Transformative Change

Although Appreciative Inquiry is a useful approach to change in any human system at any scale—individuals, dyads, the group (team or family), neighborhoods, and communities—our focus in this book is toward the use of AI in the more complex levels of human systems. We will describe a process that can be used in organizations that are multi-functional and multi-level with multiple stakeholder systems operating in unstable environments. In such complex organizations the sociotechnical architecture, the organizational culture, and the interactions of individuals are highly interconnected—conditions present in for-profit, not-for-profit, or public service organizations.

Change in the essence of such complex organizations may begin, for example, with any of the following seven areas, realizing that transformative change always impacts several or all of the other areas. The seven intertwined areas of transformative change (Beckhard & Pritchard, 1992):

1. Change in the kind of work done within the organization and how it is done in the pursuit of producing the organizations service or product;

2. Change in the roles people hold and the relationships they have with each other;

3. Change in the identity of the organization in the marketplace;

4. Change in the relationship of the organization to customers and the outside world;

5. Change in the mission of the organization;

6. Change in the culture of the organization; and

7. Change in the organizations processes for adapting to continuous shifts in the organizations environment.

## AI and the Challenge of Organization Transformation

Complex change of this sort is no small challenge whether it is in the context of a small not-for-profit or a major public corporation. In fact the Holy Grail of organizational change has long been to create sustainable, transformative change in an organization, that is, to enable quantum leaps forward in an organization's capability to deliver needed products and services and, at the same time, to enrich the quality of life for all those connected with the organization, while simultaneously embedding in the organization the capability for continuous, ongoing development.

Pursuit of rapid, sustainable, and transformative change has spawned a collective effort of almost biblical proportions considering the time, dollars, and energy that organizations have spent on the multitude of initiatives—retraining, reforming, re-culturing, reprogramming, restructuring, reengineering, redesign, merger, acquisition, etc. But attainment of OD's Holy Grail has been elusive. Short-term gains appear in one area of performance indicators such as productivity or customer satisfaction or employee engagement or market penetration, often at the expense of other indicators. Sometimes the inherent slowness of traditional change processes make organizations vulnerable to yet another shift in the environment or in leadership before the change effort can demonstrate results in even a single sector.

Traditional complex system change efforts all too often leave behind a legacy of cynicism in the organization's culture which, together with the accompanying loss of energy, make the next effort at change or transformation even more challenging. Yet there is a geometrically increasing demand for people in organizations to shift direction, make more effective use of new technologies, and respond to unpredictable crises in shorter and shorter time frames with fewer and fewer resources. At both the personal and organizational levels, an increasing number of people are floundering in this sea of new demands with consequences that we are just beginning to understand at the societal, community, and family levels. It is within this context, and in response to these challenges, that AI has emerged as a powerful framework that directly addresses the conundrum of *"People don't change unless the organization does and the organization doesn't change unless the people do."* AI provides consultants and their clients with a new "frame" or a new paradigm for the co-creation of quantum change at both individual and system levels—simultaneously and almost literally at the speed of imagination!

## Complex Change and the Two Gifts of Appreciative Inquiry

Facing the challenge of transformative change in complex systems from the perspective of an emerging paradigm gives AI the potential to flourish in areas in which many techniques have been applied that have produced only moderate success. AI's potential comes from the integration of (1) a *practical change process* and (2) *a new paradigm view of how we shape our future.* It is the integration of these two valuable gifts that makes AI a powerful shift from the deficit perspective of traditional OD practice.

The *practical change process* of AI can be described using the well-known 4-D Model that was developed in the work of the GEM Initiative (see Exhibit 2.1). In reality, we explain the model with an additional "D" (Definition) that, for OD practitioners, is roughly analogous to the contracting stage of consulting. The five "D's" are:

1. A *Definition* phase during which the inquiry goals, including the framing of the question and the inquiry protocol, the participation strategy, and the project management structure are developed.

2. A *Discovery* phase during which members from the system develop an in-depth understanding of (a) the "life-giving properties " that are present in those exceptional moments when the organization is performing optimally in human, economic, and organizational terms and (b) of the structures, dynamics and other associated conditions that allow those "life-giving properties " to flourish.

3. A *Dream* phase during which system members create shared images of what their organization would look, be, feel, and function like if those "exceptional moments" and the "life-giving properties" in the system became the norm rather than the exception.

4. A *Design* phase during which system members agree on the principles that should guide changes in the organization's

sociotechnical architecture and develop the details of whatever changes are thought to be needed, based on the previously articulated guiding principles.

5. A *Destiny* phase, sometimes called the *Delivery* phase (and more recently the "deploy" stage), during which the organization evolves into the preferred future image created during the Dream phase using the work done in the Design phase.

While this 5-D process can be reduced to a linear explanation, in fact the change in the system begins with the first questions asked in the Definition phase. We recently had a client, struggling with a Design process, exclaim in frustration that it was hard to make a plan when people were already working to bring about ideas that were articulated in the Discovery and Dream phases. This is almost inevitably the case. The change begins with the articulation of the image—change at the speed of imagination—not at the end of a linear planning process, which brings us to the second "gift."

The second "gift" of AI combines the notion of AI as a philosophy of knowledge and AI as applied to an intervention theory that articulates an *alternative view of how we shape our future*. Grounded in the theory base of social constructionism, research on the power of image, and research on the powerful effects of positive emotions, this alternative view of OD interventions emphasizes the role of language, dialogue, and ordinary organizational conversations, particularly as they influence the crucial choice of how the topic or issue for inquiry is framed, and the subsequent development of the inevitable inquiry protocol that accompanies almost all change efforts as the organizations seeks to understand what Dick Beckhard described as "the present state." Because this alternative view is not just another technique, but a total *reframing* of our current theory of practice, it leverages all that we do in organization development, design, and change consulting, rather than just adding another "tool" to our "kitbag."

# The Theoretical Basis for Appreciative Inquiry

## Social Constructionism

Appreciative Inquiry is, in its essence, rooted and grounded in the theory of social constructionism. As practitioners of Appreciative Inquiry it is essential that we have a working knowledge of the theory, its impact on our beliefs about social knowledge, and how it plays out in theories about how organizations change. Understanding social constructionism gives us a basis for the scientific research (much of it done in the current paradigm's pure science method) that points to the power of images and the way we use them to create our own realities and even our own futures. We believe that only through a solid grounding in these concepts and theories will practitioners have the knowledge needed to co-create with clients the kinds of organization change processes that will be congruent with the need of a particular client.

Social constructionism is a theory that answers the age-old question: How do we know what we know? Social constructionism calls all of our traditional answers to and beliefs about that conundrum into question. Ken Gergen, whose work on social constructionism has had a major formative impact on AI, describes the power of the idea of language as creator of reality and lists: "Social constructionist dialogues—of cutting-edge significance within the social sciences and humanities—concern the processes by which humans generate meaning together. Our focus is on how social groups create and sustain beliefs in the real, the rational, and the good. We recognize that, as people create meaning together, so do they sow the seeds of action. Meaning and action are entwined. As we generate meaning together we create the future" (Taosinstitute.net).

To enlarge on that definition, we include here a dialogue between Ken Gergen and the participants who visit the Taos Institute website:

## *Social Construction Orienting Principles: Thoughts from Kenneth J. Gergen*

"What does it mean to carry out work in a social constructionist frame? This is a topic of broad discussion, and it is important to resist the temptation of a conclusion. However, I thought it would be useful for these discussions to develop more systematically some of the views that lie somewhere toward the center of what I do.

1. We live in worlds of meaning. We understand and value the world and ourselves in ways that emerge from our personal history and shared culture.

2. Worlds of meaning are intimately related to action. We act largely in terms of what we interpret to be real, rational, satisfying, and good. Without meaning there would be little worth doing.

3. Worlds of meaning are constructed within relationships. What we take to be real and rational is given birth in relationships. Without relationships there would be little of meaning.

4. New worlds of meaning are possible. We are not possessed or determined by the past. We may abandon or dissolve dysfunctional ways of life and together create alternatives.

5. To sustain what is valuable or to create new futures requires participation in relationships. If we damage or destroy relations, we lose the capacity to sustain a way of life, and to create new futures.

6. When worlds of meaning intersect, creative outcomes may occur. New forms of relating, new realities, and new possibilities may all emerge.

7. When worlds of meaning conflict, they may lead to alienation and aggression, thus undermining relations and their creative potential.

8. Through creative care for relationships, the destructive potentials of conflict may be reduced or transformed.

9. The preceding understandings do not constitute beliefs. They are neither true nor false. They are ways of approaching life that, for many, hold great promise."

*Taos Associate News*, October 2009, The Taos Institute

It is fair to say that this statement and the nine concepts capture the core of Appreciative Inquiry as an organization change process. As the people of organizations create meaning through their dialogue together, they sow the seeds of the organization's future.

We have talked about the shifting paradigm (in Chapter 1) that is moving our understanding of the world from Newtonian linearity to quantum relational theories. This shift in beliefs about how we see and experience the world has been at the heart of academic debate that focuses on the "modernist" era (the 20th Century's paradigm) and the "post-modern" era (the emerging paradigm in the 21st Century).

To recap briefly, the "modernist" era is usually dated from the period called the Enlightenment (approximately the mid-18th Century). In reaction to the dogma of religion when the arbiter of truth was the church, the Enlightenment—no doubt influenced by the ascendancy of "pure science" typified by Newtonian thinking—shifted the focus for judgments about morality and what is real to the individual. People began to make judgments based on what was conceived to be "objective, scientific evidence" about what was real and what was true. This search for truth led to the belief that there were underlying rules and structures that defined the "right" way of doing things. There was also the assumption that this "right" way could be discovered.

This enlightened thinking and scientific focus impacted the arts and architecture, literature, the social sciences, indeed, every sector of human endeavor. The belief during this period, and by many today, is that there is one all-embracing principle that, if we could discover it, would explain the world. We are much like the scientists climbing the mountain of questions about the origins of the universe that Simon Singh (2004) describes in his book, *Big Bang: The Origin of the Universe.* He quotes American astronomer Robert Jastrow, speaking of the role that the struggle between science and religion has always played in this discussion. Jastrow describes a scientist climbing to find the answer to his conundrum: "He (the scientist) has scaled the mountains of ignorance; he is about to conquer the highest peaks; as he pulls himself over the final rock, he is greeted by a band of theologians who have been sitting there for centuries." It will not be one person or one group that discovers a predetermined truth about reality. It will be, instead, a continuous and perhaps endless dialogue among us all.

"Post-modernism" rejects the idea of an underlying structure and of an underlying truth. Instead of one grand design, post-modern thought embraces the idea of multiple and contextually determined "realities." Social constructionism is a formative theory of the post-modern idea. Social constructionists argue that our world is shaped by the many dialogues and discourses that we have with each other—conversations in which we both selectively make sense of our past and present, experience, and history and create shared images of what we anticipate in the future. Appreciative Inquiry takes this one step further into an intervention process based on the power of dialogue generated by inquiry itself, that is, the power of the questions we ask. It is with those questions that we shape our destiny.

As Cooperrider (1995) says:

> "The most important thing we do as consultants is inquiry. We try to read situations, we do organizational analysis and diagnosis. It all starts with inquiry. The key point is that the way we know is fateful. The questions we ask, the things that we choose to focus on, the topics that we choose determine what we find. What we find becomes the data and the story out of which we dialogue about and envision the future. *And so, the seeds of change are implicit in the very first questions we ask! Inquiry is intervention.*"

At the crux of AI is the choice we make in the first question we ask. For example, an organization wanting to heal the wounds of racism can (1) inquire into instances of racism in the workplace with the idea that once we are really clear on what racism looks and feels like and what causes it, then it can be eliminated, or (2) the organization can choose to inquire into instances of exceptionally good cross-race working relationships and the conditions present at those times, creating images of desirable relationships. The practice of AI is founded on the theory that the very act of inquiry causes the system to shift in the direction of the inquiry by evoking anticipatory images that are created in the dialogue that is part of any inquiry. AI chooses the positive inquiry precisely because it leads to positive images that, in turn, create a positive future.

## The Power of Image

With this understanding of the shift in the theories about social knowledge, about what is real and true, and about the power of language to create reality, Cooperrider turned to research in a wide range of social sciences to understand more fully the impact of positive images in the creation of the future. And he began to tie this into his thinking about the impact that these new theories could have on organizational change theory and practice. In his story, from our interview with him in 1999, he says:

> "I decided to refocus my dissertation on Appreciative Inquiry. Then, of course, we had to explain the 'why' of this phenomenon. We did this by bringing together a multidisciplinary group in a conference at Case. The purpose of that conference was to explore the relationship of image to action; to understand where the positive images come from and how they are developed. That conference provided the basic material for my chapter 'Positive Image: Positive Action' in the book Suresh and I edited called *Appreciative Management and Leadership*."

The information on that research and from "Positive Image; Positive Action" form the basis of this discussion of the role of image in our lives. Taking research from widely diverse fields such as medicine, sports, behavioral science, and anthropology, Cooperrider thoroughly documents the phenomena of the relationship between our images and our behavior, between what we believe to be true and what we create as truth.

For example, since the mid-1950s, Western medical science has become aware of the power of the mind to heal the body. This concept has always been the basis of healing in Eastern cultures. The split in mind and body that began with the Greeks, was reinforced by the Newtonian paradigm, and dominants in Western thought and behavior even today, is giving way to a greater understanding of the mind/body connection. Scientific experimentation and documented data are increasing and the belief in the holistic nature of the "self" is becoming mainstream in major scientific research institutions as well as in the daily press.

What does this have to do with Appreciative Inquiry? AI is, in part, the art of helping systems create images of their most desired future. Based on the belief that a human system will show a heliotropic tendency to move toward positive images, AI is intentionally focused on the generative and creative images in a system that can be held up, valued, and used as a basis for moving toward the future. The research that follows is abundant and well documented, a fact that was not the case a decade ago. As with social constructionism, our intention here is to give a very brief description to familiarize practitioners with the roots of AI while, at the same time, providing citations of resources for those who want to explore these ideas in greater depth.

In the middle of the last century, research began in earnest on the impact that the language we used and the images we created had on our mental and physical health and well-being. These studies are useful in helping us make the cognitive leap from our world of parts to a more holistic sense of the cosmos. It is hard to imagine that we are only now, in the West, taking seriously the notion that our minds are indivisibly connected with our bodies, but that has been the case. Following are examples introduced by David Cooperrider in his original writing about AI. The examples come from studies of positive images and positive thinking in four different areas.

## The Placebo Effect: The Power of Our Own Images of Ourselves

Perhaps the best-known studies of the impact of our minds on our bodies are the widely documented placebo experiments that began in the mid-1950s. Although the placebo phenomenon has been controversial, most of the medical profession now accepts as genuine the fact that anywhere from one-third to two-thirds of all patients will show marked physiological and emotional improvement in symptoms simply by believing that they are being given an effective treatment, even when that treatment is just a sugar pill or some other inert substance. Further, the effect is even more powerful if the doctor prescribing the medicine or treatment also believes that it will help (Beecher, 1955; White, Tursky, & Schwartz, 1985).

Norman Cousins (1981) popularized the notion that a person's mental state impacts health. In his book, *Human Options*, he writes of the therapeutic value of hope, faith, love, will to live, cheerfulness, humor, creativity, playfulness, confidence, and great expectations, all of which contribute to a healing system for the body. A landmark experiment was undertaken by Simonton, Creighton, and Simnton (1981) at their clinic in Texas, where they documented an unusually high rate of recovery from "terminal" cancer by patients who worked to resolve their psychological issues and practiced positive imagery. Bill Moyers created a whole series for the Public Broadcasting System on the power of the mind to heal the body. Almost daily new books and articles appear documenting studies or proposing theories about this connection between our mental processes and our mental and physical well-being.

## The Pygmalion Studies: The Impact of Another's Image on Us

A set of experiments called the Pygmalion studies, carried out in classrooms with schoolchildren, demonstrate the power that another person's image of us can have in shaping our performance. In these studies, teachers were told that one group was made up of students who were not very intelligent, tended to do poorly, and were often not well-behaved in the classroom, while the children in the second group were bright, hard-working, and successful. The teacher believed these to be the facts while, in actuality, the division of students into the two groups was entirely random. Within a very short time, however, almost without exception those labeled low potential were performing poorly and those labeled high potential were excelling.

In observations of the teacher, researchers discovered that the teachers responded to students in line with what they believed about a student's potential and ability. If the teacher thought that a student was smart and competent, body language was encouraging, verbal exchanges were supportive, and the teacher made allowances for the student when he or she did not perform well. On the other hand, the teacher's interactions with those thought to be less capable were much more terse, perfunctory, and dismissive.

Long-term follow-up to the studies showed that the effects of this image held by the teacher affected the students far into the future. (By inference, the same effect can be anticipated with images held by parents, bosses, and other authority figures.) Furthermore, it was proven that the image that the teacher held of the student was a more powerful predictor of a child's performance than IQ scores, home environment, or past performance. So damaging were these experiments to the students labeled "poor" that the scientific community discontinued them.

## Positive Thinking

In another set of studies, behavioral scientists looked at the ratio of positive as opposed to negative thought patterns in people facing major heart surgery. The studies demonstrated that those who approached the operation with a feeling that the doctor was the best, the medical techniques were proven and safe, and their chances of being well again were excellent recovered at a much greater rate than those who approached the operation with fear and concern. In these studies, it was concluded that the desired ratio of positive thoughts to negative thoughts is approximately 2 to 1 (Srivastva, Fry, & Cooperrider, 1990, p. 109). With a 2 to 1 ratio, there is a marked difference in the level of well-being that a person experiences.

## Metacognition: Using Our Internal Dialogue for Positive Impact

Evidence suggests quite clearly, especially in the arena of sports, that we can learn how to create positive images for ourselves that will impact our performance, our health, our sense of well-being, even our relationships with others.

There are many examples in the sports arena of the power of the positive image in creating success for athletes. Books such as Jack Nicklaus' *Golf My Way* argue that the positive affirmation ("I'm going to hit it down the middle of the fairway," rather than "Don't hit it into the woods") causes the whole body to respond to what the mind imagines is possible. Paradoxically, most of us believe that elimination of failures (negative self-monitoring, that is, "No, not the woods") will improve performance when exactly the opposite appears to be true.

With this kind of scientific evidence emerging, it makes sense to rethink our approach to organization development. It is not hard to make the connection between the research and people's lives in an organizational setting. The Pygmalion studies suggest that performance appraisals that focus on people's shortcomings, particularly if the appraisals come from one who has power over the person being appraised, is likely to assure that the employee will not perform well in the future. The placebo studies document ways that the power of our minds can keep our bodies healthy. It is not an unreasonable connection to make that an employee who holds self-images of competence and success is much more likely to be high-performing. And the power of our inner dialogue to impact out behavior suggests that the cynicism so prevalent in Western culture is quite likely to be a self-fulfilling prophecy. Taken to the organizational level, if we accept that there is at least a possibility that we socially construct our world and a reasonable amount of evidence that we have the power to create what we imagine, it follows that a process for facilitating organization change would consciously focus on empowering employees to believe that they can make a difference; reward leaders who know how to empower others; and focus the energy of the system on the positive, generative, and creative forces that give life and vitality to the work.

## Social Constructionism + The Power of Image = AI in Organization Change

As we know from research on the power of image (Srivastvra, Fry, & Cooperrider, 1990), human beings are strongly impacted by these anticipatory images of the future and in a myriad of ways ranging from physiological responses at the individual level to the creation of new strategies and organization architectures, we collectively create the very future that we anticipate.

This *view of how we shape our future* gives us a whole new way of understanding the process of change in an organization. Rather than being limited to the traditional view of change as an event that has a beginning, middle, and end (as in, for example, Kurt Lewin's model of Unfreezing-Changing-Refreezing), we now see change as a continuous process, ongoing in every conversation we have, in every inquiry we make, in every action we take to "know" or understand something about our organization and/or about the world. Hence the notion of AI as a philosophy of knowledge.

Within this social constructionist perspective, aided and abetted by the research on the power of image and the role of language, discourse, and dialogue in creating those images, we realize that some very significant doors open up for us as we pursue transformative change in our organizations. Specifically, since all change processes begin with framing an issue and collecting some data to give us a better understanding of the issue, we become aware that in the very act of doing these preliminary activities, we, even at that moment, are engaging in the process of socially constructing our futures through the choices we make about how to "frame the issue" and the dialogues we have as we make inquiries into those issues. For example, we can choose to frame an issue as, "What's keeping us from being able to get our innovations into production faster?" or we can choose to frame the issue as, "In those exceptional periods, when our new product development process is moving at the 'speed of light,' what conditions, factors, or contributing dynamics are present?" Our choice in this initial framing is fateful, as either frame will start a snowball of dialogues, inquiries, and the resultant anticipatory images of the future.

Social construction theory says, in essence, that we create reality through the conversations that we have. Therefore, an alternative theory of organizational intervention would suggest that a fundamental precondition for all organization change work— whether focused on process innovation, stakeholder relationships, business strategy, organizational culture, diversity, the capability to adapt and improve, team effectiveness, etc.—to shift the flow of "issue framing dialogues" in the direction of health rather than pathology. This, then, shifts the flow of dialogues that result from the inquiries from an analysis of moments of malfunction to a holistic understanding of moments of optimal performance. The choice to focus on moments of optimal performance is driven by the theory that our daily dialogues and our conscious use of inquiry are powerful interventions in and of themselves.

## What Good Are Positive Emotions?

In addition to the original research that underlies AI theory and practice, in the decade between the publication of the first edition of this book in 2001 and the research that underlies the second edition, a major body of research has emerged on the importance of positive thinking and action to our well-being as human beings. The origin of this exploration was Martin Seligman's book about the importance of positive emotions. A graduate student at the time,

Barbara Fredrickson, began to do research on the power of the positive in human behavior and won, in 1998, an award for her outstanding paper on the subject. Over the past decade, the impact of her research has legitimized the Appreciative Inquiry process in major ways. Her research asked the question: "What good are positive emotions?" and the answers she found as a result of her research have led to a major shift in how we understand the powerful positive impact that experiencing positive emotions have on our bodies and behaviors.

# Living Well with Dementia: Creating a Regional Strategy for the East Midlands

*By Julie Barnes and Jill Guild*

> "If you are saving for a rainy day, you need to recognize it when it comes."

*Heather was so relieved to have the diagnosis and to know, for sure, what was happening to her. At fifty-three, it was hard to imagine the future with Alzheimer's disease, but now she and her family could face it together and "start living again." For them, this means enjoying the time they have together, traveling, celebrating, and doing things they might never have done, while they can. Dave, her husband, left work and together they are living their life to the full, including campaigning for greater national and local awareness of dementia and better services. Creating great times and memories for their future; making a major contribution to services; and, in doing so, impacting positively on Heather's well-being and the progress of her dementia.*

## Focus of the Inquiry

Creating a vision for living well with dementia in the East Midlands, UK. This story describes and demonstrates the power of discovery and dreaming in creating compelling visions for the future.

There are currently 700,000 people in the UK with dementia whose care costs £17 billion a year. In the next thirty years, the number of people directly affected by this condition is likely to double. In August 2007, the government announced a program to develop the first National Dementia Strategy and Implementation Plan for England. Published in February 2009, this ambitious strategy aims to support people with dementia and their careers in living well with dementia.

This is an important challenge for everyone involved. Dementia can result in a progressive decline in multiple areas of function, including memory, reasoning, communications skills, and the skills for carrying our daily activities. Alongside this, individuals may develop behavioral and

*case story*

psychological symptoms such as depression, psychosis, aggression and wandering, creating risks for the individual and challenges for caregivers. Family caregivers of people with dementia are often old and frail themselves with high level of depression and physical illness, and a diminished quality of life. Dementia is a terminal condition but people can live with it for seven to twelve years after diagnosis. There are growing numbers of people of working age with dementia whose medical, social, and care needs are different from those of older people.

## The Client

The NHS Development Centre is part of the East Midlands Strategic Health Authority with responsibility for improving services and building partnerships across the multiple agencies who are delivering child, mental health, and offender healthcare. The East Midlands region covers rural and urban areas in five sub-regions including five local councils and nine primary care healthcare trusts from Northampton to Lincolnshire. Approximately 4.3 million people live in the East Midlands, with a range of minority ethnic populations and 700,000 people aged sixty-five and over.

Responsible for implementing the dementia strategy in its region, the client was committed to creating a process with people with dementia and their caregivers at its heart, not just consulting about predetermined proposals but supporting them to create and lead the development of the strategy themselves.

### Client Objectives: What Were the Best Possible Outcomes Articulated by the Client?

It is in this context that the East Midlands Development Centre decided to use Appreciative Inquiry in developing its regional strategy for helping people to "live well" with dementia. With people with dementia and their caregivers at the center of this work, it has developed an innovative and leading-edge approach to creating a vision and strategy for the region.

The regional support team planned and scoped the project with internal and external stakeholders, including people with dementia and their caregivers. The team produced data packs of the known socio-demographic characteristics of the localities and a diagnostic screening tool to help service commissioners and providers map their current activity against the seventeen key objectives outlined in the National Dementia Strategy. This work started to indicate where current resources were focused and where they might be needed in future. A plan emerged to run five commissioning workshops in each sub-region using a structured process of "strengths-based lean thinking" in which local people would work together to identify what was needed and to decide how to make it happen. This was supported by CSED, a national team at the UK Department of Health, tasked with supporting efficient working across the National Health Service.

The lead client was determined that this process would only start after the regional vision was created by those most affected by dementia. Having worked with Appreciative Inquiry before, she knew that this would be a uniquely enjoyable, creative, and powerful way to unite people in tackling this strategy together; in creating a shared, compelling vision; and making sure that every voice was heard. The team's aim was to work with people with dementia and their caregivers in co-creating a vision for living well in the East Midlands and to take this vision into the planning and commissioning of local services. Their greater wish was that, by using Appreciative Inquiry, the "living well" would begin at once, through the appreciative conversations and new ways of thinking and talking about how we live and what helps us to live well.

### What Was Done: Who Did What? A Summary of How the AI Process Was Used and What Occurred in Each Phase of the Process

Between June and September 2009, regular meetings were held with people with dementia and their caregivers to discover what it means for them to live well with dementia and to start envisioning for the future. Using appreciative questions to structure their conversations, this core group of people "discovered" and "dreamed" together, and some took the questions out to other caregivers and people with dementia in their local areas. The group co-planned a wider summit meeting for the autumn and some people spoke at this meeting, either in person or via video clips. The membership of this group changes each time, with a consistent core of people who come to every meeting.

## June 2009

In June 2009, an invited group of ten people with dementia and their caregivers, together with caregivers from third-sector organizations, came together to start talking about what this work might look like and to begin conversations about what living well with dementia means to them.

We began by inviting people to introduce themselves and say what they were bringing to the meeting—of themselves and their experience. We quickly learned that everyone had an important connection to dementia, both personally and professionally. Even the practitioners there had stories of mothers, fathers, in-laws, grandparents—people in their lives who had been touched by dementia. "We're in it together" emerged as a powerful quote from this first meeting.

We invited people to talk in pairs about what living well with dementia means to them and to tell stories about times when they experience this. Initially this was a challenge—this is not the usual kind of conversation about dementia, where people watch their loved ones "disappear," where the demands of caring are rarely matched by external support and where frustration and emotion runs high. Living well with dementia is a contradiction in terms to many.

Yet when we started to tell each other stories, we found the high points, the joy, the laughter, the love. Carol told us about a riverboat trip that she and her mother had taken, where the relief of sharing the care with others for just that afternoon meant that "we could be mother and daughter again." Stories of life in residential care homes, where elderly people who had been neglected, lonely, and isolated in their own homes were now surrounded by support, were eating well, and staying warm, so that relatives could focus on building their relationships and being with the person rather than struggling to keep him or her safe and well. Stories where having an early diagnosis and active follow-up from the consultant meant that people with dementia could start living again, managing their

*case story*

condition, learning new skills, and doing things that they had never imagined doing before.

We "dreamed" together of ways in which this campaign could be communicated to others and of what it would be like if everyone was talking about "living well" with dementia. We shared ideas about taking this "discovery" out into their communities, using the same questions and particularly the invitation to talk about times when people are living well with dementia. We talked about media opportunities to share these stories and to keep the message going out, raising awareness, which itself is one of the national strategy objectives. The seeds of an idea to have a larger day or summit meeting with professionals and stakeholders across the region were discussed for later in the year, after more work had been done with people with dementia and their caregivers.

This small group of people agreed to be the core group for this project and undertook to meet again in July, bringing with them one or two friends or colleagues so that we could continue these discussions with a larger group of people. We undertook to write up the key messages from this first meeting and to present this to the next gathering.

## July 2009

At this meeting we planned to outline our process, share the messages from the previous gathering, and continue our discovery conversations. We also planned to do some group dreaming or envisioning of what "living better" might look like, to prepare people to carry out further discovery interviews, and to plan together for the summit meeting.

Like all best-laid plans, this was a day that went its own way, responding to the needs and wishes of the people who came. Already one facilitator down, the lead client was struck by swine flu. Undaunted, the day began with about fifteen people from different parts of the region; some people had been before and many were here for the first time. As the introductions began, more and more people arrived until there was standing room only. There were people with dementia and their caregivers; elderly people caring for their husbands, fathers, and mothers; care workers and people from the voluntary (third sector). People who had been working in this area for many years, and even someone who had just heard that her mother had been diagnosed with dementia and didn't know where else to turn! Everyone listened as people told their stories and explained why they had come to this meeting.

As people left the room to carry on their conversations in pairs, we moved to a bigger room, smoothly transferring people and belongings to the comfort of a new location. Energy was high as people came back into small groups to share their stories and to draw out the common and different themes of what is at the heart—the positive core—of living well with dementia.

Here are some of the things they told us:

People with dementia and their caregivers tell us that they can live well when they:

- Are met, treated, and respected as individual people without labels

- Are accepted, listened to, and involved in what happens to us

- Have an early diagnosis with active, smooth, quick follow-up

- Have appropriate medication and monitoring

- Know what is available to us when we need it through appropriate information

- Are supported to be independent, take risks, and lead active lives

- Have choices about the quality services we can receive

- Can share our experiences with people who know what we are going through

- Have access to planned and unplanned respite care

- Focus on what we *can* do, rather than on what we can't

- Can laugh together

Amid the high energy and positive stories were some heart-breaking ones. Tears were shed of sorrow, loss, and grief at the impact of this terrible condition. Anger and frustration about the lack of resources and the hardship of caring for loved ones at home alone rose up and were respectfully heard by everyone. As the facilitator, I made the decision to stay with the stories and the emotions and to let go of the planned agenda—what was happening in the room needed to be heard and acknowledged, and this is what we did.

At the end of the day, people left with their discovery interview packs and we had barely spoken at all about the summit meeting. Aware that we had not done as much as we had planned, I was reassured by the feedback from the client's side that this had been an important meeting and they were very happy with what we had achieved. On reflection, this was one of the key learnings for me—that appreciating and valuing all the stories and all the emotions is a powerful part of the Appreciative Inquiry process. What needs to happen will happen if I, as a facilitator, can be open enough to trust the people involved and can co-create an environment in which people feel they will be listened to in their pain as well as in their joy.

## September 2009

During the summer, I heard from some of the caregivers about the additional discovery interviews they were doing and the power of these conversations in bringing people together and inspiring them to take part in this process. We set up a meeting in September to share more of these stories and to talk about how we would take these forward into the regional summit. We also told people that we would be filming the meeting and we invited people with dementia and their caregivers to tell their stories on camera. We wanted to use some of this film at the regional summit and also to create a record of the whole process for teaching and awareness-raising.

At the September meeting, we were back to fewer numbers, including some of the people who had been most vociferous at the last gathering. We had typed up the stories we had gathered and posted these around the room. We invited people to take a walk around and to talk in pairs about the stories that had most impact on them, looking for the "sticky stories"—the stories we must tell. We talked together about the structure and content of the regional summit meeting, including who should be invited and who might want to tell their stories, either in person or via the film. Through the day, individuals and couples also told their stories to the camera and it was a credit to the young camera crew who captured sensitively even the most painful subjects, and kept focusing on living well.

There was a growing sense of fellowship in the group and changes for individuals since the last meeting. One lady in particular had taken concrete steps for herself, her husband, and her family with great impact on their lives, on her feelings about her situation, and her own sense of self-esteem and empowerment. She subsequently told us that "Over the sessions and with each one being different, I feel I have gained information and confidence."

In the afternoon, we used the positive core of the stories to dream together about "living well—living better" with dementia, using creative materials to create powerful visions of the future. Here is one example of what was created that day.

## Flourishing Services—Strong Support

*This picture for the future (Figure 2.1) was created at the discovery meeting on 11 September 2009, by people with dementia and their caregivers. The person with dementia is at the heart of the tree. The solid trunk represents a consistent pathway for everyone. At its centre, the consultant is the gateway to early diagnosis, assessment, information, support, and services. Arrows in all directions show the complexity of the relationships and the importance of clear, focused communication. The flourishing services are shown as fruits of the tree, which people with dementia can access, and there is a gold star when the system works well for individuals and their careers.*

By the end of this meeting, we had planned the regional summit meeting and talked through who was going to speak and the stories we would tell. We agreed that the focus would continue to be "living well with

## Figure 2.1. A Compelling Vision for the Future

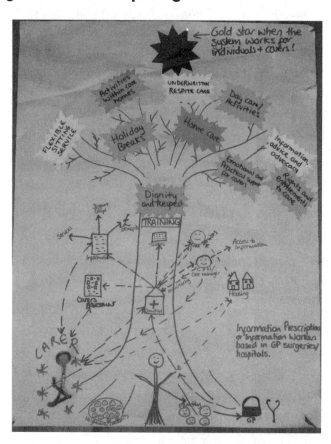

dementia" and our purpose to create a vision for the regional strategy. We agreed that our "sticky" stories would be made into posters for the summit room and that collated stories would be placed on each table so that newcomers could read about living well with dementia. Now we were bringing together a much wider group of stakeholders, including care workers and managers, commissioning managers, local counselors, medical consultants, nurses, occupational therapists, social workers, third-sector groups from across the region. Limited only by the size of the venue we knew there would be up to 150 people there and we talked about how to support people with dementia and their caregivers at such a large event and whether they wanted to speak in person or to tell their stories on the film. Both options were taken up and we undertook to edit the film so that stories could be shared during the day, as well as having two live presentations at the beginning, one from a person with dementia and one from a caregiver.

### Sharing the Story, Peer Support

Later that month, I joined an Appreciative Inquiry foundation training course in Lincoln as an apprentice trainer. There was an opportunity to present current projects for reflection with colleagues, which proved to be a great moment for this work. I told the story, and together we talked through the questions we might use for the summit. Keeping the focus of living well, the important addition was to start the inquiry with a question for everyone about what living well means to them, right now. Having widened our conversations to what is important for us all, we then focused back into what living well *with dementia* means. This felt like a really significant reminder to aspire for the best for everyone regardless of condition and to harness what we all know and experience in creating a compelling, desirable, and stretching vision for the future.

The other gem from this discussion was the introduction of table facilitators to support participants and the overall process through the day. This was my biggest summit so far, and I was working with my personal challenge of how best to facilitate the day. With smaller groups, I encourage groups to self-organize and facilitate themselves; and I build in time for feedback to the whole room, using microphones and asking groups to present their material. With this size and the diversity in the room, this wasn't so practical, and I was working on letting go of my need for the whole room (and me) to hear everything, trusting that the conversations at the tables were the important ones. The idea of table facilitators came from a desire to support these conversations as well as the people at the table and to ensure that key messages were captured by the table and posted for everyone to see.

Volunteers from the training group as well as officers from the regional support team and long-standing colleagues with an interest in finding out more about AI came as facilitators. They were briefed in advance with a written outline of their roles and expertly warmed up with humor, gifts, and minimal instructions on the morning by my co-facilitator, Lesley

Wilson. This innovation worked well, providing support to the participants who were new to AI; to the people with dementia and caregivers in keeping their voices at the centre; to me as the facilitator, freeing me up to keep seeing the bigger picture; and to the facilitators as a learning experience.

## October 2009

On 2 October 2009, 180 people from across the East Midlands and from all parts of local health, social care, and community services came together with people with dementia and their caregivers to continue this inquiry and to create a regional vision for living well with dementia.

Building on the discovery work with people with dementia and their caregivers, the summit inquired into what it means to live well with dementia and what it will mean to live even better; creating images and words for a compelling future—creating a live vision for the regional strategy. Participants worked together, telling and listening to stories about living well—powerful and inspiring stories of times when people felt most valued, most connected, and most supported.

From the stories, we identified the essential elements of living well—the things that contribute to full lives—and we used these to create our visions for the future—how it will look when everyone is living as well as they possibly can, with the information, people, and services that will support them to do this. The day was recorded by film and by photographs.

Working with this large group, we heard powerful stories from people with dementia and caregivers and impassioned pleas to improve services and make a real difference with this dementia strategy. Working with people they'd "like to know better," participants had conversations in pairs and small groups about what it means to live well and for the future. We posted table feedback about the key themes and the positive core of living well with dementia and invited people to walk and talk around the gallery. After lunch, we invited people to work in their sub-regional groups for the dreaming and design sessions in preparation for the sub-regional workshops. Here was an opportunity for local people to start co-creating together, getting to know each other better and to forge what

case story

we hoped would be constructive and long-lasting relationships that would assist them in the next stages. People who dream together, stay together, and this was how we set it up. Some sub-regions had several tables and everyone threw themselves into the creative process of dreaming for a future in which the positive core of living well with dementia was amplified, achieved, and the best it could be.

Rather than taking formal presentations of the dreams, we invited people to visit each other's tables, walking and talking, world-café style. The ensuing session was a sight to behold as people talked and exclaimed, proudly presented their dreams, and laughed and imagined together. As a concession to my longing for the whole room to catch a glimpse of the whole, we did a final run around the room with the microphone, hearing some of the provocative propositions that accompanied the visions. Here are some examples:

- *Look at me, not the label*

- *My life, my choices, my dream*

- *Pick and mix—we are with you for the journey*

- *From deflation to elation to celebration*

- *From stranded to boarded to sailing*

- *Breaking down barriers*

- *A real deal for real people*

- *The only way is up*

- *Living, achieving, holding*

- *We are as good as we are because we listen to people with dementia and their carers—they are the experts and we never forget this*

In the final session, the sub-regions reflected on what they had achieved, their next steps, and what they would be taking forward into the detailed planning and commissioning process. The day ended with a powerful call from one of the caregivers to everyone to keep up the momentum of this work, to "avoid wasting everyone's time," and to make sure that real changes were made as a result. A final clip from another caregiver asking only to be respected and supported brought the day to a silent and moving close.

**Outcomes:** *What results were achieved for the business, for members of the organization, and for customers or other stakeholders?*

> "People with dementia and their caregivers have been at the heart of our discovery in the East Midlands and will continue to lead us in creating the services and support systems for living well with dementia. This regional strategy begins with powerful visions for the future when people with dementia and their carers are living well; visions to which people in the East Midlands are aspiring and are now starting to create. The stories, pictures, and quotes that follow describe what living well means and what people with dementia and their carers value most." (Regional Strategy November 2009, p. 5)

The visions, provocative propositions, and key messages from the summit were collated into the regional strategy report—a document intended to inspire and set direction for the sub-regional workshops and local commissioning. It has been sent to everyone who came to the summit and to the key commissioners and senior staff in the sub regions.

Rather than picking one vision, the report contains five or six key pictures (Figure 2.2) that express powerful successful futures and lives lived well with support for all.

One particular statement (Figure 2.3) was chosen by the client to represent their whole work and this now appears on everything that is connected to the ongoing work.

Over the next six months, these powerful images and words are inspiring local commissioners, practitioners, people with dementia, and their caregivers as they come together for the sub-regional workshops, to design and start creating local services based on what people with dementia and their caregivers value most in living well. This work is being filmed and will be made into a complete DVD of the whole process, and

## Figure 2.2. Simply the Best—Created at the Regional Summit

there are still discussions about creating a book of the stories we have gathered and a traveling exhibition of the visions that were produced in order to keep raising awareness about dementia and inspiring conversations about living well. This is just the beginning...!

And the core group of people with dementia and their caregivers continues to meet to review their progress and to tackle specific design topics, for example, recently creating prototypes for information packs. As well as participating in the commissioning workshops in their own areas, they are keeping an eye on the whole process and are central to decisions about the strategy and the next steps. They have given their blessing for this story to be submitted as a case study.

**case story**

### Figure 2.3. Vision Statement Created at the Regional Summit, October 2009

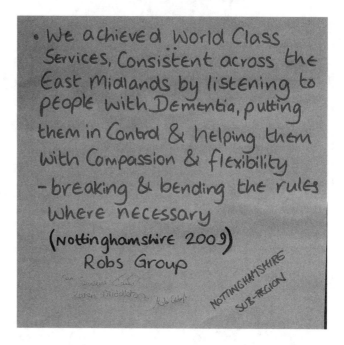

**Learnings:** *What worked especially well? What wishes do you have for the next time?*

Reflecting on this story has been a moving reminder of how much can be achieved in the most unexpected ways from working with Appreciative Inquiry, at personal and professional levels, as well as for the whole systems that step forward to work together. It is a way of working and being that liberates people, unleashing their talents, creativity, resources, and best selves to the common good. As a facilitator, I follow the Watkins mantra of "planning tight, hang loose"—co-creating the conditions and environment for people to work together and then "getting out of the way" so that they can do it for themselves. As with every AI I have ever been involved with, I stand enthralled and humbled by what is created and designed.

I have been particularly struck by the determination of the client to keep people with dementia and their caregivers at the heart of this work. Her energy and leadership in bringing together the project, the people, and the mission has been crucial to its success.

The courage and generosity of the people with dementia and their caregivers in talking together, in sharing some of their most difficult stories, and in trusting us with a process they were sometimes unsure about has been inspiring; what has been achieved is a real tribute to them.

I particularly liked the way that this project created its own momentum while giving time for the people with dementia and their caregivers to build their confidence through the series of meetings and the development of their stories and visions. This was important modeling for the professionals and practitioners who work with service users and caregivers all the time, but rarely keep them central to such an important planning process.

I have observed first-hand the powerful impact for individuals of working in this way, as change really does begin from the first questions we ask. The appreciative questions and our focus on the positive created an energy and momentum for this work, which in itself was healing and nurturing. Friendships have been formed and individuals empowered to take charge of their own situations.

I learned again about the value of appreciating every contribution, especially the anger and frustration, and the importance of working flexibly so that everyone can be heard and acknowledged. When we look for the best in AI we are not turning away from the difficult and the painful—we want to learn from them and understand what helps us to survive the tough times too.

Finally, I learned about letting go of my need to know what is happening in the room and to trust that the conversations that are happening are the important ones. The people in the room are responsible for taking this forward so it is what they are saying to each other that is important. What I need to contribute is co-creating and holding the creative space in which they work in the best ways they know.

Wishes for next time? Maybe to create something even bigger and better—an aircraft hangar rather than a ballroom for the summit, with

*case story*

greater numbers and representation from the whole system? To not be limited by my own imagination, trusting that this process brings the right people with the necessary energy and creativity to the table and then generates a whole lot more momentum for change and action.

**Author's Contact Information**

Julie Barnes
Appreciative Inquiry Facilitator
143 Abbey Road
West Bridgford
Nottingham, NG2 5ND
0115 914 3830
Julie.barnes@yahoo.co.uk

**Client's Contact Information**

Jill Guild, Strategic Relationships and Programme Manager
NHS East Midlands Development Centre
Pleasley Vale Business Park
Mill 3 Floor 3, Outgang Lane
Pleasley, Mansfield
Nottingham NG19 8RL
Telephone: 07827 895908
jill.guild@eastmidlands.nhs.uk

# CHAPTER 3

# Appreciative Inquiry as a Perspective for Organization Change

"Modern management thought was born proclaiming that organizations are the triumph of the imagination. As 'made and imagined,' organizations are products of human interaction and social construction rather than some anonymous expression of an underlying natural order. Deceptively simple yet so entirely radical in implication, this insight is still shattering many conventions—one of which is the longstanding conviction that bureaucracy, oligarchy, and other forms of hierarchical domination are inevitable. Today we know this simply is not true.

"Recognizing the symbolic and relationally constructed nature of the organizational universe, we now find a mounting wave of socio-cultural and constructionist research, all of which is converging around one essential and empowering thesis: that there is little about collective action or organization development that is pre-programmed, unilaterally determined, or stimulus bound in any direct physical, economic, material or deep-structured sociological way. Everywhere we look, seemingly immutable ideas about people and organizations are being directly challenged and transformed on an unprecedented scale. The world, quite simply, seems to change as we talk in it."

David Cooperrider, Frank J. Barrett, and Suresh Srivastva, "Social Construction and Appreciative Inquiry: A Journey in Organizational Theory," 1995, p. 91.

**THIS CHAPTER BEGINS WITH A DISCUSSION** of the "DNA" of AI. It then moves on to explain the five core principles of AI and the five core generic processes that differentiate AI from other approaches to organization change. Finally, we outline a description of the skills needed by those (either internal or external, either staff or line) who seek to lead and/or consult to any AI-based change process.

## The "DNA" of Appreciative Inquiry

As with any new approach to organization change, the question is asked, "What are the essential components of this approach?" Or, "What are the basic building blocks that make a process Appreciative Inquiry rather than some other kind of organization change approach?" In other words, "What is the DNA of AI?"

The DNA building blocks (essential ingredients) of AI are:

1. First, the beliefs and values that emerge from the five core principles plus the additional principle of wholeness, a concept added to the list as the powerful impact of AI as a theory of change became better understood:

   (1) Constructionist

   (2) Simultaneity

   (3) Anticipatory

   (4) Poetic

(5) Positive

(6) Wholeness

2. Second, the five generic processes or phases of AI practice:

   (1) Focus on the positive as a core value;

   (2) Inquiry into stories of life-giving forces;

   (3) Locating themes that appear in the stories and selecting topics from the themes for further inquiry;

   (4) Creating shared images for a preferred future; and

   (5) Innovating ways to create that preferred future.

Like everything in Appreciative Inquiry, even these basic building blocks are constantly being transformed, redefined, and used in creative ways. (For example, in Jackie Kelm's 2008 book *The Joy of Appreciative Living* there are several additional principles.) However, for the sake of building a platform of knowledge from which to practice and innovate, we will take those listed here as the current DNA of AI. Taken in tandem, these two building blocks—five plus one principles and five core processes—constitute the basic DNA of an AI approach to an organization development process for change in a human system.

To broaden this perspective, Gervase Bushe (Bushe & Coetzer, 1995) describes five different ways of thinking about how an appreciative inquiry can create change in social systems. These five are: (1) the social construction of reality, (2) the heliotropic hypothesis, (3) the organizational inner dialogue, (4) paradoxical dilemmas, and (5) appreciative process theories of change. He points out that each of these directs us to different ways of thinking about and implementing an Appreciative Inquiry when our purpose is developmental change. Further, he notes that the key data collection innovation of Appreciative Inquiry is the collection of people's stories of something at its best. He writes: "If we are interested in team development, we collect stories of people's best team experiences. If we are interested in the development of an organization, we ask about their peak experience in that organization. If enhanced leadership is our goal, we collect stories of leadership at its best. We need to embrace different ways of inquiring appreciatively while recognizing that for an OD intervention to be offered from an appreciative perspective, the whole process needs to reflect this articulated mindset."

Thus, one does not "do AI" for organization development; one does an organization intervention from an AI perspective. In addition, it is also essential to have a sense of the theoretical and research foundations underneath the DNA of AI—the soil out of which the five core principles, plus the principle of wholeness, and the five core generic processes emerge. The theoretical and research foundations for AI come from:

1. Social constructionist theory and practice

2. The new sciences (quantum physics, chaos theory, complexity theory, and self-organizing systems)

3. Research on the power of image

4. Research on the power of the positive

Standing on this foundation of theory, research and the "DNA building blocks" is the current practice of change in human systems from an AI perspective, that is, that constantly evolving set of steps and activities within each of the five generic processes (phases) that enable organizations to search and build upon the best of what is and to create a future focused on the best that can be.

Figure 3.1 shows how the "practice" of AI rests on the "DNA" of AI, which in turn emerges from the "soil" of AI.

With a good understanding of the five core principles, the additional principle of wholeness and the five generic core processes, AI practitioners can adapt and/or create appropriate steps and activities for using an AI approach in virtually any situation or context in which human beings play a key role. For example, there is a "case story" in this book about using an AI approach to a currently popular intervention models called "Six Sigma" and "LEAN." In that

## Figure 3.1. The Structure of AI

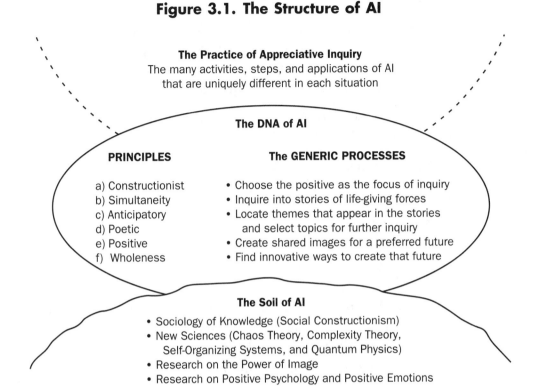

**The Practice of Appreciative Inquiry**
The many activities, steps, and applications of AI
that are uniquely different in each situation

**The DNA of AI**

**PRINCIPLES**                    **The GENERIC PROCESSES**

a) Constructionist          • Choose the positive as the focus of inquiry
b) Simultaneity             • Inquire into stories of life-giving forces
c) Anticipatory             • Locate themes that appear in the stories
d) Poetic                       and select topics for further inquiry
e) Positive                 • Create shared images for a preferred future
f) Wholeness                • Find innovative ways to create that future

**The Soil of AI**
• Sociology of Knowledge (Social Constructionism)
• New Sciences (Chaos Theory, Complexity Theory,
   Self-Organizing Systems, and Quantum Physics)
• Research on the Power of Image
• Research on Positive Psychology and Positive Emotions

example, the principles and practices described in this chapter are
applied to models of change management that are usually applied
from the perspective of a search for problems to be solved, while
the exact same process can be applied from an AI perspective with
a search for what works and creates new knowledge. Without
an understanding and translation of these principles into practice,
AI becomes just another tool or technique, thereby severely limiting
its power.

# The Core Principles of AI

## Are Principles Important?

While the 5-D cycle for applying Appreciative Inquiry is presented
here as a systematic approach to organization change, it is important

to understand that variations on or even alternatives to this model will inevitably emerge as each system takes the AI approach and makes it their own. Once grounded in the principles of AI, organizations inevitably become generative and creative, which leads to even more innovation in the application of AI.

In the original work of Appreciative Inquiry, five principles are articulated:

1. Constructionist

2. Anticipatory

3. Simultaneity

4. Poetic

5. Positive

The sixth, wholeness, was added later. (Several authors have added other principles to this list, but the one that almost all agree on is an overarching principle of Wholeness.) Following are brief descriptions of each of the principles.

## The Five Original Principles Plus Wholeness

**1. The Constructionist Principle.** An understanding and acceptance of the *social constructionist stance* toward reality and social knowledge, that is, that what we believe to be real in the world is created through our social discourse, through the conversations we have with each other that lead to agreement about how we will see the world, how we will behave, what we will accept as reality. *Knowledge and organizational destiny are interwoven; the way we know is fateful. Awareness of this concept enables change. We create what we can imagine.*

The Constructionist Principle states that knowledge about an organization and the destiny of that organization are interwoven. To be effective leaders in any situation, we must be skilled in the art of understanding, reading, and analyzing organizations as living, human constructions. What we believe to be real in the world is created through our social discourse, through conversations we have with each other that lead to agreement about how we will see the world, how we behave, what we accept as reality. The first task of any organization change process is Discovery—learning and making sense of what is believed and said about the system. Thus, the way we know *is* fateful.

**2. The Principle of Simultaneity.** A realization that inquiry is change, that the first question we ask is fateful in that the organization will turn its energy in the direction of that first question, whether positive or negative; and, as a result, the seeds of change are embedded in it. Inquiry is change! The seeds of change are embedded in the first questions we ask. The Principle of Simultaneity recognizes that inquiry and change are not separate moments, but are simultaneous. Inquiry is intervention. The seeds of change—that is, the things people think and talk about, the things people discover and learn, and the things that inform dialogue and inspire images of the future—are implicit in the very first questions we ask. One of the most impactful things a change agent does is to articulate questions. The questions we ask set the stage for what we "find," and what we "discover" creates the stories that lead to conversations about how the organization will construct its future.

**3. The Anticipatory Principal.** The impact of anticipatory images, that is, understanding that behavior and decisions about actions are based not only on what we were born with or learned from our environment, but also on what we anticipate, what we think or imagine will happen in the future. Habits of the collective imagination, habits of the mind, habits of the heart, guide images of the future. Images are relational, public property, dialogical. The Anticipatory Principle says that the most important resources we have for generating constructive organizational change or improvement are our collective imagination and our discourse about the future. It is the image of the future that in fact guides the current behavior of any person or organization. Much like a movie projector on a screen, human systems are forever projecting ahead of themselves a horizon of expectation that brings the future powerfully into the present as a mobilizing agent. Organizations exist, in the final analysis, because people who govern and maintain them share some sort of shared discourse or projection about what the organization is, how it will function, and what it is likely to become.

**4. The Poetic Principle.** A valuing of storytelling as a way of gathering holistic information that includes not only facts, but also the feelings and affect that a person experiences and the recognition that stories (like all good poetry) can be told and interpreted about any aspect of an organization's existence. An organization's past or present or future is an endless source of learning, inspiration, interpretation, and possibility. We can inquire into anything and any living human organization. The Poetic Principle acknowledges that human organizations are open books. An organization's story is constantly being co-authored by the people within the organization as well as by those outside who interact with it. The organization's past, present, and future are endless sources of learning, inspiration, or interpretation, just as a good poem is open to endless interpretations. The important point is that we can study any topic related to human experience in any human system. We can inquire into the nature of alienation or the nature of joy. We can study moments of creativity and innovation, or moments of debilitating stress. We have a choice!

**5. The Positive Principle.** A belief that a positive approach to any issue is just as valid as a basis for learning and that it is just as contagious as a negative approach, which makes taking the positive stance an antidote to cynicism. Positive affect is just as contagious as negative affect. There is power in positive questions; the affective side of transformation; the dynamic of hope. Positive and grounded inquiry is an antidote to cynicism. The Positive Principle grows out of years of experience with Appreciative Inquiry. Momentum for change requires large amounts of positive affect and social bonding—things like hope, inspiration, and sheer joy in creating with one another. AI demonstrates that the more positive the questions used to guide a group process or organizational change effort, the more long lasting and effective the change effort (Bushe & Coetzer, 1995; Gergen, 1995). Human beings and organizations move in the direction of what they inquire about. Widespread inquiry into "empowerment" or "being the best organization in the field", will have a whole different long term sustainable impact for positive action than a study into "low morale" or "process breakdowns" done with the idea that those conditions can be cured.

**6. The Overarching Principle of Wholeness.** Appreciative Inquiry, rooted as it is in that which is strong and positive, leads to a "new manner of thinking." AI unleashes the imagination and provides a process for human beings to join together and experience the idea that "Wholes precede parts!" as articulated in the book *Presence: An Exploration of Profound Changes in People, Organizations, and Society* (Senge, Scharmer, Jaworski, & Flowers, 2005).

Speaking of Albert Einstein, one writer noted: "He marveled at magnetic fields, gravity, inertia and light beams. 'Something deeply hidden had to be behind things,' he said. He retained the ability to hold two thoughts in his mind simultaneously, to be puzzled when they conflicted and to delight when he saw an underlying unity."

The challenge of these times is for each of us to realize that what we label dichotomous is caused by our limited ability to realize that what we see in parts is always some small piece of a larger whole, and that it is our choice about whether to see the part or to embrace the whole.

For example: We want to play a game of football, a sport known for being highly competitive. So we go to an agreed-on location; we suit up in agreed-on gear; we locate an agreed-on ball; and we play a game by agreed-on rules and regulations. Is this a "competitive" process? Or a cooperative one? To have a football game, cooperation and competition are part of a whole, essential to the game's success.

Further, to understand "wholes" and realize that "wholes" precede parts, we might reflect that we are not born a piece at a time. We arrive in the world with everything attached to everything else. It is possible for us to learn to hold dichotomous ideas in our heads at the same time (a process that Don Beck calls "second tier thinking" in Spiral Dynamics theory) and we can come to see the world anew. We can approach these seeming differences with an "Isn't that interesting!" approach in place of an "I don't agree with that" framework.

Appreciative Inquiry is all about "wholes":

- Getting the whole system involved in imagining their preferred future

- Getting all voices in the system into the room

That is the challenge for an AI consultant—to help organizations begin to understand the interconnectedness of every part of the organization and to see it as an interconnected whole.

> "With Appreciative Inquiry, it becomes apparent that what we defined as 'problems' can be resolved by looking forward toward a dreamed-of future rather than by looking backward to what was broken and needed fixing. It helps us understand that human systems are different from mechanical systems, and that the way forward is not by becoming the admired leader; rather, it is by empowering all of human kind to tap into their gifts and talents together 'to create not just new worlds, but better worlds?'"
>
> David Cooperrider from the film "Fusion of Strengths."

## Example: Principles as Guidelines for Organizing

example

In the late 1990s a group of twenty-two AI practitioners began to meet regularly to explore the possibility of creating an organization based on a clear statement of purpose and a set of organizational principles to guide the work of the organization. The organization, Appreciative Inquiry Consulting, is an experiment in creating a global organization that operates as a loose confederation of people and groups who practice AI and are united in the purpose and principles of the organization. It took the group of twenty-two over two years of regular meetings to create this document and to formulate organization structure and form to fit this purpose and these principles. It is a model that other organizations are now beginning to adopt. Below is the list that, while it may seem simple

example

and easy to new readers, was a long and dialogue-filled process that led to agreement and enthusiasm in the founding group.

### Appreciative Inquiry Consulting

*Purpose and Principles*

**AI Consulting Purpose:** Our purpose is to create a positive revolution in change by using Appreciative Inquiry (AI) to engage the "positive core" of all people and all living systems and to expand that rich potential, creating organizations that are themselves agents of world benefit.

## Principles of Co-Ownership

1. *Advancement of AI:* At the heart of the co-ownership is a commitment to the conceptual and practical advancement of Appreciative Inquiry including its constructionist, scientific, and spiritual foundations.

2. *Transformational Organizations:* Co-owners in AI Consulting commit to the development of organizations, industries, and individuals working in a positively correlated way toward a future of (1) sustainable economic enterprise; (2) human and ecological prosperity; and (3) a global awakening of the heart to the kinds of life-giving ways of being, relating, and doing that we believe our world is calling us to express. Co-owners in AI Consulting are committed to noticing, connecting, and combining the transformational energies they see in the world and advancing significant work of enduring consequence.

3. *Creative Synergies:* As a community we realize that AI is in a constant state of evolution and as long as the "inquiry" part of AI is alive it will continue to break new ground. Therefore, as a community we constantly seek creative links and synergies with related and diverse approaches that share in the search for new frontiers of positive change.

4. *Generosity and Entrepreneurship:* Co-owners in AI Consulting advance our shared purpose in ways that enhance the capacity of the whole, as well as each owner. We work in

the spirit of generosity, creative excellence, and individual entrepreneurship. We practice the highest level of collaboration, mutual support, and transparency.

5. *Spirited Learning Community:* AI Consulting is a spirited learning and sharing community in which co-owners dare to help each other think and dream in new ways, to acquire new knowledge and skills, and to advance the state of the art of positive change. High-quality work is ensured and advanced through high-quality learning, research, action, and writing.

6. *Sharing Learning:* Each co-owner in AI Consulting is committed to share with the whole—information, knowledge, or materials—that will enhance the quality of learning and practice of the other co-owners while honoring client desires for confidentiality.

7. *Promoting the Individual and Collective Good:* Co-owners in AI Consulting believe in building trust and transparency into each member and client relationship. We understand trust to be sincerity, competence, and reliability. It manifests as a profound concern for the good of the whole and for individual entrepreneurial freedom. We see the world as a place of abundance and are committed to presuming and treating each other with good intentions.

8. *Integrity:* Each co-owner maintains the highest standards of integrity and seeks an increasingly higher quality of AI practice. We are committed to delivering on what we promise, saying what we mean, doing what we say, and staying in dialogue about the meaning of integrity.

9. *Acknowledgement:* Co-owners in AI Consulting support one another's creativity and profitability in terms of new product development, while simultaneously fostering a wide sharing of the new creations by referencing and acknowledging the work and contributions of others.

10. *Co-Ownership:* Co-ownership in AI Consulting is open to all AI practitioners, organizations, and associations that fully

*example*

subscribe to the purpose and principles and demonstrate the commitment and learning to pursue them constructively. Each member is committed to developing personally and organizationally the highest level of excellence in AI theory and practice.

11. *Freedom to Organize:* When co-owners are representing themselves as a centre of AI Consulting, they are empowered to organize and do business in any manner, at any scale, in any area, and around any priority that is relevant to and consistent with the purpose and principles.

12. *Local Authority and Decision Making:* Authority is vested in and decisions are made at the most local level possible that includes the relevant parties. Decisions are deliberated and made at every level by bodies and methods that represent a diversity of voices and are not dominated by any single view.

13. *Autonomy and Resources:* Every part of AI Consulting surrenders only such autonomy and resources as are essential at the governing level of the whole in pursuit of the purpose and principles.

14. *Support of AI Writing and Theory:* AI Consulting is committed to make linkages and support students, researchers, and scholarly practitioners making next generation advances in AI writing and theory. We recognize that there is nothing quite so practical as a good theory and theory building warrants mindful attention. We are committed to building, publishing, and disseminating new theories that reflect and inspire innovative practice.

15. *Honoring Diverse Voices, Languages, and Cultures:* We honor the richness of diversity and support the right and responsibility of co-owners around the world to translate and interpret the charter, bylaws, and related documents in accordance with the purpose and principles, and the spirit of AI Consulting.

16. *Living AI: Humility as Our Strength:* We realize, with a profound sense of humility and a stance of ongoing curiosity, that we are just beginning to understand the enormously rich potential of appreciative ways of knowing, relating, and changing. In this spirit, we are committed to the Gandhian principle: "We must become the change we wish to see in the world." This organization is still in existence and open to all who agree with the Purpose and Principles.

For further information, go to: www.AIConsulting.org.

The question arises: "What will organizations that are aligned with AI Principles and practices look like?" Some of the answers to that question have emerged over the past decade, and as we approach the next decade, it is apparent that the speed of change in organizations is accelerating given the rapid development of new forms of technology and communication. The following list highlights some observable changes that are already taking place. And the list is continually evolving at accelerating speed!

**New Paradigm Organizations**

1. *Multi-locational:* The global organization will be at least multi, and sometimes "non" locational. Coordinating units will take the place of "Headquarters" and may move about as required.

2. *Shared leadership:* Leadership is a function, not a position. People step forward to assume leadership when it is needed and appropriate to their skills and interest. Areas of expertise are clearly identified and opportunities to expand roles and expertise are provided when possible. Traditional roles such as "director" are selected in a collaborative environment and are often rotational.

3. *High tech/high touch communications:* Global organizations will depend on electronic technologies for communication, doing their work through e-mail, fax, phone conferencing and teleconferencing. Large amounts of the budget are used for travel, meeting, and electronic communications to ensure collaboration and partnership at every level.

4. *Partnerships and alliances:* Global organizations have multiple cooperative arrangements not only for programming and program delivery, but also for mutual learning, shared physical space and facilities, representational activities (that is, one person attends a conference for several organizations and reports back).

5. *Learning organizations:* Global organizations are continuous and self-conscious learners. They embrace the changing rate of change and set up flexible systems and plans to accommodate change as required by circumstances, additional data, etc. They constantly study their work and develop grounded theory about their field and their work processes. They give adequate time to share what they are learning and factor new knowledge and theory into their ongoing projects and processes.

6. *Task competent; process focused:* Global organizations are made up of people highly skilled not only in their areas of expertise, but also in the human processes of organizing and work. A high priority is given to communication skills and the ability to work together for win-win solutions.

7. *Values and vision centered:* Finally, global organizations are held together by the power and clarity of their shared values and vision. Tasks change, transform themselves, multiply, all in harmony with the values and vision agreed on by the organization's community at large—staff and stakeholders at every level.

These are some of the ideas that we have explored and observed. We have also observed that change these days is rapid beyond documentation. It is certain that what seems true in one moment is likely to be different in the next. The purpose of these observations is to encourage each of our readers to embrace this process of fascination with the changes that are happening and to track the content of such changes.

Once grounded in the purpose and principles of Appreciative Inquiry, the next step is to understand shifts in the ways that human systems organize and thrive and to develop flexible ways of being and thinking that enable people and organizations to ride the waves of change at constantly accelerating speeds! It is abundantly clear that mechanistic models will no longer be able to survive. In the next part of this chapter, we will introduce some existing and some past ideas about organizations and how they change, examining the theory and methods in ways that enable you to dismiss, adapt, or adopt as appropriate to the rapidly changing times in which we are living.

## The Five Generic Core Processes for Guiding AI-Based Change

In partnership with the core principles of Appreciative Inquiry are several popular processes for working with organizations and other human systems. We call these the other half of the DNA of AI and begin with what we call "the five generic core processes for applying AI as a framework for organizational change." We use the term "generic processes" very intentionally—as a way of drawing attention to the essence of what AI is about while also emphasizing the flexibility of these processes. The five generic processes are:

1. Focus on the positive as a core value;

2. Inquire into stories of life-giving forces;

3. Locate themes in the stories and select topics from the themes for further inquiry;

4. Create shared images for a preferred future; and

5. Innovate ways to create that preferred future.

The limitations of this medium for communication (books and the written word) impose certain constraints on our description of the core processes. For example, for ease of comprehension, we have listed them above in a linear, sequential format. But in the world of client work the core processes don't begin and end neatly. Instead, they overlap and repeat themselves without predictability, which is another reason that we emphasize so much the importance of being grounded in the theory, research, and principles of AI as you begin translating these core processes into practice. A somewhat more descriptive view of the five core AI processes is shown in Figure 3.2. Each process is part of a larger whole. Each process overlaps with other process. Chapters 4, 5, 6, 7, and 8 describe some of the kinds of things that happen in each of these processes.

### Figure 3.2. The Five Core Processes of AI

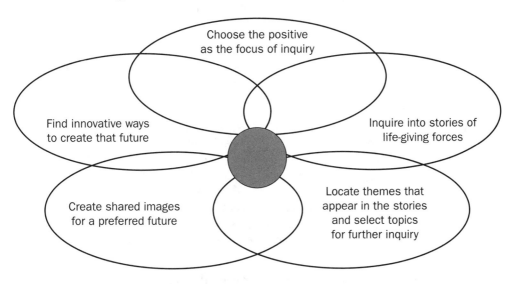

## Multiple Models of the Five Generic Core Processes of AI

In fact, these generic processes have already taken on the form of "AI process models" (the 5-D model, the 4-I model, the original AI model, etc.). Each of these existing "process models" draws attention to different parts of the five generic processes in a way that is helpful in seeing the variations that are possible.

### The Original Cooperrider/Srivastva Model

When first introduced (Cooperrider & Srivastva, 1987) this "model" was part of the transition from thinking about AI as purely an

## Figure 3.3. Dimensions of Appreciative Inquiry

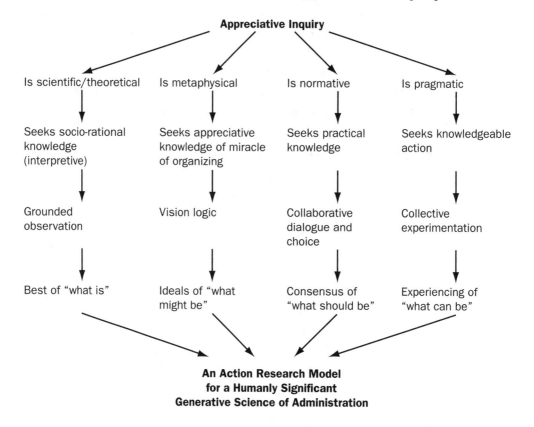

approach to the building of generative theory to thinking about AI more directly as a process for intervening in and changing organizations. The model is shown in Figure 3.3.

This same model was later depicted more explicitly as an AI process model in a way that also served to contrast what Cooperrider and Srivastva called Paradigm 1 action research versus their Paradigm 2 model. In Paradigm 1 the root metaphor is "the organization as a problem to be solved." In Paradigm 2 the root metaphor is "the organization as a mystery to be embraced."

The two contrasting processes are shown in Figure 3.4. Also in the early days of expanding the theory of AI to apply to organization change processes, Cooperrider created an overview of the process

that remains even today as a comprehensive depiction
of the whole of AI theory and practice.

**Figure 3.4. Two Contrasting Processes for Organizational Change**

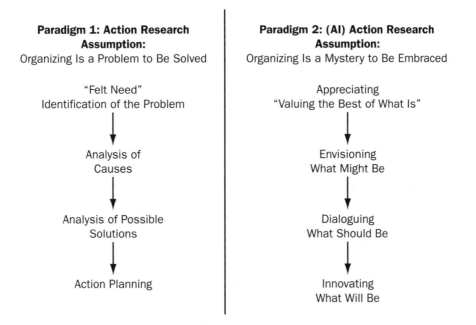

| Paradigm 1: Action Research Assumption: Organizing Is a Problem to Be Solved | Paradigm 2: (AI) Action Research Assumption: Organizing Is a Mystery to Be Embraced |
|---|---|
| "Felt Need" Identification of the Problem | Appreciating "Valuing the Best of What Is" |
| Analysis of Causes | Envisioning What Might Be |
| Analysis of Possible Solutions | Dialoguing What Should Be |
| Action Planning | Innovating What Will Be |

## The GEM Initiative Four-D Model

The Four "D" model (Discover, Dream, Design, Deliver) began as
a sequence of sentences that described the phases of an AI process.
Ada Jo Mann and David Cooperrider were working on a GEM
Initiative project in Zimbabwe when they realized that the
complexity of the language in describing the steps of the AI planning
process was confusing for some of the participants. In place of the
long explanatory sentences, Ada Jo suggested the 4 D's as a more
comprehensible process that would work better in their projects
around the globe where English, if spoken at all, is a "second
language."

The 4-Ds became the "gold standard" as the most comprehensible
way to use AI as a perspective for organization change processes.
Based closely on Kurt Lewin's "action research" model that focused

on the problems and deficits in a system that needed to be "solved," the 4-D model (shown in Figure 3.5) launched what has become a global phenomenon—action research from an appreciative and positive perspective!

### Figure 3.5. The GEM Initiative's 4-D Model

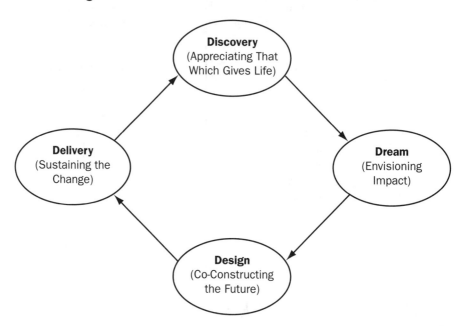

## A Fifth D—Define

Sometime after the publication of the first edition of this book, we began to add a fifth D to the traditional 4-D Model. The fifth D—Define—describes the first process that consultants and other AI practitioners use to clarify what in traditional OD is called the "contracting" phase—that time when the consultant negotiates with the client about what they want to have happen and how they will proceed; who will be involved; and other details required to have a clear understanding of roles and responsibilities in the project. By adding this Define stage to the 4-D model, we ensured that the preparation and planning for the project would be seen as an integral part of the overall process.

Following is a description of each of the tasks in each circle of the "traditional" Four D's. (The Define stage is discussed in detail in Chapter 4; Discover in Chapters 5 and 6; Dream in Chapter 7; and Deliver in Chapter 8.)

**Discover (Appreciating That Which Gives Life).** The core task of the *discover* phase (or process) in this model is to appreciate the best of "what is" by focusing on times of organizational excellence when people have experienced the organization as most alive and effective. In order to understand the unique factors that made the high points in an organization possible, people deliberately let go of analysis of deficits and carefully inquire into and learn from even the smallest examples of high performance, success, and satisfaction. They tell stories about all aspects of their organization—inspired leadership; generative relationships and partnerships; technologies that make work go more smoothly or facilitate better service; structures that support innovation and creativity; planning that encompasses new ideas and diverse people; opportunities to learn; and so on.

In the discover phase of the model people share stories of exceptional accomplishments, discuss the core life-giving factors of their organizations, and deliberate upon the aspects of their organization's history that they most value and want to bring to the future. Members come to know their organization's *history as positive possibility* rather than a static, problematized, eulogized, romanticized, or forgotten set of events.

**Dream (Envisioning Impact).** The dream phase involves challenging the status quo by envisioning a preferred future for the organization. This is the time when the organization's stakeholders engage in possibility conversations about the organization's position, its potential, its calling, and the unique contribution it can make to global well-being. For many, this is the first time they have been invited to think great thoughts and create great possibilities for their organization. As the various stories of the organization's history are shared and illuminated, a new historical narrative emerges, one that engages those involved in re-creating the organization's positive history which, in turn, gives life to its positive future. Thus, the dream phase is both practical, in that it is grounded in the organization's history; and generative, in that it seeks to expand the organization's potential. As images of the future emerge out of grounded examples from its positive past, compelling possibilities emerge precisely because they are based on extraordinary moments from the organization's history.

By creating possibility statements that make clear the shared visions for the organization's future, there is created a beacon, a set of unique statements that paint a picture of the group's vision of the organization's most desired future.

**Design (Co-Constructing the Future).** The design phase includes the creation of the social architecture of the organization and the generation of *possibility statements* that articulate the organization's dreams in ongoing activities. These two processes ensure that everything about the organization reflects and is responsive to the shared vision of the organization's future created in the dream phase.

As stakeholders create the organization's social architecture, they are defining the basic infrastructure. Constructing an organization requires careful consideration and widespread dialogue about what the structure and the processes of the organization will be. Possibilities for the organization are raised by the kinds of questions asked: What kind of leadership structure is needed and what is the preferred behavior of the leaders as they do their work? What is the organization's strategy and how does will it be formulated and carried out? What are all of the structure elements needed?

Once there is agreement on the myriad possibilities for structuring the organization and an image of how they will function in relationship to the each other and to the organization as a whole, the task of the group is to articulate those decisions in possibility statements. These statements make explicit the desired qualities and behaviors that will enable each part of the organization to function in a way that moves it toward the higher visions articulated in the dream phase.

This creation of the social and technical architecture of the organization and aligning it with the overall organizational vision insures that everything about organizing reflects and is responsive to the dream. Both the dream phase and the design phase involve the collective construction of positive images of the future. In practice the two often happen in conjunction with each other.

**Deliver (Sustaining the Change).** The final phase creates ways to deliver on the new images of the future, both the overall visions of the dream phase and the more specific possibility statements of the design phase. It is a time of continuous learning, adjustment, and improvisation, much like a jazz group, all in the service of shared ideals. The momentum and potential for innovation are extremely high by this stage of inquiry. Because of the shared positive images, everyone is included in co-creating the future.

The deliver phase is ongoing. In the best case, it is full of continuing dialogue; revisited and updated possibility discussions and statements; additional interviewing sessions, especially with new members of the organization; and a high level of innovation and continued learning about what it means to create an organization that is socially constructed through poetic processes in a positive frame that makes full use of people's anticipatory images.

Over the years since the 4-D model emerged, others have created innovative processes and ideas for ways to work from an AI perspective. Below is an alternative model as an example of the kind of innovation and creativity that is an integral part of what we refer to as "living" AI.

## The Mohr/Jacobsgaard Four "I" Model

In addition, to demonstrate the flexibility and innovation encouraged in AI, we have included one of the many models for practicing AI that are being created and used by practitioners and leaders around the world. The 4-I model is an example of how Appreciative Inquiry can be adapted and used in a wide variety of models and approaches, affirming the fact that AI is a perspective and theory rather than a prescribed "model."

As with the development of the four "D" model, it was the need to create something in the field which would fit a certain situation that led to the development of the four "I" model (Initiate, Inquire, Imagine, Innovate). During an advanced NTL Institute AI workshop (a field practicum) Bernard Mohr and Mette Jacobsgaard found themselves asking two questions:

1. "How can we graphically highlight the critical phase of foundation building—the work of educating the client system so they make an informed choice about proceeding with AI as well as the work of putting into place the necessary management structures to support the change process and also of course the fateful choice of inquiry focus and topics?"

2. "How can we graphically spotlight the terribly important phase of moving from the dreams and provocative propositions to reconnecting and modifying the socio-technical architecture of the organization to bring the dream and propositions to life?"

Mohr and Jacobsgaard were also concerned with the need of the "client managers" (with whom the program participants were working) to have language in the model which spoke to their experience of "initiating" something and the need of the "consultants" (the program participants that we were training) to have a model that covered all key processes of an AI-based change effort. The model they created is shown in Figure 3.6.

All the models have within them the core processes of AI. Each of the models emphasizes something a bit different, depending on the context in which they were created.

## Figure 3.6. The Mohr/Jacobsgaard Four-I Model

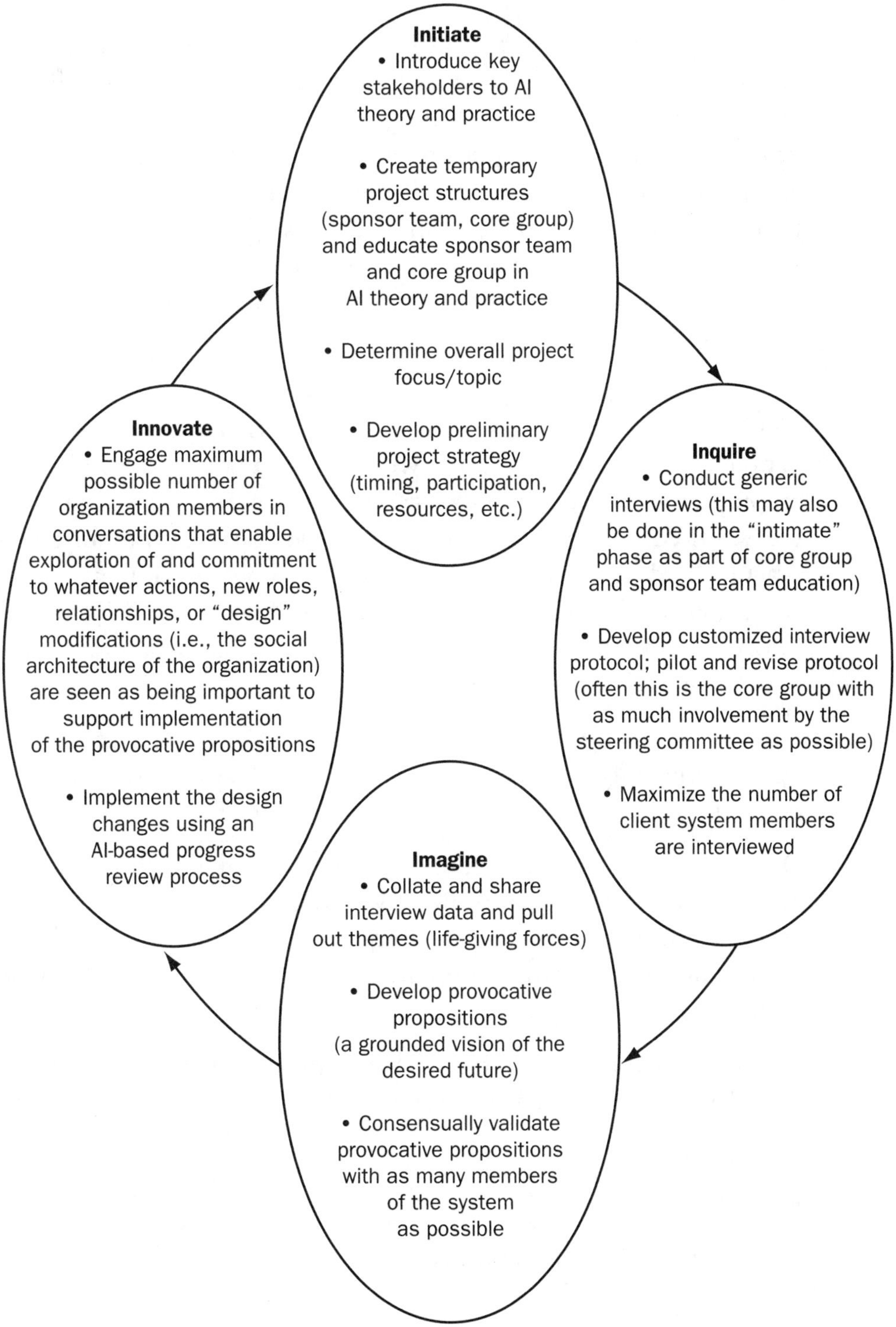

**Initiate**
- Introduce key stakeholders to AI theory and practice

- Create temporary project structures (sponsor team, core group) and educate sponsor team and core group in AI theory and practice

- Determine overall project focus/topic

- Develop preliminary project strategy (timing, participation, resources, etc.)

**Innovate**
- Engage maximum possible number of organization members in conversations that enable exploration of and commitment to whatever actions, new roles, relationships, or "design" modifications (i.e., the social architecture of the organization) are seen as being important to support implementation of the provocative propositions

- Implement the design changes using an AI-based progress review process

**Inquire**
- Conduct generic interviews (this may also be done in the "intimate" phase as part of core group and sponsor team education)

- Develop customized interview protocol; pilot and revise protocol (often this is the core group with as much involvement by the steering committee as possible)

- Maximize the number of client system members are interviewed

**Imagine**
- Collate and share interview data and pull out themes (life-giving forces)

- Develop provocative propositions (a grounded vision of the desired future)

- Consensually validate provocative propositions with as many members of the system as possible

## Skills and Knowledge Needed to Lead AI Processes

Once practitioners grasp the idea that AI is not a method in the traditional OD sense, it becomes clear that they need solid skills in experiential education methodologies and in organization development theory and practice, as well as in-depth knowledge about and experience in the field of human behavior and group process. This kind of skill and knowledge is critical for those who want to use AI in their practice since a major characteristic of an AI intervention is that it is co-created with the client. There is no AI "cookbook"!

We do not mean to imply that AI can be used only by long-time, highly skilled practitioners. Indeed, one of the wonders of AI is that people can begin to experiment with its use after only a small amount of exposure to the theory and practice. However, in order to use AI for complex systems change, we have learned from our own practices and from participants who come to our consultant training workshops that those with a broad range of consulting skills and long experience with OD practice will be more likely to undertake large-scale change projects using AI.

In response to participants in our workshops who asked what training they might want or need to equip them to use AI as the basis of their practice, we created the following chart.

Our thoughts here are intended to provide useful guidelines for the professional development of those wishing to work as facilitators and practitioners in Appreciative Inquiry. We see these guidelines as evergreen—always a work in progress, as we all gain more experience with this evolving practice.

We might usefully differentiate between professional development at three levels. These we have named:

- AI Facilitators;

- AI Practitioners, and

- AI Meta-Practitioners/Trainers

## Role Definition: AI Facilitator

AI facilitators are internal staff or line people whose development could come from internal two-to-five-day workshops conducted by AI practitioners. AI facilitators are folks who would work collaboratively *under the guidance of an internal or external AI practitioner or meta-practitioner.*

## Competencies for This Role

After a workshop, AI facilitators would be comfortable in:

a. Co-facilitating (with an AI practitioner) the development of customized protocols;

b. Conducting interviews;

c. Co-facilitating (with an AI practitioner) the writing of Provocative propositions;

d. Co-facilitating (with an AI practitioner) for members of their organization, a variety of large group processes for systemic/structural changes (as needed).

## Role Definition: AI Practitioner

AI practitioners are "consultants" (internal or external, either in staff or line management roles) who are competent at guiding client systems through the whole appreciative inquiry process, including:

- Advising the client on how/where to get started;

- Conducting training of internal facilitators/ interviewers;

## Competencies for This Role

AI practitioners function best when they are comfortable in the following areas:

1. Competence in articulating the concepts and research behind:

   a. Social constructionism;

   b. Image-action connection;

   c. Role of language and inquiry in image creation;

   d. People and organizations as mysteries to be embraced;

   e. The emerging paradigm as context for AI;

- Working with internal teams in topic selection and protocol development; and

- Co-designing with the client a variety of processes for consensual validation, processes for redesigning the systems and structures of the organization to support the propositions, etc.

f. A wide range of AI "applications" (e.g., strategic planning, organization and business process design, quality improvement, career counseling, mergers and acquisitions, team building, diversity initiatives, evaluation etc.).

2. Competence in coaching clients in the following Appreciative Inquiry processes:

a. Identifying topics (life-giving forces) from generic interviews;

b. Crafting customized protocol AI questions;

c. Conducting interviews;

d. Identifying themes from the customized protocol interviews as prelude to PPs;

e. Writing provocative propositions (PPs);

f. Consensual validation and possibilities for expanding appreciative conversations throughout the system;

g. Innovating the sociotechnical architecture of the organization (the structures, roles, processes and systems) so as to support and help bring to life the PPs; and

h. Helping the system to build ongoing internal capability.

3. Competence in collaborative skills:

   a. Experiential Education;

   b. Use of self as instrument (being personally congruent with AI theory);

   c. Contracting/client relations/project management; and

   e. Integration of AI with large group/interactive methods (e.g., Open Space, Future Search, Whole System Design, etc.).

| Role Definition: Meta-Practitioner | Competencies for This Role |
|---|---|
| Meta practitioners/ trainers of practitioners are people who can run extended in-depth professional development events. | In addition to the proficiency in the same areas as a practitioner, a meta-practitioner would typically: <br><br> a. Have extensive experience in a variety of AI applications and settings; <br><br> b. Be actively participating in an ongoing forum for peer consultation and development during the course of whole system AI change processes; and <br><br> c. Be steeped in the theory and research, models of practice and what is going on worldwide in this field. |

During the decade since the first edition of this book appeared, we have learned much about what people need and want in order to feel competent to use AI in their work internally in organizations or as consultants to groups and organizations.

First, there is now a certification process established by the NTL Institute of Applied Behavioral Science and Case Western's School of Organization Behavior. This program has trained and certified a large number of AI practitioners equipping them to be not only master practitioners, but also to be able to train others in the skills and knowledge needed to become master practitioners.

Second, we have also learned that there are skills required by the changing environment in which we live and work. The following ideas come from the final chapter written by Jane Watkins in *Practicing OD* (2009).

## Competencies Needed in OD Consulting Today

In a world where, according to Einstein, "our technology has exceeded our humanity," it becomes the job of OD Consultants to help human beings in organizations "acquire a new manner of thinking." If OD Consultants heed the warnings of Einstein, there are important competencies that must be added to the traditional human relations skills of well trained OD practitioners. These competencies include:

1. OD Consulting in the Post-Modern Era requires consultants to have a deep understanding of the phenomena of wholeness— the intimate connectedness of every part of the organization. Consultants need the ability to examine and challenge their own assumptions about their work and about how human systems really function. They must, themselves, shift from traditional beliefs in dichotomous reality and the idea that we can study "parts" of a system, to an understanding of the concept of "whole systems," interconnected in complex ways that make it impossible to change one part of the system without affecting the whole.

2. OD Consultants need to know how to transfer that knowledge of wholeness to the clients so that they, too, understand the

impact of their individual actions on the whole; and, further, to understand that an intervention in any one part of the organization will ripple out to affect all other parts. This understanding on the part of those in the organization will lead to greater collaboration and stronger commitment to each other as they observe and learn from the impact of their own behavior on multiple parts of the organization.

3. OD Consultants need to know how to enable people within the system to develop the skills needed to help their own organizations become high performing, interconnected systems and to empower the people in the system to create ways of working creatively and effectively in an environment of continuous and accelerating change. It is essential that the people within the organization feel ownership for the process of managing continuous change. The consultant's task is to empower the system to know itself and to trust that by seeking to identify the strengths and the positive core of their enterprise, they will collectively imagine and then create their best possible future.

4. OD Consulting in the Post-Modern Era requires that consultants themselves have the capacity to engage multiple ideas and possibilities without judging, and the ability to facilitate the development of that capacity in those with whom they work.

5. OD Consulting in the Post-Modern Era requires that consultants step aside as clients develop the understanding, skills and abilities to function creatively and independent of outside guidance. Ideally, the OD Consultant facilitates the process so the role of consultant is almost invisible.

6. Finally, in this Post-Modern Era, as in the past, OD requires that consultants understand and act congruently with the values and beliefs that are reflected in the theory and practice of Organization Development. From its inception, OD has focused on helping consultants understand themselves and

the impact of their behavior on the groups with whom they consult. It is from the consultants "way of being" that client systems are able to observe, learn from, and eventually emulate the behavior of the consultant through an experiential learning process. Master OD consultants are the embodiment of the kind of behavior needed to facilitate and empower the people of an organization to become successful change agents within their own systems.

With these competencies, OD Consultants can move easily into complex and daunting situations comfortable in the knowledge that within any system there resides all of the knowledge and expertise needed to create a successful enterprise.

As we continue to participate in the spread of AI theory and practice, we all share the challenge of making this work, this thinking, accessible to many without either trivializing it or making it overly complex.

We assume that all initiatives that people undertake to alter, develop, or in some way shift their world, have, in their beginning stages, some form of "data gathering"—that is, some form of collecting information about the current status or functioning of the system which we are seeking to alter, develop or change in some way. In AI, we refer to this data gathering as "inquiry." Within the framework of Appreciative Inquiry, the "data" which is gathered comes in the form of stories from people in the system since we hold the dual assumptions that: (1) people in the system are able to provide the richest responses to our questions and (2) the very act of asking and answering the questions begins to shift the system in the direction of the questions asked. Master AI Consultants are comfortable with the idea that this work is "Not about me!"

*case story*

# Using the SOAR Framework at Aerospace Alliant International (AAI)

*By Jacqueline M. Stavros*

## Focus of the Appreciative Inquiry

Strategic planning (SOAR framework), cultural transformation, and alignment were the focus of the AI. (SOAR is the AI version of the traditional SWOT analysis of Strengths, Weaknesses, Opportunities, Threats.)

## Case Overview

SOAR is a profoundly positive framework used for strategic thinking, dialoging, and analyzing that allows a person, team, or organization to create a strategy and/or strategic plan to construct its future through collaboration, shared understanding, and a commitment to action. SOAR stands for Strengths, Opportunities, Aspirations, and Results.

In this case study, the SOAR framework integrates Appreciative Inquiry (AI) 5-D process (Define, Discovery, Dream, Design, and Destiny) and an AI Summit to create a successful transformation process when a U.S. organization was acquired by a large European organization. As you have learned in this book, AI is one of today's most successful organization development and change philosophies that engages the whole system in shaping the organization's future for change and builds on the life-giving forces of the organization (also referred to as the positive core). This organization combined the SOAR framework with the AI 5-D approach because it provided in the midst of an acquisition a "cooperative evolutionary search for the best in people, their organization, and the relevant world around them" (Cooperrider, Whitney, & Stavros, 2008, p. 1).

## Client Organization

Aerospace Alliant International (AAI) Division (formerly a U.S.-based company of 6,100 employees with revenues over $1.2 billion) was acquired by a global aerospace organization with over 88,000 employees and $25 billion in revenues.

case story

## Client Objectives

This story started with the divisional general manager, who was very familiar with AI but also searching for a specific approach where the AI 5-D process could be applied to create a whole-system strengths-based strategic management process and strategic plan for the recently acquired AAI division.

The organization development (OD) manager knew about the SOAR framework and AI, so he suggested to the general management that they use the SOAR framework with the AI 5-D process. Another member from the management team had recently seen a video of how the U.S. Navy had successfully applied AI 4-D process to build leadership at all levels (visit the AI Commons at http://appreciativeinquiry.cwru.edu). This U.S. Navy project resonated with the organization because the U.S. Navy is one of their major customers. The leadership team hoped to bring the strengths and a proposed strategy of the acquired AAI division to the parent organization, and the SOAR framework seemed like a good strategic fit to create a strategic growth plan that brings the division in alignment with corporate. At the time, the general manager said:

> "Let's have a pilot program first like the U.S. Navy. If it succeeds, then we will apply it to the entire division. We are not good at strategic planning; we are great at execution and especially at fire-fighting. Let's call this a strategic growth plan, not a strategic plan."

The metaphor and language of the SOAR framework was a fresh positive approach to traditional strategic planning that used SWOT. The acquisition already experienced a lot of negativity and the acquired division felt threatened by the acquisition. SWOT looks at strengths, weakness, opportunities, and threats. The AAI employees' energy had been drained by the whole acquisition process and they wanted a strategic planning process that would create positive momentum to identify strengths and opportunities that would align with the corporate vision and mission plus produce results, rather than dwell on the problems, weaknesses, and threats. The SOAR framework does not ignore weaknesses and threats;

instead, "they are reframed and given the appropriate focus within the opportunities and results conversation" (Stavros & Hinrichs, 2009, p. 13).

## What Was Done

A pilot program was assigned to the program manager of Vehicle Maintenance Series (VMS) program. The VMS program manager, OD manager, and an external consultant created a core strategic growth team that laid out a four-phase plan connecting to the SOAR framework and following the AI 5-D process:

Four Phase Plan: Plan → Implement → Plan a Strategic Growth Summit →

## Implement the Strategic Growth Summit

### Discovery Phase

Thirteen VMS leaders participated in a three-day strategic leadership meeting to define and initiate the process and carry out the "discovery phase" of AI through the lens of the SOAR framework. The focus was the VMS business. Thirty-five interviews were completed with key stakeholders: executives, program managers, business development, functional managers (human resources, controllers, engineering, operations), and customers. The main objective was to gather information in the form of stories to develop a five-year strategic growth plan that would include the major areas for growth and competitive advantage. The strategic discovery phase started with strengths-based possibility questions:

### Strengths: What can we build on?

Q. What are current vehicle maintenance systems strengths?

Q. What are the strengths of our current program management group? Please share a story.

### Opportunities: What are our stakeholders asking for?

Q. Is there an innovative way to convert our systems to non-surface-based usage? How can you imagine this to be done? Create a story of how this can be.

case story

*case story*

Q.  How do we expand our business base with new customers/new businesses?

Q.  How can our technologies be expanded?

Q.  What new opportunities might we consider to develop/grow our business? If we achieved these opportunities what would it look like?

## Aspirations: What do we care deeply about?

Q.  What can we do different in business development to increase our market share in five years?

Q.  What do you do to ensure customer satisfaction and engagement while we embark on an aggressive growth plan?

Q.  We have a lean organization; how do we continue this organization as we grow?

Q.  What do we want to be? What do our customers want us to be? What new capabilities do we need?

## Results: How do we know we are succeeding?

Q.  In order to achieve what we and our customers desire (major goals), how will this team need to be different?

Q.  How do we improve the leverage that we have in our own supply base to achieve optimal results?

The VMS program used responses to these questions to identify core capabilities, opportunities, and the most preferred future. These responses also helped to further develop a value set, current mission (clear and compelling purpose), goals, and guiding principles from which to best operate. A values set and mission statement were co-created, as follows:

## Core Values

We...

- Maintain the highest standards of integrity and ethical behaviors

- Exceed customers' and shareholders' expectations

*case story*

- Promote individual and team responsibility
- Value each other, our common mission, and our individuality
- Commit to individual and organizational excellence through continuous improvement
- Work safely, effectively, and efficiently while maintaining environmental responsibility
- Enjoy the interaction of working together to achieve our goals

These values demonstrated what the organization most values in its internal stakeholders. It defines the expected behaviors and culture. Then mission was co-defined:

*Mission:* We are the recognized premier global vehicle maintenance system supplier because we provide innovative and integrated solutions that meet customer requirements with on-time delivery at the lowest achievable costs.

The mission is "what" the organization is all about and what it does to best serve its customers.

The team decided to create guiding principles to support the value set and mission:

- Empowerment
- Act on all ideas—accept ideas from anyone
- Innovation-to-reality roadmap
- Innovation in all aspects of the business
- Entrepreneurship
- Risk management

These principles became the substance of everyday interaction in a highly dynamic global work environment virtually over numerous sites. This formed the intentionality, feedback, and daily teaming that cause this group to execute so extraordinarily. The performance development structure supports them by measuring performance to objectives daily.

## Dream and Design Phases

The dream phase co-created the following vision:

> *Vision:* We will strive to be the premier innovator of vehicle maintenance systems solutions for a sustainable world.

An overarching strategic goal was also defined in support of the vision: to be the premier global vehicle maintenance systems supplier and go from $100M to $200M in sales by 2015.

The design phase occurred in a three-day AI summit with cross-functional stakeholders from six operational units. An AI summit is a three-to-four day application of the AI 4-D process for which the whole system (or representatives of the whole system) are brought together to create large scale change and can include hundreds to thousands of stakeholders. This group of 128 participants identified eight strategic objectives to align with the strategic goal, vision, and mission. These eight objectives were to be achieved within the five-year strategic growth plan:

1. To collaborate with other corporate groups for the purpose of creating new products, opportunities, technology, and customers to reach their goals.

2. To identify and understand our customers and users by proactively educating our current and future customers about us, by developing and maintaining awesome customer relationships, and by seeking strategic partners in the global vehicle maintenance system business.

3. To be a state of the art systems engineering organization that optimizes product solutions as an integral part of the design process.

4. To be a center of excellence for vehicle maintenance systems by empowering our employees.

5. To be an innovative manufacturing operations team by ensuring our customers' success by delivering quality products, on time, at the lowest achievable cost and using high-performance work teams.

6. To continually evaluate all products that serve the entire cycle life by discovering innovative ways to apply these to create new

case story

products (20 percent of revenues come from products new to the market in the last five years).

7. To be best in class by seamlessly flowing information throughout the organization, encouraging risk taking, fostering innovation, developing our people and focusing on the long-term sustainability.

8. To challenge boundaries that prevents us from accomplishing our goals by having the leadership team step up and get the job done!

## Destiny Phase

In this phase, strategic tactical plans were created through dialogue with fifty key program professionals from three levels. This dialogue created ownership of the planning and implementation responsibilities to achieve the eight strategic objectives and provided the continuity and sustainability of the project. The planning and implementation teams met monthly for course corrections and presented results. During this phase, sales increased by $18M.

The team continued to discover, dream, design, and pursue both the existing and emerging vehicle maintenance systems opportunities in the world market. The team leader said:

"The SOAR framework along with the AI 5-D process provided an environment that placed emphasis on building a supportive culture that demonstrates inclusion and collaboration in creating a strategy in an environment that generates positive enthusiasm and ownership by the entire strategic growth plan."

## Outcomes

The outcomes for each phase of the AI 5-D process for this case study were explained in each phase above. To reflect back through the process, during the phases from discovery to destiny, respect, engagement, and ownership were evident. The SOAR framework called for a positive and collaborative environment in which people felt safe to suggest new opportunities and improvements and to take shared risks. The five-year

case story

growth plan was created and its objectives were translated into tactical plans with yearly goals that were clear, actionable, and measurable. The participants accepted accountability. The members from the executive level to staff are continuing to have a positive spirit because they are asked for their ideas. They see the connection of their ideas to action plans.

At the close of the Strategic Tactical Planning Summit (fifty participants) the general manager and four executive directors were given the final presentations. Their focus was evident since no one left the room nor used personal communications devices. Employee engagement and commitment were also evident in the walls posted with documentation of who committed to doing what by when. A spontaneous standing ovation for the program manager and the planning team punctuated the final presentation.

A positive spirit and powerful teamwork were enhanced since the groups commended each other and provided very specific feedback. The division continues to work with strategy and strategic planning as an evolving process. They also learned that it is important to provide more follow-on and through consulting and accountability measures. To that end, the whole group wants to do additional brainstorming on "ingredients for success" to ensure sustainability.

The SOAR framework blended well with the division's lean manufacturing principles and applications, business process model, process integration, and monthly reporting. As a result, the VMS program director wants to use a SOAR framework and AI approach, and the general manager wants to continue using the SOAR framework to drive a division wide growth process. There is also another person that wants to study how the SOAR framework can be used to build strategic capacity in the organization.

A final impressive outcome is the general manager's decision to use the process for the entire division. What especially impressed him was the obvious enthusiasm and positive momentum of the VMS workforce. A one-year review is planned, using an AI summit. It will be expanded to include the whole business, which includes: Navy programs,

*case story*

succession planning, leadership development program, development of the diversity program, and continuous follow-up for the VMS program. AASI found the power of the SOAR framework and AI 5-D approach contagious!

## Learnings

The creation of a core team with leadership support gave the project the momentum and support it needed to be defined, planned, executed, and sustained. Through the use of positive lens and strengths-based framework like SOAR and the AI 5-D approach, anything is possible when you let go and trust the stakeholders to do the work.

The SOAR framework emerged through the DNA of AI. Based on this DNA, it is hard to imagine creating any future strategy or strategic plan without "considering where it is strong, what the opportunities are, what we really want to happen, and what would indicate progress and success" (Stavros & Hinrichs, 2009, p. 43). As problems and challenges are presented in any AI-related case study in this book, reframing the ones related to strategy and strategic planning seem quite natural through the SOAR framework and becomes automatic.

### Author's Contact Information

Jacqueline M. Stavros
Graduate College of Management
Associate Professor
Lawrence Technological University
21000 West Ten Mile Road
Southfield, MI 48075-1058
248-204-3063
Jstavros@comcast.net
http://mgt101.ltu.edu/

# The Results of Appreciative Management by a Corporate Manager

*By Daniel Saint*

Beginning in 2005, the Michigan office of a global consulting firm began using Appreciative Inquiry when a new managing director (MD) joined the team. Appreciative Inquiry was first used by the MD as an intentional way to enter the organizational system. The MD, working closely with the director of human resources, set out to meet each of the nearly three hundred employees and approximately forty clients.

They asked the employees to tell of their peak experiences since joining the firm and what the employees valued most about themselves and the firm. The MD and HR director also asked employees to imagine what a best possible future would look like for the office. The leadership team asked clients to tell of the best experiences working with the firm and to imagine what the ideal relationship with the firm would look like.

The initial inquiry was designed to uncover a positive core upon which to build, to identify and amplify what was already working well within the system, and to begin consciously to co-construct a positive future as members of the team.

In 2006 the leadership team used Appreciative Inquiry to develop their annual operating plan and update their strategic plan. Through a series of group meetings culminating in a summit, the entire team of consultants was able to contribute. Some excellent ideas emerged, but more importantly, there was a positive flow of energy and engagement. Everyone in the organization had some degree of ownership and pride in the future direction of the firm locally. Dissemination and implementation had begun simultaneously with the research and planning phases of the planning process. Appreciative Inquiry allowed the organization to tap the wisdom and passion of all employees.

Over the three-year study, the Michigan Office more than doubled in size to become the firm's largest and most profitable office. Employee retention improved from an annual employee turnover rate of 32 percent at the beginning of 2005 to a low of 7 percent in 2007, moving the office from

*case story*

**Table 3.1. Change in Position Within Firm: Relative Rank in Firm of Michigan Office (Thirty Operation Centers Globally)**

|  | '04 | '05 | '06 | '07 |
|---|---|---|---|---|
| Income | 12th | 7th | 2nd | 1st |
| Revenue | 8th | 5th | 4th | 1st |
| Employee Retention | 6th | 3rd | 1st | 1st |
| Employee Engagement | 6th | 1st | 1st | 1st |
| Client | 8th | 6th | 2nd | 1st |

sixth place in the firm to first place. As you can see from Table 3.1, Employee engagement (measured by a global survey) and client satisfaction (measured by a survey after each engagement) also improved similarly. Michigan moved from twelfth place to first place in producing income and from eighth place to first place in generating revenue.

Client satisfaction, employee retention, an employee engagement as measured in a global survey also significantly improved. The results show the positive impact of creating sustainable value by leveraging social and economic considerations within strategy.

**Author's Contact Information**

Daniel K. Saint, Ph.D.
Partner
Innovation Partners International
(248) 565-5056/(704) 528-5659
saint@innovationpartners.com

# CHAPTER 4

# Choose the Positive as the Focus of Inquiry (Define)

**THIS CHAPTER AND THE NEXT FOUR** will each focus on one of the core processes of Appreciative Inquiry. We present a detailed explanation of each process followed by Appreciative Inquiry intervention stories that demonstrate designs, handouts, sample tasks, and hints to help you work with a group using AI.

## Define: Focusing on the Positive

Significant organization change is often catalyzed by some form of external pressure or opportunity (for example, decreasing customer satisfaction, emerging technologies, new government regulations, shifts in the competitive landscape, unforeseen market opportunities, changing stakeholder expectations, or, more generally, a desire to increase collaboration and to share knowledge, ideas, and successes). As an organization begins to contemplate systematic and deliberate change in response to these pressures or opportunities, one of the first activities is generally a situation analysis: "Where are we right now in relation to 'issue X'?" In other words, faced with some impetus for change, the first conscious step undertaken by human systems is to study the situation and to generate "data"—that is, "knowledge" about the situation. This critical first decision to search for data/knowledge starts a chain of events that is "fateful." Ways of changing the organization's relationship to the identified catalyst of "issue X" are defined in this first chain of events.

The AI perspective suggests that before the first question is asked, the client organization is faced with the most important choice of the whole change process. Appreciative Inquiry begins when the organization consciously chooses to *focus on the positive as the focus of inquiry.* As a result, the first choice point is not *whether* to collect data about an issue, but rather what the *focus* of the data collection process will be. In our experience, many organizations choose a negative focus ("What's wrong with this issue?") without even realizing that there are other alternatives open to them.

If clients follow the traditional approach, they will focus on the obstacles they face, the problems they have, the malfunctions that have caused them to be in their current situations, and so on. The Appreciative Inquiry approach shifts that focus. The search becomes a process of sharing stories about the positive history of the situation, that is, to generate knowledge by exploring moments in the organization's present or past when the "issue" being studied has given life to their organization. For example, if the focus is on "customer dissatisfaction," the choice is between the traditional questions: "What are we doing wrong that is causing customer dissatisfaction? What do we need to do to decrease customer dissatisfaction?" and the AI questions: "When have our customers been really happy and satisfied with our company? What were we doing then that we can learn from and build on? What images and ideas come from these success stories that lead us to new ways to increase customer satisfaction?" Thus, the choice of questions is based on the realization that we will find more of what we look for, the outcome of which in the deficit search is more and more information about what is wrong, undesirable, and troubling. In the positive-focused inquiry (the AI approach), the outcome is a clear understanding about what the organization wants in the area of customer satisfaction and how they have gotten that positive outcome in the past.

## Raising the Choice Point

The following examples describe opening dialogue with client systems that clearly differentiates the first core process of AI—focus on the positive as a core value. Although it is simple enough to suggest that organization interventions for solving problems can be approached from a positive rather than a deficit frame, it is quite another matter to convince clients or your own organization that this positive frame will work. Remember that, from the point of view of our current paradigm, we are taught in all of our cultural institutions that analysis of deficits will lead to future success. AI suggests that the most productive way to address any situation defined as a "deficit" is to look at the same or a similar situation when the outcomes have been positive and successful. So your first conversations with the organization are critically important, and the choice of focus will determine how the whole process will unfold. *Remember, however, that you are not selling AI as an intervention. Rather, you are proposing to facilitate whatever intervention the client requests by approaching it from an AI perspective.* The following two examples—a gender project and an evaluation—demonstrate how the opening dialogue might go.

## Example 1: Increasing Gender Equity

The international division of a large corporation was facing regulatory, outside stakeholder, and employee pressure to deal with an organizational culture that limited the contributions women could make to the health and vitality of the corporation. There was also concern that women were rarely able to reach the higher levels in the company's management structure. The "problem" was defined as a male dominated culture in the

*example*

company because of the history, tradition, and beliefs that defined the behavior of men and proscribed the role of women. The company decided to move globally toward gender equity in all parts of the corporation.

In the international division described in this example, managers were ready to address the "problem." Their first thought, and the advice of some consultants who regularly worked with the company, was to collect information about the breadth and depth of the "problem." They called in a consulting team known for its work on gender issues and outlined for the consultants the "problem" and their readiness to address it by finding out what was wrong and figuring out how to fix it.

The response of the consulting team went something like this: "*We all agree that the first step is to understand more about what's really going on around here. This means we have a big choice to make here. We can search for evidence of sexism, incidents of discrimination, in order to see how widespread and deep this problem really is. And when we find them we can analyze the factors and dynamics that allow this sort of behavior to flourish.*" The division managers nodded their heads in recognition of this traditional approach.

The next statement from the consultants, however, raised some eyebrows and led to some doubts and skepticism, as well as many questions: "*Or,*" the consultants continued, "*we can search for examples of exceptional cross-gender relationships. We can search out stories and examples of moments when both parties in the relationship felt fully valued and very productive together, and we can use that data to determine what conditions and factors were present in those instances that supported such a good relationship. Our choice is whether we focus on moments of breakdown in cross-gender relations in this company or focus and learn from moments of excellence—no matter how rare they may or may not be.*" By choosing to focus on the positive in this case, two years later the company won the Catalyst Award granted annually to honor companies for innovative organizational approaches with proven, measurable results that address the recruitment, development, and advancement of all women.

## Example 2: Evaluation Becomes Valuation

We received a call from the OD/HR department of a transnational pharmaceutical company. The company had just spent a large amount of money and a lot of corporate "goodwill" on putting their top four hundred research managers and scientists through an intensive workshop using a computer simulation to give participants experience with the company's portfolio and process management model. The question to us as consultants was whether we could provide an outside evaluation of the degree to which the workshop had been a good investment of corporate resources, human and financial. The HR representative indicated that, depending on what we found, a decision would be made to continue or to cancel the training program.

After some reflection on the request, we called back and said, *"We know you want to collect information from within your organization about the impact of the workshop and we know that you need to decide whether and how to proceed. You could do this in two ways. The traditional 'scientific' way would be to determine through external judgment whether or not your program had any impact on behavior at all and just how much the participants in the program actually understood. From this traditional perspective we could help you focus on the gaps and how to bridge those gaps in future program design. Or we could study together the assumption that participants had some degree of learning and that they have, to some degree, translated that learning into changed behavior in the workplace. In other words, you could chose to search for, understand, and then find ways to enhance examples of times when participants successfully learned the company's approach to portfolio and process management. And you could find moments of high transfer of learning from the classroom to the workplace and determine what conditions contributed to that success. You could then find ways of creating those supporting conditions more frequently."*

In the two examples given above, we see the beginnings of the first core process in AI—*focusing on the positive as a core value.* Since clients, like the rest of us, have been educated in a deficit-oriented problem-solving approach that emphasizes looking for the obstacles, the gaps, or dysfunctions in a situation, they are often taken aback by any suggestion that solving their problems could be done more effectively by focusing on the positive as a core value.

## Explaining and Demonstrating AI

Whether you are an external consultant, internal staff person, or line manager responsible for a particular operating group, one of the very first challenges in beginning an AI-based change process is to introduce the concepts and research underlying AI. Of course, it is also desirable to connect this first introduction of AI with some sort of participative decision making as to the applicability of AI and next steps for the system. Key questions to ask are:

- Is this approach right for you and this situation?

- If this approach feels right to you, what will the topic of the inquiry be? And how shall we phrase the topic in a manner congruent with a choice to focus on the positive as a core value?

- If we proceed with this approach, what are the essential elements that need to be present for the change to be successful?

- If we proceed with this approach, who should be involved in developing the customized protocol and in designing the overall "inquiry architecture." Should there be a "core team" of people to do this design work and, if so, what group in the organization will guide and support the work of the core team?

(To add a personal note, in all of our work with client systems we request a core team made up of a diverse cross-section of the organization. In most cases we have been successful and this group becomes the "co-creators" of the AI process for their organization. Often, we have found, they are also the people who imbed AI in the organization so that it thrives long after we are gone. We have come to believe that just as the first questions we ask are fateful, this first group—its composition, enthusiasm for the project, and commitment to the organization—can be "fateful." A really first-rate core team has a powerful positive effect on the success of the AI process in the organization. We will talk more about the role of this team in subsequent chapters. Suffice it to say that the earlier you can have the organization identify such a group and the more they are involved from the very beginning, the more you will be able to co-create an AI process that will be unique and appropriate to that organization.)

In any case, clarifying and agreeing on this first core AI process typically calls for many dialogues between the AI practitioner and the representatives of the organization. Sometimes these dialogues happen over the phone or in conjunction with face-to-face meetings with the decision being made through those conversations.

In some cases the potential client may ask for a brief, formal presentation by the consultant to some decision-making group from the organization. An outline for a forty-five-minute presentation is included here. We consider forty-five minutes to be the very minimum, to say the least. Clearly, it is too short a time to expect that all the questions about AI will be answered. However, the forty-five-minute introduction is presented here because of its utility in building a base for the longer sessions—and because forty-five minutes is sometimes all we have to work with.

## Sample Forty-Five-Minute Introduction to AI

The goal of this introduction to AI is to introduce the concepts and research underlying AI in a way that is both energizing enough for people to want more while being sufficiently comprehensive so that people get a sense of AI's full potential as a framework for whole systems change rather than seeing it as just the process of asking a few nice questions or looking at the world with an appreciative eye.

### What Is Appreciative Inquiry?

- Appreciative Inquiry is a practical philosophy of being in the world at a day-to-day level, and it is also a highly flexible process for *engaging* people to build the kinds of organizations and world that they want to live in.

*example*

example

- As a practical philosophy of being in the world at a day-to-day level, AI invites us to choose consciously to seek out and inquire into that which is generative and life enriching both in our own lives and in the lives of others, along with an exploration of our hopes and dreams for the future.

- As a process for *engaging* people in building the kinds of organizations and a world that they want to live in, AI involves collaborative, inclusive discovery of what gives a system "life" when it is most effective and capable in economic, ecological, and human terms and the weaving of that new knowledge into the fabric of the organization's formal and informal infrastructure.

- Appreciative Inquiry is not another OD intervention; rather, it is a new approach to existing OD interventions such as strategic planning, business process redesign, team building, organization restructuring, individual and project evaluation, coaching, diversity work, and so on.

### The AI Process May Look Like This

Choose a model from Chapter 3. Put the model on chart paper or on an overhead and use it to give a brief explanation of the overall AI process, making it clear that there is no formula for using AI, just guiding principles and some models created by practitioners who are explaining approaches that have been tested and adapted.

### An Inquiry Mini Experience

After you have presented your introductory comments, tell participants that they will now take part in a brief inquiry experience. Ask the participants to form pairs. (A threesome works fine if you do not have an equal number of participants.) Tell them that one partner will interview the other for five minutes and then switch roles for another five minutes.

Tell the interviewers that their goal is to encourage a vivid description of events and to help the interviewees tell very descriptive and detailed stories. Encourage expansion of the stories' richness by using comments such as, "Tell me more about the part when...."

*example*

Post the following two interview questions on a chart and tell the participants to begin.

## Interview Questions

1. Think about a time when you were really engaged in and excited about your work. Tell me your story about that time. What was happening? What were you feeling? What made it a great moment? What were others doing that contributed to this being a great moment for you? What did you contribute to creating this moment?

2. If you had three wishes for your organization, what would they be?

After the interviews are complete, debrief the interview process by asking participants, "What was that experience like for you?"

### *Two Intertwined Ideas Under-Girding the Practice of Appreciative Inquiry*

*1. The Image—Action Connection*

A. What happens when:

- You tell a three-year-old, "Don't go near the pool"?

- You give your golfing buddy, just before she swings the club, the following advice: "See those trees on the right? Be really careful not to hit your ball into those trees!"

- You are on your way to meet with someone who always makes you feel very good about yourself, someone with whom you find yourself laughing frequently and behaving in an unguarded, spontaneous manner?

B. Mini-Lecture

- Using your own knowledge and the information on the scientific theories about positive image and positive action presented in Chapter 2, explain to participants the connection between positive and negative images and human behavior.

- If you have time you might ask the audience for examples from their own lives.

*example*

### 2. Social Constructionism: The Role of Conversations in Creating Social Reality

THE TRADITIONAL VIEW OF "REALITY," particularly as it applies to human behavior, is that:

- Reality only exists externally to us;

- The eye is a neutral mirror of the reality that is "out there";

- The function of language is *to describe* the "given" reality of the world;

- THE SOCIAL CONSTRUCTIONIST PERSPECTIVE holds that through language and social discourse, we are constantly evolving and creating new realities;

- The images of things that we anticipate (like the anticipation of seeing someone who makes you feel really good about yourself) are a powerful reality in and of themselves;

- These images lead to actions/behaviors; and

- Conversations (particularly inquiry) continuously create new images that in turn lead to new actions, which in turn create "new realities."

Since we can decide what to focus on in our conversations we have a choice. If we are focused on "improving" an organization, a team, a family, or a relationship, for example, we can choose to focus on what is broken, what is a problem, what is frustrating us, or we can choose to focus on that which is life-giving, energizing, and valuable to us. The choice is fateful!

### In Summary

AI is an approach to the development of human systems that recognizes that we can choose to approach human systems with the view that either:

1. Human systems are primarily constellations of problems/obstacles to be analyzed and overcome, or

2. Human systems contain mysterious life-giving forces to be understood and embraced.

example

AI recognizes that whichever assumption we make about the nature of reality, that choice will lead us to a certain focus in our conversations. And those conversations will lead to certain images being dominant in our minds and those images will in turn lead to action at both the conscious and unconscious level.

Appreciative Inquiry uses the power of inquiry to engage our imagination, which in turn influences our actions. By focusing through Inquiry on that which is life-giving, that which is energizing, that which is joyful and fun—and amplifying those qualities by involving the "whole system" in co-construction and co-innovation based on the findings of the inquiry, AI enables systems to transform themselves.

If there is time left, people generally have a lot of questions!

## Identifying the Focus for Inquiry

In the process of choosing to focus on the positive, the early dialogues must also include explorations leading to a decision on topic choice—the primary area of focus for the upcoming inquiry described in Chapter 5. The topic choices are guided by the overall purpose of the project (such as gender equity and evaluation in our previous examples).

These discussions about the focus of the work and the resulting topics to be explored are governed by the Principle of Simultaneity. As we seek to understand a situation by gathering data, the first question we ask is fateful. The organization will turn its energy in the direction of that first question, whether positive or negative. The seeds of change are embedded in that first question. Careful, thoughtful, and informed choice of topic(s) is important as it defines the scope of the inquiry, providing the framework for subsequent interviews and data collection.

Since AI begins and ends with valuing that which gives life to organizations, during their preparation work inquirers choose affirmative topics based on bold hunches about what gives life to their organization and formulate questions to explore those topics. They also write questions that encourage conversations about the

desired future of the organization. The topics and questions focus
the organization members on what they most want to see grow and
flourish.

Without the client system making the choice to focus on the positive
as a core value, it is not possible to proceed with an AI process of
change. In making this choice, the client needs to understand that
choosing to focus on the positive does not mean excluding any
reference to difficulties or obstacles. In fact, truth telling in
Appreciative Inquiry is just as valued as it is in the traditional deficit-
based problem-solving approach. And it is a great deal easier to tell
the truth about positive experiences! The choice about how to
resolve difficult situations lies in both the choice of the primary
focus for inquiry—positive or deficit-based—and in whether
difficulties are seen as immovable obstacles or as sources of insight
into strategies for effective forward movement. AI is at its most
powerful when it is used to seek out the ray of light in what seems
to be a totally dark and dismal situation!

As in all things with Appreciative Inquiry, there are multiple ways to
proceed once you are asked to go forward in an organization. Topics
are sometimes chosen by the client who brought you into the
organization or, if you are an internal consultant or manager, by
your own understanding of a situation. In time-limited and subject-
focused processes—team building, conflict resolution, etc.—the topic
is clear. Often your task in those situations is simply to help create
AI questions about that topic: "Tell me a story about the very best
team you ever worked or played with," and so on. However, in
complex system change (the major focus of this book) the second
part of imbedding the positive core value is to facilitate a group—
ideally a core group assigned to you, as we suggested—to identify
key topics that are affirmative. For example, an AI topic to study
might be "excellent customer service" rather than "improving
customer service." This process of topic selection goes from the
simple naming of the topic to be studied all the way to large system
involvement in identifying the topics that are most important to
people in the system. Following is a detailed example of an actual
four-hour workshop that led to topic choices.

example

## Example: A Four-Hour Design to Initiate an AI-Based Process

This design was used at the initial meeting of an eight-person leadership team at a school recently formed through the merger of three schools. The response to the merger ranged from hostility to confusion to apathy to a sense of loss to moderate support for the merger. The hoped for change was the creation of a new culture that would contain the best of the past cultures.

The meeting included the school principal who was our primary client and his eight-person leadership team, which included representatives of all sections of the school. Prior to this four-hour meeting, the principal, an internal evaluation specialist, met with one of us for a two-hour session to explore the possibility of working together using AI as a framework for the work. During that two-hour meeting, the principle explained the following:

- The school size was about six hundred students and fifty staff, including faculty administrators and educational technologists (teachers' assistants). It was a "new" school in the sense that about 30 percent of the faculty had moved there from other schools.

- The principal, in his first year at this school, was also new.

- Both the faculty who had come from other schools and the original faculty felt as if they had lost something. In the case of the original faculty, they felt a sense of loss of the "old family," including a much-liked previous principal; in the case of the new faculty, they were missing the schools they had left behind.

- The time available for the involvement of school faculty in the determination of the school's future educational environment/culture and their roles within it was very limited (six hours in two-hour increments over a period of six weeks).

By the end of the two-hour meeting, the author, the principal, and the evaluation specialist had concluded that an appropriate next step was to gather the existing leadership team at the school for four hours in order to:

*example*

1. Obtain support for proceeding with this process

   - By introducing how Appreciative Inquiry is a process for positive change

   - By describing the phases of the process and the choices available; the role of this group in supporting and guiding the process; and the role of an interviewer group

2. Agree on an overall project focus and scope (future of the school? or something more specific?)

3. Agree on preliminary project strategy, including

   - Timing of various phases/steps

   - Participation—who needs to be involved in which phases/activities and how will we involve them?

   - What resources are available to draw on throughout this process and what other activities are underway to which we should link this process?

4. Clarify next steps and individual responsibilities

Table 4.1 is the design of the actual four-hour meeting, along with key "lecturette" notes:

### Table 4.1. Sample Four-Hour Design

| Time | Activity | Lecturette Notes |
|------|----------|------------------|
| 8:00–8:15 | Introductions: goals and participants' hopes for this session | • How we got to this point<br>• Principal's hopes for this process and the school's future<br>• Agenda for today |

*example*

## Table 4.1. Continued

| Time | Activity | Lecturette Notes |
|---|---|---|
| 8:15–8:25 | Micro Overview of Appreciative Inquiry | Over the last thirty years of working in both the public and private sectors, my experience has been that people are usually willing to talk about what's wrong, but as they talk about it, there seems to be a downward spiral or despair. Instead of being energized, people became de-energized. David Cooperrider reviewed research on the connection of image and action, research from medicine, education, and psychology, and developed Appreciative Inquiry—the idea that there is a connection between the images we hold of what is possible and the questions we ask about our past and present. The AI approach to change can be applied to your family, your team, your school. The approach is like a journey that engages people in creating the sort of school or team or family or community that they want to live in. It focuses people on what happens when things are at their best. The rationale is twofold: (1) When you focus on the positive, it becomes a spring-board (energizer) for the future and (2) it also generates exceptionally useful information about what to enhance and build on as you move into the future together.<br><br>"Very briefly: the phases of an AI-based change process are initiate (this meeting); *inquire* (find out what contributes to moments of greatness so we can expand this in the future; we want to articulate profound knowledge of a system when it is operating at its best); *imagine* (collectively imagine what could be, how it would be if the moments of greatness are the norm, rather than the exception); and *innovate* (What changes do we want to make so that what we imagine can happen?)" |

**Table 4.1. Continued**

| Time | Activity | Lecturette Notes |
|------|----------|------------------|
| 8:25–9:15 | Paired "exceptional moment" interviews | Form the participants into pairs (if the number is uneven, form one group of three). Ask the pairs to take turns interviewing each other using the following questions. Each interview should last twenty minutes. |

1. What first attracted you to your work, to your profession? What were your initial impressions? What excited you?
2. In each of our lives there are special times when we just know that we have made the right career choice, moments when we feel really good about the work we are doing and what we are contributing to others. As you think back over the last four or five years, can you *tell me a story* about one of those special moments when you felt most alive, involved, and excited about your work and when you were affirmed in your commitment to being part of the teaching/learning?
   • Who were the significant others and what made them significant?
   • What was happening at that time in your life?
   • What made it a peak experience?
   • What factors in the school (in your environment) made it a peak experience?
3. Without being humble, tell me what you value deeply
   • About yourself?
   • When you feel best about your work?
4. What is the single most important thing your work has contributed to your life?
5. What is the *core factor* that gives vitality and life to this school—the one thing without which this place would just not be the same?

example

### Table 4.1. Continued

| Time | Activity | Lecturette Notes |
|------|----------|------------------|
| | | 6. If you had three wishes to spend on creating a participative change process that would load to the best possible learning and working environment, an environment that would be a significant expansion of the best that you have experienced in your past, what would you wish for? |
| 9:15– 9:20 | Debrief of the interview process | What was the process like for you? |
| 9:20– 9:30 | BREAK | |
| 9:30– 10:30 | Exploration of interview content | • Sharing of interview high points: identification of what gives life to this school. What stood out for you in the interview with your partner? What sparked your imagination? What made your heart sing?<br>• Pairs draw pictures of what the "new" school would be like and share.<br>• Identification of criteria for a good participative change process at this school. |
| 10:30– 11:30 | Description of and dialogue about the proposed journey/AI process and the choice points, plus… | • Initial thoughts on how widespread the participation in this process should be<br>• Decision on whether they want to be the interview team or whether they think a fifty-person paired interview process in a large-group setting is better<br>• If we have time, what do you have enough curiosity about so that we should include it in the final customized protocol? |
| 11:30– 11:45 | Clarify next steps | Create an act on plan for:<br>• Developing a customized protocol<br>• Communication of the decisions from this meeting |

**example**

### Table 4.1. Continued

| Time | Activity | Lecturette Notes |
|------|----------|------------------|
| | | • Designing/planning the large-group meeting (if that is the choice) |
| 11:45–12:00 | Appreciative debrief of today's meeting and meeting closure | • Which part of today's meeting most intrigued or engaged you?<br>• What part of today's meeting should we try to build on as we meet with others in the future?<br>• What wishes do you have for the next time we meet? |

In larger, more complex organizations, this topic-selection process is often embedded in a longer workshop that leads to the second core process of AI—*inquiry into stories of what gives life to the organization.* We offer clients an exploratory workshop (see the two-day preparation workshop in Chapter 5) for a decision-making group in the organization. The workshop clarifies the difference between the AI approach and that of more traditional approaches to change. It includes an introduction to Appreciative Inquiry, a discussion of the shifting paradigm, and an examination of the theory of change that underlies this approach. It often includes identifying topics and writing questions for the Appreciative Inquiry protocol used in the inquiry phase of the second core AI process. The outcome of this exploratory workshop can be a go/no go decision. Alternatively, this can be the kick-off event to an already agreed-on AI change process. In this case, the workshop includes creation of a customized interview protocol and decisions on inquiry architecture. We will describe both of these more in the next chapter.

Overall, the first core AI process can be considered complete when:

• The client system makes an informed choice to focus on the positive as a core value, and

• The choice of topics for the AI process are inquired into in ways that are congruent with the decision to focus on the positive.

*case story*

# AI Stories from a Training and Technical Assistance Center (T/TAC): New Possibilities for Improving Outcomes for Students with Disabilities

*By Denyse Doerries, Donni Davis-Perry, and Lori Korinek*

## Client Organization

T/TAC at The College of William and Mary (W&M) is part of a statewide technical assistance system of seven T/TACs funded by the Virginia Department of Education (VDOE). The centers are managed by universities in the Schools of Education to help bridge the gap from research to practice. The T/TACs provide quality professional development and technical assistance to increase the capacity of school personnel, service providers, and families to meet the needs of children and youth with disabilities through consultation with school-based teams, information services (including periodic newsletters), linking and networking resources, a lending library of multi-media resources and technology, long-term technical assistance, workshops, and follow-up coaching. T/TAC W&M is comprised of one faculty member from the School of Education who is the principal investigator on the grant, two co-directors, and ten specialists, hired for their expertise as educational practitioners, three office support staff, and two graduate assistants.

This story involves one of the seven T/TACs and how Appreciative Inquiry was employed to enhance the organization and provide new possibilities of ways to work with educational professionals and school divisions. T/TAC W&M's primary focus is to support schools in implementing and sustaining long-term change initiatives designed to improve outcomes for students' with disabilities. Because T/TAC W&M is immersed in continuous improvement, the leadership team became intrigued with the possibilities of AI for enriching and deepening the understanding of organizational change.

*Note*: Support for T/TAC was provided by a grant to The College of William and Mary from the Virginia Department of Education (VDOE). The opinions herein do not necessarily reflect those of the VDOE and no official endorsement should be inferred.

## Objective

Approaching and defining problems through a positive inquiry seemed to have great potential for T/TAC W&M's work with schools in need of improving student outcomes. As educators, we realize that in order to apply a new strategy, one must understand the content at both a cognitive and experiential level as well as be able to determine the best ways to communicate the material to practitioners. The leadership at T/TAC wanted to experience the Appreciative Inquiry (AI) process and apply the process to a real issue in the organization as well as learn how to embed it in trainings and consultations with schools. This was accomplished through the following objectives to:

- Apply and embed AI in our organization in order to understand the process and its potential for transformation and change;

- Improve the organization's processes for continuously updating staff skills in research-based strategies and technology during a time of monetary constraints;

- Envision ways to continue to provide quality training and technical assistance to schools given the current economic conditions;

- Explore the possibilities for the use of advances in e-learning with our constituents, our staff, and other T/TACs;

- Envision new ways to collaborate with The College of William and Mary School of Education faculty and projects to enhance T/TAC services;

- Create a stronger organization that empowers all of its members to share their strengths and promotes shared leadership;

- Focus our efforts from the possibilities we create to improved outcomes for students with disabilities; and

- Integrate our knowledge of adult learning with the application of the AI process with schools and educational professionals without de-railing the process.

*case story*

## What Was Done and the Impact

T/TAC W&M participated in multiple Appreciative Inquiries, received ongoing coaching from consultants, and networked with AI practitioners including the University of Virginia Medical School. What was done and its outcomes were both internal to T/TAC and external as it became infused as a part of how T/TAC interacts with its constituents.

### Phase 1. Introduction to the Appreciative Inquiry Process (Spring 2008—Fall 2008)

The T/TAC journey began with a reference to research on a positive change model that significantly impacts school culture with which a W&M faculty member was involved. Because of restrictions on conference travel, T/TAC was exploring alternative avenues for professional development for the staff. T/TAC invited the professor to provide an overview of her research on AI and non-violent communication. As part of this presentation, an inspiring video, *Celebrate What's Right with the World*, by DeWitt Jones, was shared. This presentation provided the impetus and motivation to the staff to learn more about the AI process. T/TAC staff members also started to embed this video in their trainings with schools to set the stage for change.

Because the T/TAC staff wanted to learn more about applying the AI process, the W&M faculty member connected T/TAC to consultants Jane Magruder Watkins and Ralph Kelly of Appreciative Inquiry Unlimited, who are experts on AI and who could help chart the next part of this journey. During the summer of 2008, a small leadership group in collaboration with the local consultants planned a one-day AI event that allowed the participants to experience the 4-D process of Discovery, Dream, Design, and Deliver. Because of the enthusiasm of the staff about the potential of AI and the generous support of our consultants, T/TAC opened this event to W&M School of Education faculty, the T/TAC staff at Old Dominion University, and to a Virginia Department of Education staff member who worked closely with T/TAC W&M on a complex change initiative.

As a result of this AI event, the T/TAC staff re-discovered what we valued, what energized us, and what we wanted to do more of at an individual level. This event further motivated staff about the AI process, provided a shared experience and language, and helped to establish new partnerships with our fellow participants. However, the event was not designed to focus specifically on the T/TAC organization or to implement the Design phase, so there was more work to be done.

## Phase 2. T/TAC Appreciative Inquiries and More (Fall 2008– Spring 2010)

As a result of the fall 2008 introductory AI events, there was a heightened awareness among the leadership team of a need to apply the 4-D process with an inquiry around how our T/TAC organization might enhance its own processes and practices. A pressing question about sustainability of change produced by this process was also discussed. The consultants suggested a number of actions: expand the leadership team from two to six in order to set a foundation for sustainability; network with other AI practitioners within the state and beyond to discover lessons learned in the implementation process; and plan a T/TAC-focused AI event.

The leadership team was formed with four additional enthusiastic volunteers. One of the first actions of this team was to have each member network with a different AI practitioner whose name was provided by our local consultants or found on the AI commons website. We were particularly looking for practitioners who were applying AI with schools as well as AI practitioners in Virginia.

The networking proved to be very fruitful. AI practitioners are generous with their time and resources. T/TAC conferred with a consultant working with a school system in Canada and developed an ongoing partnership with the AI coordinator at the University of Virginia Medical School, which afforded additional training in planning AI Summits. The partnership with the W&M faculty AI researcher was enhanced by a shared experience in an AI Colloquy during the summer of 2009. T/TAC W&M will also be involved in an AI "Evocative Coaching" pilot training, which was to occur in the spring of 2010. Connecting with other AI

*case story*

practitioners and organizations employing Appreciative Inquiries fostered new learning and insights into the possibilities for the process. The leadership team also began a book study that is ongoing and helps to root the practices in a knowledge base, providing rich discussion for the group.

After much study and many conversations with the local coaches, in January of 2009, T/TAC W&M held their own AI "mini-summit" with the seventeen people in T/TAC. This summit was led by the AI leadership team using the 4-D process to determine how T/TAC W&M can continue to provide quality effective services to our schools. Two themes emerged from this inquiry—T/TAC W&M wanted to: (a) be on the "cutting edge" of best practices and (b) become more connected and integrated in our work among projects, staff members, and faculty. There needed to be a shift in roles of staff members to have a greater share in the leadership and a change in the relationships among the staff in order to feel less isolated in their 'project silos'.

The following activities resulted from the 4-D AI January 2009 experience:

> Two AI subgroups formed to lead the way in creating interconnections among staff members and the content of the projects and in providing avenues for the staff to learn "cutting-edge" interventions to improve student outcomes.

### Interconnectedness Theme

An AI subgroup emerged and committed to leading the change in the format and processes for our twice-monthly staff meetings to incorporate professional development, help integrate projects, and increase interpersonal connectedness. This group's membership brought people together from across work groups and projects to analyze the issues and make recommendations for ways to improve our meetings.

Other efforts to increase the "connectivity" or cross-pollination of projects included intentionally assessing ways to integrate the content of projects and having specialists cross-train each other. For example, the Effective Schoolwide Discipline project embedded parts of the Self-Determination project in their trainings. The inclusive practices work group worked with the AI leadership team to embed questions to help adminis-trators focus on "what is currently working" around inclusive practices.

Infusing AI into workshops and team facilitations through storytelling, wishes, and dreams helped to make this new initiative a part of best practices. School-based concerns were approached by reframing them into positive possibilities.

In order to enrich further the culture of T/TAC, the management team revised the performance evaluation of the staff to an AI "valuation" process. As a result, the roles of the office support staff expanded to include areas of strength and increased their collaboration with the specialists to support the T/TAC mission. The specialists volunteered for more opportunities for leadership.

Another initiative that increased the connectivity and integrative practices across the T/TAC and provided leadership opportunities was the develop-ment of two "graduation summits" that examined ways to improve gradu-ation outcomes for students with disabilities. The complex nature of this issue afforded opportunities for integration of information across all of the T/TAC W&M projects.

The specialists spontaneously implemented a "soup sipping" working luncheon on the second Monday of the month to encourage connectivity among the staff and an exchange of ideas and plans. Staff activities outside of work hours have also increased as a result of a desire for connection among staff members.

Staff expressed feeling more connected to T/TAC and their work. The working atmosphere and interactions have improved. On any given day, you can see specialists and office staff consulting and working with each other across projects to improve the quality of their work. Everyone touches base with the office, no matter how far away he or she may be on fieldwork days.

## Cutting-Edge Theme

A technology leadership subgroup was formed composed of both office staff and specialists with the purpose of examining use of technology to

*case story*

provide quality professional development and technical assistance. Knowledge and skills in the area of technology were shared across work groups, roles, and assignments. The technology work group created a professional development plan that included partnering with W&M faculty to provide workshops and ongoing coaching on cutting-edge skills in the use of technology to support quality services to our schools. Because of this support, two new discussion boards, one on behavior and one on inclusive lesson plans, are being used as a follow-up to training. The specialists are receiving coaching from the faculty to implement these discussion boards.

- A hybrid course on inclusive practices was developed and has tentative approval from the College.

- New strategies to determine the best match between content and technology are being studied.

- The technology leadership subgroup initiated a book group focused on e-learning.

- The specialists, with the help of the support staff, are embedding the technology in T/TAC workshops in order to provide educational professionals with hands-on experience in developing e-learning products and to cross-train staff.

- The AI process has resulted in renewed enthusiasm, understanding, and commitment of the office support staff to the T/TAC mission. Their contributions have emerged in new ways such as the development of Excel documents for tracking data to inform our work and helping schools to manage their data. A new web page was developed collaboratively between office support staff and specialists.

## Unintended Outcomes

One of the unintended outcomes of AI was the addition of "more work" due to the energy and enthusiasm of staff for working across projects. Everyone wanted to take advantage of any new opportunity to learn and network. A general sense of being overwhelmed by too many opportunities began to emerge. In response, the AI leadership team held a one-day

**case story**

meeting in the fall of 2009 to address this issue. The purpose of the meeting was to further define and re-commit the staff to identify and focus on specific areas to deepen their understanding. The objective was to determine where to focus energy and resources. The AI leadership team and the meeting process subgroup led this inquiry.

As part of this re-focusing meeting, the AI subgroup working on team meetings, provided training to staff on new team meeting processes and purposes. In order to make better use of our work time, the AI subgroup proposed changing the processes and purpose of staff/specialists' meetings. The meetings would now include time for professional development, work integration, and connecting to each other and to faculty.

- One team meeting each month will be focused on integrating our work on our separate projects. The emphasis will be on finding the connections and cross-training staff in order to develop more integrated approaches.

- The meeting process will continue to include a format for AI stories and wishes within the celebrations part of our meetings.

## Learnings

As a result of infusing AI throughout our practices, T/TAC W&M experienced a culture shift that enhanced the quality of collaboration among the staff and resulted in the development of new tools for providing services to educational professionals and school divisions. Re-discovering the values that enliven us created opportunities in our work that we could not have predicted. Committing to our value of interconnecting has motivated us to reach across projects to collaborate and create exciting opportunities for ourselves and those we serve. Dreaming of providing cutting-edge training and technical assistance for our schools has motivated us to learn new ways to support our sites. By looking for the positive, we uncovered reasons to celebrate instead of criticizing, unleashing enthusiasm instead of focusing on barriers.

Our journey of learning and applying what we learned is exciting. We moved from awareness of a different way to inspire change to applying

case story

the process of AI. We transformed our internal work groups, our meeting process, our yearly valuation, and the ways in which we approach concerns. Our organization may be unique in that we use AI to transform our internal organization as well as our external educational practices with schools.

We reflect on our changing practices and notice pieces and parts of AI cropping up in unexpected places— in our workshops, in schools requesting the AI process, in our conversations with our families. We continue to wonder: "Have we arrived?" "Are we doing all we can?" In living AI, we created hybrid professional development sessions using what has worked well in the past and activities we learned through the AI process. By sharing stories, daring to make wishes for our future, and approaching situations with enthusiasm and positive curiosity, our organization brings hope to itself and those with whom we collaborate.

## AI Scenario

My first time applying parts of the AI process in a school resulted in such dramatically different outcomes that I was hooked and determined to learn more about AI. I was consulting in an inner-city middle school that was struggling to meet accreditation standards. My partner and I met at a table in the school's library with teams of teachers at each grade level to talk about including students with disabilities in their classes. I noticed right away that the teachers seemed angry at giving up their much-needed planning periods to meet with us. In our first group, one teacher sat at a separate table, reading the newspaper and refusing to join our conversation. Typically, we would have used a traditional problem-solving approach, looking at their current practices of including students with disabilities, brainstorming all the barriers they were experiencing, and continuing to focus on what wasn't working in order to identify the changes needed to do things differently. But this time we asked the teachers to tell us their best stories of positive experiences of including students with disabilities in their classes. I noticed the teacher at the other table lowering his newspaper and listening as his colleagues began recalling times when things were going well in their classrooms. He joined us, recounting his own positive story about his co-teaching relationship with

*case story*

a special educator. At that point, with the help of sharing stories, our group had "cooked up" enough positive energy to keep the momentum focused on remembering what worked in the past. We ended our short session by having the teachers write down three wishes for including students with disabilities in their classrooms. Without using AI, this session might have ended differently. With AI, the teachers left smiling, energized, remembering why they became teachers and committing to their future dreams for themselves and their students.

## Authors' Contact Information

The College of William and Mary T/TAC
Denyse Doerries: dbdoer@wm.edu
Donni Davis-Perry: ddperry@wm.edu
Lori Korinek: lkorinek@wm.edu

## External Consultants' and Coaches' Contact Information

Appreciative Inquiry Unlimited
Ralph Kelly: ralph@appreciativeinquiryunlimited
Jane Magruder Watkins: jane@appreciativeinquiryunlimited.com

## From Deficits to Strengths: Six Sigma from the AI Perspective

*By David Shaked*

### Part One: Problem-Solving Experience Built, AI Discovered—Now What?

Over several years of experience, I had built a great track record in the corporate world. I was solving many business challenges and concentrating on improving inefficient and wasteful processes. I was using the well-tried business improvement approaches such as Six Sigma and Lean thinking. I also regularly used many analytical approaches such as gap, SWOT, and Force-Field Analysis to support the change efforts and balanced scorecard, KPIs and control charts to monitor the progress. Waste and defects were everywhere I turned! All my efforts to eliminate them impacted on our customers and the bottom line in a really positive way. At the same time, I was teaching others how to use these approaches so that they could hunt out waste.

Then one day, I discovered AI.

Being so used to identifying the problems in each situation, I was intrigued by the completely different focus AI had. The focus was on how to achieve our dreams by focusing on what was working well and exploring how good we could get? I found myself torn between two seemingly different worlds. While I knew how to methodically solve problems by the traditional approaches, I could see how the positive approach of AI unleashed an enormous potential within organizations. My big question at that stage was how to integrate this fantastic new approach with everything I was doing before. At that stage, I felt that my work with Six Sigma and Lean thinking was "bad" and that AI was "good." I felt I had to throw away everything I had learned and experienced until then and re-start a new learning journey. All my experience to date seemed to fundamentally clash in style, language, process, and logic with AI. For example, how could I connect AI's 5-D process with the DMAIC (Define, Measure, Analyze, Improve, and Control) process from Six Sigma and its specific emphasis on finding root causes for problems through analysis? How

case story

could I continue my efforts to eliminate waste while inquiring into what gives life to my organization? These questions kept confusing me for a while. On the one hand, I loved the energy and creativity AI brought by focusing on the strengths and high moments. On the other hand, I didn't want to lose the familiar world of process mapping with Post-it Notes and deep statistical analysis.

## Part Two: Appreciating All My Skills and Building Bridges Between Them

Over time I learned more about AI. The experience I gained offered a potential solution to my challenge. For example, I learned that the 5-D model, which is very solid and versatile, is not the *only* way to apply AI. Being driven by my desire to be a better AI practitioner, I gained a much deeper understanding and strong connection with the principles behind AI and their importance. I realized then how important it was to apply these principles to everything I did, both professionally and personally. The conversations I had around the AI principles changed the way I look at my work and my life. It made them both more meaningful and alive. I also started appreciating my strengths and best experiences to date. This included the strengths and best experiences I had while practicing deficit-based techniques. It meant that I started asking myself different questions. Instead of asking how to "fix" my problem-solving skills in order to create a bridge between my two internal worlds, I started exploring my own strengths. What do I do well when I work with Six Sigma and Lean thinking? What were the most powerful problem-solving experiences I had? What were the best insights I gained when analyzing data? What did I like the most? Which tools worked best? What did people I worked with like about these methodologies? What worked well for the organization when I applied them? What was so unique and attractive in my view with these methodologies? In other words, *What gave life to my traditional way of solving problems?*

The shift of my attention toward what gave life to my way of solving problems generated the breakthrough I was yearning for. All of a sudden, I could see potential bridges and new ways to work with the old methodologies people are so familiar with. At the same time, I also referred back to the guiding principles behind Six Sigma and Lean thinking. These principles were actually, to my surprise at the time, very strength-oriented. For example, the reason why Six Sigma is focused so much on defect identification and elimination is actually the pursuit of quality. The guiding principle behind Lean thinking is the desire to deliver the best value to the customer as quickly as possible. All of a sudden there didn't seem to be such a dichotomy between the two worlds!

The next stage in this journey was to take the tools and techniques from Six Sigma that I liked the most and apply an appreciative approach (or a "lens") and the principles of AI to them. I also had to rethink the questions I used as part of these approaches. For example, I used to enjoy facilitating groups through process mapping exercises to gain clarity around a given process. I realized that instead of focusing the group's attention on the waste and issues in the process, I should apply the positive principle by focusing them on the parts of the process whereby value is created and good performance is achieved. Waste naturally disappears if people orient themselves (in other words, the anticipatory principle in action) toward ways of increasing the value they generate in any process. The questions I ask managers, employees, and customers as part of the Six Sigma Define stage are focused on trying to find when the process has worked well in the past or what they wish to see *more of* instead of reduce/eliminate.

Another example is the use of the powerful statistical tools and rigor that Six Sigma and the DMAIC model provide to identify root causes of success and amplifying them instead of studying defects. I also apply the principle of wholeness by involving a wider representation of the system I work with. Finally, I also realized that the value of data and statistics is not in the numbers or charts we produce but rather in the conversations we hold around them. We can choose to discuss them in any way we wish. Previously, in most cases I used to focus on the gaps, the weak performance points, the "red-colored" indicators and the data about customer complaints. This is not absolutely necessary! Being critical doesn't mean being objective. Most of these critical observations were a result of my habits. There is a lot we can learn from any chart and spreadsheet if we seek the strong points and the cases of stellar performance.

I choose to look at these data points and inquire about them not because I want to ignore the problems but rather because I am truly curious about them and believe they hold useful information. Bad data and weakness points are also very useful. However, their usefulness is not so much in understanding what caused the problem. Focusing on what we wish would be different or what we want to change is the key. This unique focus drives different conversations with other members of the organization and allow improvement teams to socially construct their desired future. (This means that one can apply the AI principle of social construction to analysis, data and statistics.)

These ideas may seem challenging to many successful problem solvers. We were trained under the assumption that in every organization and its various processes there are problems waiting to be identified and solved. What would happen if we approached our improvement efforts with an underlining assumption that every organization and process is a result of an originally great idea and that in every organization or process something works well and delivers value? After all, we can almost always point out areas in which our current problems were once a good solution to another problem. This cycle of problem solving results in laying the foundations of the next problem and is not necessary at all. If we dare to suspend our basic suspicion about every organization or process, we may find and access more creative ideas, greater motivation for change, and the innovation that is so essential for survival in the marketplace.

## Part Three: Appreciative Lean Thinking and Problem Solving in Practice

Perhaps one of the best examples I have to date of the Simultaneity Principle in action was a recent client project I worked on. The client, a rail company, asked my colleague (Gill How of Buonacorsi Consulting) and me to facilitate a process improvement workshop to reduce the delays to rail services that occurred when faulty coaches were exchanged with serviced ones. The exchange, when not done correctly or in a timely fashion, causes delays to the rail service and a chain reaction of further delays to other services. At our first meeting, the head of the department

case story

in charge of rail performance provided us with plenty of data points about the delays, their frequency, root causes, and their great financial impact on the company. After a while, I asked our sponsor how often the organization changes coaches successfully and on time? A powerful moment of silence followed. The answer our sponsor provided was "I don't know. I don't think we ever measured it." From that moment on, our conversation took a completely different direction. We were all curious to find out how often the process works well, what contributes to this success, and how we can do more of what already works well.

This single powerful question was the basis of the workshop we delivered. The workshop followed a new and innovative design following Lean thinking process improvement workshops (kaizen event) I have delivered in the past but run with an appreciative, strength, and value focus. We inquired about best experiences, mapping the process when it works, collecting stories and data about the process at its best, and asking participants what would make it even better. The questions asked, the evidence sought, and the analysis conducted were all different from the normal Lean approach and more powerful. The great ideas the participants came up with came from good practices they were already doing or had done in the past. It was an exciting process to facilitate and observe. It also felt very satisfying personally to reach this point in my own professional development and to be able to connect my ideas and knowledge in this approach. A new, more appreciative and life-giving way for Lean thinking process improvement was born!

To summarize my experience so far, I can offer other practitioners a wider and deeper look at AI and its implication on deficit-based approaches. As I learned from my own journey, there is no need to look at the two as opposites. AI can benefit from the variety and rigor of some of the deficit-based models that worked for us so well for such a long time. At the same time, successful practitioners of the various deficit-based models that have been developed during the 20th Century could bring a lot of energy and exciting new innovations by applying AI principles to their strengths and great experiences. If you need further advice how to apply this thinking to your particular situation or organization, get in touch.

case story

**Author's Contact Information**
David Shaked
Almond Insight
23 Devonshire Road
London, W4 2EX
United Kingdom
www.almond-insight.com
david@almond-insight.com

# CHAPTER 5

# Inquire into Stories of What Gives Life in the System (Discover)

"The universe is made of stories, not of atoms."

Muriel Rukeyser, American poet and writer

"We can tell people abstract rules of thumb, which we have derived from prior experiences, but it is very difficult for other people to learn from these. We have difficulty remembering such abstractions, but we can more easily remember a good story. Stories give life to past experience. Stories make the events in memory memorable to others and to ourselves. This is one of the reasons why people like to tell stories."

Roger C. Shank, *Tell Me a Story*

**THE PRIMARY WORK IN THE SECOND GENERIC AI PROCESS** is conducting the interviews that constitute the research into the topics that have been identified in the previous process.

The Appreciative Inquiry interview is a process for exploring the "life-giving" factors of the organization. It is a process of discovery. The data collected in the interviews helps you to locate, illuminate, and understand the distinctive strengths that give your organization life and vitality when it is functioning at its best.

The AI interview represents the core of the inquiry process. This interview—in no way a traditional interview seeking facts and opinions—is a mutual learning process. Both the interviewer and the person interviewed learn as together they explore the values, peak experiences and wishes for the organization by sharing stories.

In preparation for this core process of inquiring into stories, the client system (usually with help from an experienced AI practitioner) must:

- Understand and support the rationale for collecting "data" in the form of stories rather than in the more traditional quantitative, analytic, and reductionist methods;

- Develop a customized interview protocol focused on the primary topic chosen for inquiry during the first core process; and

- Agree on the inquiry process: Who will be interviewed? By whom? When, how, where? And how will the information be collected, saved, used to make decisions about the future of the organization?

In this chapter, we explore each of these points in more detail. At the end of this chapter we also deal with the question of training for interviewers.

## Rationale for the Use of Stories

The interview serves as the starting point for dialogue that is core to the Appreciative Inquiry theory of organization innovation and change. In traditional action research or organization development processes, the data collected is thought of as an objective reality. It is assumed that the data, which is information, stands apart from the people involved and from the process through which it is gathered.

Alternatively, in the process of the Appreciative Inquiry interview we do not seek "objective data," per se. Rather, the AI interview seeks to explore and bring alive the appreciative stories of the organization. This kind of data collecting stimulates participants' excitement and delight as they share their values, experiences, and history with the organization and their wishes for the organization's future. Appreciative Inquiry catalyzes the thinking and dialogue about positive possibilities that are often forgotten in the social and organizational patterns of deficit language so common in traditional organization development practices. This collective surfacing of such memories through appreciative stories enables forms of organizational innovation possible in ways usually not associated with deficit-focused methodologies.

The use of the story as the primary format for conducting an Appreciative Inquiry is intentional. Stories have a depth and breadth in them that conveys meaning much more effectively than a list of key points or other reductionist reports of a human experience. Stories have power to engage the imagination in ways that diagnostic discussions cannot.

### The Power of Story

| | |
|---|---|
| Universal | All cultures use story to share knowledge, custom, tradition, and learning. Remember the Griots of West Africa who carry the oral history of the tribe, and pass it down from generation to generation. It is only through the story that a tribe knows its history. |
| Engaging | Stories create relationships; they connect teller and listener and create a shared reality. |
| Memorable | They are personal, dynamic, memorable, and transmit images and affect. |

| Dynamic | Stories are continuously changeable; multidimensional; and capable of multiple interpretations. |
| Stimulate Creativity | Story causes the suspension of our inclination to sort things into categories and causes us to search backward to earlier examples or parallels in our own experience. Stories create the possibility of new acts of creation. One story leads to more stories. |
| Moves Us Toward the New | While a story causes us to look backward toward a territory we think we have left behind, we also are thrown forward to new possibilities and realities. |
| Is a Living Thing | As the story is remembered, recounted, and received by the listener, it becomes a living thing. The "aliveness" of the story energizes listeners to pass it on and remains reborn in the storyteller and gives new insight and life. |

## A Preparation Workshop to Develop the Customized Interview Protocol and Decide on an Inquiry Process

In actual client work both (1) the development of a customized protocol and (2) decisions about how to create the inquiry process are often done during a one- to three-day "preparation workshop." This workshop typically takes place after the client system has decided that AI is the right approach for them. The attendees at this workshop are, ideally, a microcosm of the larger organization—reflecting as many of the different voices and constituencies that make up the organization as possible, including but not overemphasizing senior management. This group, often called the "core team," will have been identified and selected as part of the concluding work of the first core AI process of "Define." Whether this "core team" reports to and is supported by some senior steering group is a function of what was determined in the Define process when the question was asked: "What are the essential elements and conditions that need to be present for this change process to succeed?" Although AI is an energizing and exciting process, in larger organizations we have found it helpful to have some formal linkage between the "core team "and the existing senior management group, if only to ensure that the core team has the resources and support needed from the rest of the organization when necessary.

Typical goals of the preparation workshop are:

- To clarify the difference between the AI approach and the traditional change processes that focus on individual skill building and/or deficit-based problem solving;

- To help participants create their own AI interview guideline (customized protocol) for gathering information;

- To develop a plan (inquiry process) for collecting information from the interviews and for working with it after it has been collected, including:

  ○ Who should be interviewed and how?

  ○ Who should conduct the interviews and what training, if any, is needed?

  ○ Who should be involved with the information after the interviews?

  ○ Who should be involved in developing the image of the preferred future?

  ○ Who should be involved in creating the "design" of the new organization?

Because the work that is done in this preparation workshop sets the foundation for the rest of the change process, selection of members of the core group is a critical task.

**Seven Steps to Develop a Customized Interview Protocol and Plan an Inquiry Process**

Step 1: Select a Core Group and Possibly a Steering Team

Step 2: Orient Participants to the Goals of the Workshop and to Their Role in Meeting the Goals

Step 3: Quickly Get Participants into an Experience of Al

Step 4: Debrief the Mini-Al Experience

Step 5: Share Highlights of the Interviews and Select Topics for Further Inquiry

Step 6: Create Questions to Be Added to the Four Generic Questions

Step 7: Develop the Inquiry Process

The rest of this chapter provides detail about each of these steps as well as notes, sample designs, handouts, and typical task sheets.

## Step 1: Select a Core Group and Possibly a Steering Team

With the contact person from the organization, decide whether a formal steering team, composed of the internal and external consultants, along with a few other critical people with influence and/or control of resources is helpful or whether an informal working group is enough. Then select a core group to attend the preparation workshop. This core group is typically a small group and may or may not include all the members of the steering team or informal working group. The core group is selected whenever possible from representatives of each part of the organization and each staff level. Ask them to attend a meeting that will be the beginning of the Appreciative Inquiry process. The meeting can be done in one day; however, if you are working with multiple languages or a complex system, two to three days is much better.

At the beginning of an Appreciative Inquiry process with an organization, it is very important to talk about the inclusive and democratic nature of the work. Encourage the client to involve, as quickly as possible, people from all parts of the organization. The more diversity you have in the core group, which is your planning team, the more you will be working in the spirit and philosophy of AI.

The task of selecting members of the "core group" usually falls to someone in the organization. When possible, work with that person and explain the importance of multiple perspectives and voices. A "diagonal" slice of the organization works well.

The "core group" is the group that creates a Customized Interview Guide and plans the inquiry. It is helpful to have a core group of a few people who will work with you throughout the process to link you to the organization and to co-create the steps in AI. Planning groups can be as small as three or four and as large as twenty or thirty, although in the latter case it is wise to have a core team or three or four who are primary contacts.

## Step 2: Orient Participants to the Goals of the Workshop and to Their Role in Meeting the Goals

Begin the preparation workshop by explaining the purpose of the workshop, the agenda, the way you want to work together, and with an introductory exercise. Discuss any logistical issues like location of Rest Rooms, information about the site, etc. Allow time for questions and answers. Using information from the sheet titled "Topic Choice: A Fateful Act" from Chapter 6 explain to the group the importance of the work they will be doing in this step of an Appreciative Inquiry.

### Actual Goals and Agenda for a Two-Day Preparation Workshop

This example is drawn from our work with a transnational pharmaceutical company that had asked us to "evaluate" the impact of a major training program that had been conducted by their internal HR/OD division. In attendance at this workshop were members of the staff (both internal OD staff and scientists) who had designed the program.

The five goals of this two-day preparation workshop were:

1. To clarify the difference between the AI approach to valuation and traditional evaluation approaches.

   - Introduce Appreciative Inquiry

   - Discuss the shifting paradigm

   - Examine the theory of change that underlies this approach (leave time for discussion and Q&A)

   - Present Appreciative Inquiry principles and practices

2. To agree on desired outcomes and critical success factors for this evaluation process and how we will get there.

   - Discuss the desired outcomes and critical success factors

   - Discuss the major phases of the Al Valuation approach and agree on a way forward

3. Jointly develop a customized draft interview protocol for gathering stories using this approach and to practice it.

   - Importance of how we capture data and what data to record

   - Create a draft customized interview protocol

   - Practice AI interviewing skills

4. Jointly create a plan for collecting and making meaning of the evaluation data.

   - Identify stakeholders

   - Key steps in data collection

   - Collect, organize, and compile the information

5. To agree on next steps (actions, responsibilities and dates) for all on the team.

The design of the preparation workshop is shown in Table 5.1.

## Table 5.1. Design for Two-Day Preparation Workshop

| Time | Day One | Time | Day 2 |
|---|---|---|---|
| 8:00 | Gather for coffee | 8:00 | Gather for coffee |
| 9:30 | The AI Evaluation Process: Context, assumptions, approach, desired outcomes of the evaluation process, steps, roles, and critical success factors for this process | 9:00 | Step 3b: Test Protocol Draft 1. *Test Interview 1*—Design team members or simulation participants are interviewed by workshop participants one-on-one. |
| 10:30 | BREAK | 10:00 | BREAK |
| 10:45 | Create Customized Protocol and Data Collection Strategy: Step 1: Conduct Generic Interviews. Workshop participants interview each other using the four generic AI questions | 10:30 | *Test Interview 2*—Design team members or simulation participants are interviewed by workshop participants one-on-one. |
| 11:45 | What Is Appreciative Inquiry? Overview of theory, research, and principles | 11:30 | Interview Debriefing. Questions, comments about the interview |
| 12:30 | LUNCH | 12:15 | LUNCH |
| 1:15 | Step 2: Identify Topics: From the generic interviews identify key topics and language to be used in developing the customized protocol | 2:00 | Step 3c: Create Draft 2 of customized interview protocol. Revise the protocol based on results of test interviews1 and 2. |
| 2:00 | Step 3a: Create first draft of customized interview protocol. Combine themes emerging from the generic interviews with research into a first draft | 3:00 | Step 4: Develop plan for data collection and analysis. Identify key stakeholder groups. Plan the interview process, Preliminary plan for data compilation, analysis, and presentation |
| 3:30 | BREAK | 3:45 | BREAK |

## Table 5.1. Continued

| Time | Day One | Time | Day 2 |
|------|---------|------|-------|
| 4:00 | AI Interviewing Skills: Interview tips. Practice introducing AI. Practice conducting interviews. Documentation/note-taking guidelines | 4:00 | Next Step Planning: Conduct pilot interviews. Final protocol revision. Company-wide embedded evaluation interviews |
| 5:30 | Review of the Day: Questions. Preview of Day 2. Interview assignments for Day 2 | 5:30 | Debrief: Workshop Debriefing and Closure |
| 6:00 | ADJOURN | 6:00 | ADJOURN |

### Introductions for a Mini-AI Interview

- Choose a partner you don't know or that you want to know better. Ask the following questions of each other. You will have five minutes each for the interview.

  ○ Tell me a story about a time in your life when you have felt particularly joyful, creative, successful—a real high point. Make yourself the hero/heroine of the story. Give me the details about what happened, who was there, what you did, etc.

  ○ Without being humble, tell me what it is that you value most about yourself.

- After everyone has finished this mini interview, introduce your partner to the group by sharing a high point in his or her life and one thing that he or she values about him- or herself that you learned from your interview.

## Step 3: Quickly Get Participants into an Experience of AI

Introduce the generic interview (that is, the four generic questions) by giving a simple explanation of AI as a different approach to understanding organizations (five minutes). These four questions form a useful preliminary protocol which exemplifies the spirit of AI, while also being easily modified to fit whatever topic the organization has chosen to focus on. For example, in the four-hour workshop presented in Chapter 4, the questions were modified for an academic setting. The people involved in that workshop, having interviewed each other using these questions, went on to work with the data from their own responses to (1) design an overall inquiry architecture which engaged, students, parents, school faculty and staff, school board members, and senior administration within this school system and (2) to develop not one but three customized interview protocols—one for faculty and staff, one for students, and one for other key stakeholders such as parents, senior administration, and school board members. Assign the interview task and review the tips on how to do an Appreciative Interview.

*example*

## Sample Language for Introducing the Generic Interview

"Appreciative Interviews differ from traditional interviews in that the questions are simply guidelines that lead the person being interviewed to delve into the most creative, exciting, life-giving experiences that they have had in their life and work. It is not as important to answer every question as it is to tell a complete story, evoking the situation complete with details of what happened and the feelings involved. The goal is to help the person doing the interviewing experience as much as possible the situation being described. The interviewer's role is to LISTEN, occasionally prompting the interviewee to be more descriptive or to enlarge the story. *This part of the process is like a monologue by the person being interviewed.*"

### The Four Generic Questions

The development of the customized interview protocol is frequently done by having core team members in the preparation workshop interview each other using a slightly modified version of the Four Generic Questions shown below:

1. *Best Experience:* Tell me about the best times that you have had with your organization. Looking at your entire experience, recall a time when you felt most alive, most involved, or most excited about your involvement. What made it an exciting experience? Who was involved? Describe the event in detail.

2. *Values:* What are the things you value deeply; specifically, the things you value about yourself, your work, and your organization:

a. Yourself: Without being humble, what do you value most about yourself -as a human being, a friend, a parent, a citizen, and so on?

b. Your Work: When you are feeling best about your work, what do you value most about it?

c. Your Organization: What is it about your organization that you value? What is the single most important thing that your organization has contributed to your life?

3. *Core Life-Giving Factor or Value:* What do you think is the core life-giving factor or value of your organization? What is it that, if it did not exist, would make your organization totally different than it currently is?

4. *Three Wishes:* If you had three wishes for this organization, what would they be?

## Sample Task Statement for the Paired Interview Using the Four Generic Questions

*Note:* Prior to giving this explanation, you should display a flip-chart page showing the four generic questions, which will be used as the basis for this exercise.

"Select a partner you do not know well or someone you'd like to know better. Participant 1 of the partners will interview Participant 2 for thirty minutes (or up to one hour, depending on the time available) using the questions shown on the flip chart. The interviewer's role is to ask the questions, to encourage the interviewee to be very descriptive and to expand his or her story. The person being interviewed is encouraged to tell the story in language that evokes the feelings and the experience so that the interviewer can feel that he or she really understands the event.

After the allotted time, the partners change roles and Participant 2 conducts the same interview with Participant 1.

Everything we do from here on in will depend on the data from these interviews, so please listen intently and make note of words, phrases, and ideas that are present when the person being interviewed is telling an exciting story of a creative and successful experience."

*example*

## Step 4: Debrief the Mini-AI Experience

After the paired generic interviews are completed, bring the group together and conduct a short discussion about how it felt to do this process. Make your own comments about what you noticed— the high energy level, the buzz of excitement in the room, the way people were interacting with each other. Give the group a presentation on "What Is Appreciative Inquiry" using the material from Chapter 4 (although you can skip the mini inquiry experience described in Chapter 4). Answer any questions the group has.

### Hints on Debriefing the Paired Generic Interview Experience

Ask the group to brainstorm "What was that experience like for you?" It's very important to keep the group focused on debriefing the "process" of the experience rather than getting into the "content" of the questions or the responses. They will have plenty of time to do that later. It's also useful to write the short one- to three-word brainstorm responses on a flip chart. This honors all the responses— even those that are not overly positive. Don't worry if you get a few responses that say the interview was difficult, etc. Remember that this sort of interviewing is counter-cultural for most people and generates a level of closeness between interviewer and interviewee that is not comfortable for some people.

Be patient and highlight the affirmative responses while acknowledging this is a different sort of interview process and they will have a chance to modify it later.

## Step 5: Share Highlights of the Interviews and Select Topics for Further Inquiry

Have the groups share the highlights from the stories they heard and select topics. After compiling a list of the major topics in the stories, the group decides on three to five topics that they want to know more about. (If the group is eight or fewer, you can work in one group.) Break larger groups into small groups of two to four interview partners (six to eight people) and have each group do the task.

In a small group, these decisions can be made through dialogue and consensus building. If there are several small groups doing the same task, you can have each group's work posted on a wall and create a "scatter gram." To do this, you will need either stickers such as dots or colored markers. Ask the participants to study all of the lists, decide on their three most important topics, and put a sticker or a mark on each of those three. This will give you a visual image of which topics are most important. Then the group can discuss and decide upon the final three to five topics from those that have the most marks.

## Sample Task Statement for Topic Identification

"For each question, each person shares what he or she heard—the best story, things that were the most meaningful, good ideas, etc.—as descriptively as possible. (Be careful not to share stories that were told to you confidentially. Ask your partner's permission if you are unsure.)

"As you listen to the stories, make notes of important topics that seem to be present when people are living into their values as demonstrated in the stories.

"Using your notes, create a list of the topics that have emerged from all the interviews.

"Decide on several topics that the whole group thinks are very important and make a list of those. A recorder captures the topics, ideas, and high points on the flip chart. Have a group discussion about this list.

"At the end, discover the most important overall topics that are the core factors that have given life and vitality to the organization and its work in the world. These will be the topics that you will be asking questions about in the interview guide that you will create for your organization."

## Sample Topics from a Variety of Organizations

### From an African NGO

• Spiritual Values

• Commitment to Grassroots

- Development of Human Potential
- Teamwork

**From a Financial Institution**

- Being the Best
- Shared Ownership
- Cooperation Across Boundaries
- Integrity in Customer Service
- Empowering People

**From a Health Delivery Organization**

- Winning Organization
- Excellent Service and Quality
- Sense of Ownership

## Sample Handout on "Topic Choice—A Fateful Act"

Topic selection is the next step in the Appreciative Inquiry process. Careful, thoughtful, and informed choice of topics is important, as it defines the scope of the inquiry, providing the framework for subsequent interviews and data collection. Topic choice is a fateful act. Your organization will move in the direction of the topics they inquire about.

In choosing topics, you are encouraged to be imaginative and creative. Select topics that are positive affirmations of the strengths of your organization and the powerful entity it seeks to become. Remember...

- Topic choice is a fateful act
- Organizations move in the direction of inquiry
- Involve those who have an important stake in the future in choosing the topics to explore
- Two days or more may be required to identify the additional topics
- Everyone is an active participant

example

*example*

○  Diversity is essential

○  Vocabulary is not 'just semantic"—words create worlds

○  People commit to topics they have helped develop

**Other General Guidelines**

- Encourage participants to choose a reasonable number of topics so there will be a manageable number of questions in the customized protocol.

- Topics are phrased in affirmative terms.

- Topics are driven by curiosity—spirit of discovery.

- Topics are genuinely desired—people want more of these in the organization.

## Step 6: Create Questions to Be Added to the Four Generic Questions

Using the selected topics that the group wants to know more about, write interview questions about those topics. Use those questions, plus questions from the Generic Interview Sheet to construct an interview guide for your organization.

*example*

### Sample Task Statement for Creating Additional Interview Questions

"Using the chosen topics, create additional questions for the Interview Guide. Make the questions appreciative and affirmative, focused on stories, details, feelings, words that evoke the situation as the person actually experienced it in all of its excitement and creativity.

"Put a complete interview protocol document together as you want to use it in your data gathering. The question formulated for each topic is added to the four generic questions to form a complete Interview Guide that will be used to interview stakeholders in your organization. You may want to write some introductory material to explain the project and the purpose of the interview."

example

## Sample Handout "Creating the Interview Guide, the Customized Protocol"

Creating the interview guide is an exciting task: What we ask determines what we "find." What we find determines how we talk. How we talk determines how we imagine together. How we imagine together determines what we achieve.

There are typically five parts to the interview guide, as follows:

1. Stage-setting questions

2. Best experience question focused on the general area of inquiry, such as best learning environment or best cross-gender relationships or best team experience, etc.

3. Values question focused on what people value most about themselves, their work, and their organization

4. Additional questions using topics identified in the topic selection process

5. Concluding questions—somewhat more open, externally focused and offering a place in the interview for identifying things the person wants to change. For example:

   • What are the core factors that give life to this organization?

   • Looking toward the future, what are we being called to become?

   • What three wishes do you have for the future of the organization?

## Sample Handout "Key Considerations in Crafting Questions for an Appreciative Inquiry

Effective questions...

1. Are stated in the affirmative and describe what is wanted, rather than what isn't wanted.

2. Build on the assumption that "the glass is half full" (not half empty!). Because Appreciative Inquiry is based on the belief that positive affect is as contagious as negative affect, AI questions are consciously and

example

intentionally in search of the generative, the creative, the moments of achievement and of joy. Therefore, questions can be preceded by an explanation of the positive intent of the question. AI is seeking the half-full vantage point.

3. Give a broad definition to the topic. (This is OK. Broad definitions give room to "swim around.")

4. Are presented as an invitation to tell stories—rather than an inquisition about "facts," for example, "Tell me a story about a time when...."

5. Value "what is." They spark the appreciative imagination by helping the person locate experiences that are worth valuing.

6. Convey unconditional positive regard of the person and his or her involvement.

7. Evoke essential values, aspirations and inspirations.

Following are some examples of "half-full" questions.

**Leadership.** People in this organization have described leadership as the act of facilitating people to come together to accomplish the things they want to do. By assuming leadership, a person or organization helps the people focus and realize their desires and goals that reflect their highest values for achieving the common good. We like the following quotations:

> "The best leader is the one that when the job is done the people say, 'We did it ourselves.'" Lao Tsu

> "Here are my people going; let me follow them because I am their leader." Ghandi

Describe a time or occasion when you experienced this kind of leadership. Tell us a story about it. Be very descriptive. What happened? Who was involved?

**Shared Vision and Ownership.** Based on actual experiences in this company, members of our core group have concluded that organizations work best when everyone thinks, acts, and feels like an owner of the business. That sense of ownership is highest when there is a shared vision for where the business is heading in the future, when people are involved in major decisions that are relevant to them and their work, when appropriate information about the business is shared openly, when people know the whole picture in terms of other's tasks or jobs, and when people feel they are at the center of things rather than on the outside.

Tell me a story about a time when you felt most involved in the "big picture" of the organization, a time when you felt most like a partner or even owner of the business. What can we all learn from this experience?

Think about the future, what could this organization do *more of* to create a shared vision of the future and a heightened sense of ownership at all levels?

## Examples of a Complete Customized Protocol

*Note:* This protocol begins with the opening statement for the customized protocol from the "valuation" project with the transnational pharmaceutical company.

"Thank you for giving time to participate in this evaluation study. We are coming to the end of the rollout of the discovery simulation in its current form. So the purpose of this evaluation study is to gather information on:

- How people have made connections from the simulation experience to their everyday work

- How we might follow up and further leverage the simulation in the company

- How we might enhance our use of simulations within the company in the future

"Before we start. I would like to explain a little bit about what we are going to do because it may be different from what you are used to. This is going to be an 'appreciative interview.' I am going to ask you questions about times when you see things working at their BEST. Many times

*example*

interviews such as this ask questions about things that aren't working well—the problems—so that we can fix them. In this case, we're trying to find out about things at their best—the successes—so that we can find out what works and do more of the things that work.

"I'm interested in identifying and understanding those areas and situations where your participation in the discovery simulation has helped you in your work. I'm interested in you and your work and in understanding more about those times when you feel you are excelling and any connections that you might make between that and the discovery simulation.

"All the information provided will be treated as anonymous and will be used to ensure that the company is capitalizing on its investment in the discovery simulation. My interest today is in learning from you and your experiences. I will be summarizing the information I capture today with data from other interviews. No names (unless permitted) will be associated with the overall summary or report. Please let me know if you are interested in receiving the summary and we will make sure to send it to you. The probable time frame is two to three months from now.

"I'm confident that it is through these collected comments, experiences, and suggestions that we will find what enlivens the Discovery organization and how the simulation contributes to making it a better place to work. The interview takes approximately one hour. Do you have any questions?"

**Actual Interview Protocol for Participants in Discovery Simulation**

1. Before we get to the questions about the discovery simulation, I'd like to know a bit about your experience here at (the company) and I'd like to do it in the style of Appreciative Inquiry. Could you tell me a story about a time at [this company] when you felt particularly excited, creative, productive? What happened? Who was involved? What part did you play?

2. Now I'd like to ask you about your participation in the discovery simulation. Can you tell me a story about a high point when you felt excited and engaged in the course of participating in the discovery simulation? Looking back at that experience, what made

it exciting? Who was involved? Describe the event in detail. Are there other high points? Probe: What did you learn that you valued?

3. One of the purposes of the discovery simulation is to provide opportunities for you to learn about both the Discovery process and about your style of working with a team. The desired outcome is for you to feel that the things you experienced during the workshop are useful in your work in the organization and in your life in general.

   a. In that context, can you tell me some examples (stories) of ways that the things you experienced during the simulation workshop have had a positive impact on your work and/or the quality of your life at work? Tell me a story about that. What happened? Can you tell me another story (example)?

   b. [Give a copy of the list below to the person you are interviewing.] As you look at this list, are there any stories that come to mind on any of these areas?

   • Your leadership style and skills

   • Your interaction with other departments

   • Your membership on a project team

   • Your ability to champion your research effort

   • Ability to manage projects

   • Planning/strategy of your existing research effort

   • Willingness to take risk

   • Make decisions, that is, termination; go, no-go; phase change, etc.

   • Managing in the context of the discovery portfolio

   c. If you had three wishes for how we leverage our investment in the discovery simulation program, what would they be? (Future simulations? Things that would be helpful to you on

your job in the future? Ideas for further use of this
simulation? Etc.?)

4. Now, I'd like to ask you a few questions about the discovery
   organization itself:

   a. What is it that you value most about the discovery
      organization?

   b. In your opinion, what is the core value (driving force;
      essence; underlying principle; life giving force) of the
      discovery organization. What is it that, if it did not exist,
      would make the discovery organization totally different
      than it is now?

   c. The future of organizations is greatly impacted by the images
      we hold. Our images are often expressed in our desires
      and hopes for the future. In that context: if you had three
      wishes for the future of the discovery organization, what
      would they be?

## Step 7: Develop the Inquiry Process

Create a stakeholder scan—a list of individuals or groups you know
to have a stake in the outcomes of the change process. Decide
whether you want to have core group members conduct multiple
interviews or whether you want to bring large groups of people
together in an AI Summit meeting—or some combination of both.
Create a plan for how the data will be synthesized and who will be
involved in the development of the image of the preferred future
and the "design" phase of the AI process.

Successful data collection/narrative exploration requires the
identification of key stakeholders in your organization—those who
have a vested interest in or strong impact on the organization's
growth and future and who can supply you with valuable insights
into your selected topic area(s). After identifying the stakeholders,
you will need to make arrangements for preparing your interview
questionnaire, collecting the data, recording the information, and

collating or distributing the data. The data you collect at this stage will serve as the basis for the next stage—creating the organizational dream.

## Sample Handout: "The Stakeholder Scan"

Stakeholders are those people who have a stake in the organization's future. They may be inside or outside the formal boundaries of your organization. Categories of stakeholders might include:

- Employees (various segments and levels)

- Board of directors

- Funders

- Regulatory agencies

- Neighbors of the organization

- Unions

- Vendors/suppliers

- Alliances/partner organizations

- Clients/customers

- Family members

- Competitors

- Etc.

**Task:** Once the group has finished writing their Interview Guide, have them brainstorm all of the possible people who could be interviewed. It is fun to make a large chart of this and to write names in different areas or colors according to their connection to the organization. Once they have all possible names, you will need to help them decide how many interviews they can reasonably do and to identify those people on their list that are the most important to be interviewed. Remember that the same guidelines apply to those interviewed as to the team itself—maximum diversity!

**Task:** Create an assignment sheet that lists:

| Person to Be Interviewed | Contact Information | Person Doing the Interviewing | Time and Place | Comments |
|---|---|---|---|---|
|  |  |  |  |  |

**Task:** Finally, create a report sheet for the interviewers to fill out after each interview. An example of such a sheet follows. However, there are many ways to organize the information from the interviews and it is important that the members of the organization be clear on what they want to capture and how.

## Example of an Interview Summary/Report Sheet— Pharmaceutical Company Valuation Project

**Task:** Ask interviewers to fill this sheet out *immediately* after their interview.

Interviewee name:

Department:

Years of experience in this company:

Current roles in the company:

Past roles in the company:

Date/location of simulation attended:

DMC/team member/other in the simulation:

Interview location (US/UK):

Interviewer name:

Date of this interview:

### Stories

- What were the most compelling stories that came out of this interview about the simulation workshop?

*example*

- What were the most compelling stories that came out of this interview about how the learnings were applied?

**Learnings**

- What were other learnings/applications reported in this interview?

**Wishes**

- What were the three wishes for the discovery simulation?

- What were the three wishes for the discovery organization?

**Values**

- What were the individual values?

- What was the core value for the discovery organization?

**Quotes**

- What were the most quotable quotes that came out of the interview? (What questions do these relate to?)

**Implications**

- What did you learn through this interview that will make a difference in how you/your company plans and manages other training designs?

## Creating a "Report" of the Interview Data

There are many ways to use the information from the interviews at this point. The important thing is to make it available to the whole community, especially to that part of the community that will be working on the Dream and Design phases. Of course, it is always preferable to have as much of the organization as possible involved at every phase. Work with the people who are available, and always build into any planning some ideas for ways to gain consensual validation from the whole organization.

If you create a summary sheet for each interview (see the example above), it is possible to compile all of that information by category. Another possibility is to create a "story" book that captures the most compelling stories and quotes. Another way is to have continuing dialogue in many different places with a wide cross-section of the organization.

The important thing at this point is to understand that the information gathered and compiled is the raw material for the dreams for the organization, those visions that people in the organization create based on the best of what is as told in the stories (*continuity*) to inspire the articulation of the best of what will be (*novelty*). The Design and Delivery stages create the *transition* processes that create the desired future.

The final work of this second core process is the generation of an agreement on the process (plan) for the inquiry. The core team, during the preparation workshop, typically does this work once the rationale for the use of stories is understood and the customized protocol has been developed. In the event that the core team reports to a guidance group, it is obviously advisable to have ongoing connections between the core team and that group as the core team works out its plan to move the AI process forward. These connections might be as formal as having one or more members of the guidance group be a part of the core team's deliberations during the preparation workshop or the connections might be as informal as having core team members "buddy up" over lunches or coffee with their counterparts on the guidance team.

The role of the consultant here is to co-create with the client system in a manner that continues to ensure that the change process is "owned" by members of the client system and not the consultant. This may mean helping the client system (in this case the core team and others) explore the various choices and scenarios for each of the five questions relating to the development of an Inquiry Architecture. It may also require the consultant/AI practitioner to help client system members apply the five core principles of AI to their discussion of the inquiry process. For example, the traditional guideline for determining how many people to interview revolves around the concept of "representative sampling," getting the minimal number of people identified from whom you could create a so-called "accurate picture of the situation." Our five AI principles, however, suggest an interviewing strategy that is as inclusive as possible, a strategy that recognizes that by engaging as many people as possible we are creating a highly unusual but positive form of energy, a form of critical mass moving in the direction of the inquiry questions.

For example, the Constructionist Principle reminds us that it is through dialogue that we learn about and make sense of our world. The Principle of Simultaneity reminds us that through our act of asking questions we shift the focus of the dialogues. The Anticipatory Principle reminds us that we are drawn toward the images we create in our dialogues—particularly when they are attractive images of the future. We also know from the Poetic Principle that when people are involved in story telling, they will be involved not only at the level of their heads but also at the level of their hearts. In addition, we know from the Positive Principle that as people start to talk about life-giving forces during the interviews, the positive affect created will be highly contagious.

## Interviewer Training

There is a paradoxical relationship between the high importance we attach to the interview and the relatively minimal quantity of training that the "interviewer" receives during many AI-based processes. Within traditional approaches to organizational change, interviewers are engaged in extensive practice and feedback sessions on "good interviewing." It is important to remember that this traditional approach to interviewer preparation sees the notion of the interview more as an attempt to uncover some guarded "truth" which the interviewee is reluctant to share. By contrast, the AI interview, partly because of its storytelling format and partly because of the positive nature of its questions, quickly leads to an interpersonal rapport between the interviewer and the interviewee—a rapport not easily created within the more traditional "investigative" or "assessment" oriented interview. Consequently, it has been our experience that good clarity about the goal of the interview, the role of the interviewer, and a review of a few interview tips is all that is needed in most cases, and particularly when the interviews are done within a large group meeting where each person functions both as interviewer and interviewee. The guidelines we provide are as follows:

- Choose someone whom you do not know or would like to know better.

- Using the interview guide as your script, interview each other for [times are flexible depending on the situation. Allow as much time as possible.]

- Chose a location where you both feel comfortable.

- When you interview, write down key words/phrases you hear.

- Introduce and ask the questions as they are written.

- If necessary, use the probing questions provided in the interview guide.

- Let the interviewee tell his or her story. Try to refrain from giving yours. You will be next.

- Listen attentively, be curious about the experience, the feelings, and the thoughts.

- Allow for silence. If the other person does not want or cannot answer a question, it is OK.

- Have fun.

- At the end of the two interviews, take some time to talk with your partner about what the interview was like for you.

In the case of an organization choosing to have all interviewers conducted by a small group of people (such as the core group), we often spend time with them going over the following:

### Key Characteristics of an Appreciative Interview

- The interview is based on an assumption of health and vitality. What is sought are incidents and examples of things at their best.

- The connection between the interviewer and the person being interviewed is through empathy. Questions are answered in a way that evokes the feelings in the listener.

- Personal excitement, commitment, and care are qualities that are present when the interviewer and the person being interviewed are sharing stories of their personal peak experiences.

- Intense focus by the person listening to the stories leads to the experience of being heard fully and understood—a desirable effect from the close sharing that takes place.

- Generative questioning, caring, guiding make up the role of the interviewer. The skill is to encourage and question without interrupting the storyteller.

- Belief, rather than doubt, is the proper stance. This is not a time for skepticism or for questions that imply a need for "proof." The trust that develops from simply listening with interest and acceptance is a major positive effect of this process.

- Remember that these are stories being shared, not reporting of facts. Detail is always useful, as is allowing for the person's unique individual expression of his or her world.

- Additionally, when a small group undertakes to conduct multiple interviews per interviewer, it is very helpful to build in an early meeting for the interviewer group. The purpose of this meeting is to discuss "what we are learning about how to conduct great interviews." Of course, a mini-appreciative inquiry interview is the basis for this meeting.

## Conclusion

This second core process of AI can be considered to be complete when the client system has:

- Understood and accepted the rationale for collecting "data" in the form of stories rather than in the more traditional form of analytic and reductionist quantitative ways;

- Developed a customized protocol based on the selection of the primary topic chosen for inquiry in the previous core process;

- Agreed on an "inquiry architecture" (who shall be interviewed, by whom, when, how, where, and how the data will be synthesized and used to make decisions about the future of the organization); and

- Completed the actual interviews.

## Appreciative Living: Using AI in Daily Life

*By Jacqueline Kelm*

> "The real voyage of discovery consists not in seeking new landscapes, but in having new eyes."
>
> Marcel Proust

Mahatma Gandhi said we need to *"be the change we wish to see in the world."* But what does it mean to "be" Appreciative Inquiry? How do you "walk the talk"? How do you integrate AI so completely into your personal experience that it becomes who you are, rather than simply the 5-D process you follow?

I'm Jackie Kelm, and I've devoted the past ten years researching, applying, and writing about Appreciative Inquiry as it applies to personal living. It has transformed every area of my life from improving difficult relationships to creating the business of my dreams. If you have witnessed Appreciative Inquiry in action, you know its incredible power to transform the bleakest of organizational situations. When you apply this philosophy to your own life, the results are even more astounding! You not only gain the ability to transform personal issues and move toward your dreams, but your natural perspective and outlook shift to see the world anew "through appreciative eyes." This new perspective will allow you to experience greater joy than ever before, while simultaneously opening new possibilities for how you can apply AI organizationally beyond the 5-D cycle.

In this case story I'm going to explain a three-step process you can use to integrate AI into daily living. I will also share stories of how two different people used this process to deal with two common life challenges: grief and job stress. But first, let's take a look at the theory underlying this approach.

### The Principles of Appreciative Inquiry

My exploration into applying AI at the individual level began by intensely researching, practicing, and personally applying the five original AI principles created by David Cooperrider under the guidance of Suresh

Srivastva (Cooperrider, Whitney, & Stavros, 2003). I then expanded into complementary fields such as positive psychology and the new sciences and summarized it all in my first book, *Appreciative Living: The Principles of AI in Personal Life* (Kelm, 2009). Below is a summary of each principle and the essence of what it means to apply it individually.

## The AI Principles Applied to Personal Living

### The Constructionist Principle: Reality and Identity Are Co-Created

- We construct stories together with our thinking about what happens and who we are.

- Our story is one perspective, and there are an infinite number of perspectives.

### The Poetic Principle: Whatever We Focus on Grows

- We have poetic license to create, interpret, and focus our stories, and whatever we focus on expands.

- There is always a positive side to any situation or person, but we have to choose to find it.

### The Simultaneity Principle: Questions Ignite Change

- We anticipate what the future will be like by forming pictures in our minds, and then we live into those images.

- We can deliberately change the future by visualizing what we want.

### The Anticipatory Principle: We Live into Our Future Images

- The moment we ask about something we simultaneously begin to move toward it.

- Questions are a powerful tool for positive change.

**case story**

### The Positive Principle: Think Good to Feel Good

- Focusing on positive aspects creates positive upward spirals.

- Building on strengths provides greater leverage for change than fixing weaknesses.

From the Appreciative Living Learning Circle Participant Guide, page 9.

These five AI principles form the theoretical foundation on which Appreciative Living is based, and the underlying concepts are extensive. In order to make it easy for people to apply these principles practically in daily living, I created the AIA three-step model.

There are two examples I want to share that illustrate the use of the three-step model and the AI principles. Below is an overview of each story to give you some context for detailed discussions that will follow. The first one is from Brenda:

"My mother very unexpectedly passed away in May of last year. She was scheduled to move into our mother-in-law suite in three weeks, so the shock of her death was a major part of my grieving process. I attended grief workshops, read books on grieving, prayed to God, and talked to our friends and family. However, nothing could relieve the pain of my suffering.

"When we signed up for the Appreciative Living Learning Circle through our church this year, I had no idea that it would be the solution I was seeking to understand this dynamic woman's death. By applying the principles and doing the exercises in Jackie's *Joy of Appreciative Living* (Kelm, 2009), I was forced to examine the positive elements of Mom's death instead of focusing on the loss. While I admit it took several attempts to do this, both sides of the curtain did 'open up' and give me a full 'view' of both sides of the loss.

"This brought the peace I had been seeking and the understanding that you can accept the loss of a family member you loved with all of your heart. These principles are the keys to having joy in your life again."

case story

The second story is from Gene:

"I have been having excruciating problems at work with a new administration. This negative style has turned a largely happy institution into one where morale is down, people are leaving, and many are just plain going through the motions.

"The Appreciative Living exercises have kept my spirits higher and my joy greater than I would have ever expected under the circumstances. The daily reflection on what brings me joy got me to consciously focus on my level of joy and to make a commitment to do something about it.

"I am now in my last few days of work at this institution. I will leave at the end of the month, and I am delighted by the prospects."

Gene wrote this passage two years ago, and ended up starting his own business after leaving the company he worked for at the time. He credits the appreciative exercises for helping him make the move, and his business continues to do well two years later despite the troubled economy.

Both Gene and Brenda were able to use Appreciative Living to transform very different situations, and next I'll share the details of what they did and how the process works.

## The AIA Three-Step Process

The Appreciating-Imagining-Acting (AIA) Process shown in Figure 5.1 is a simple way to integrate the principles of AI in personal life, and has been used by hundreds of people to create more joy. The steps are not linear and can be worked in any order. A summary follows (Kelm, 2005):

## Appreciating What Is

For ease of understanding, it is helpful to think of the steps in order. To this end, I speak of the first step in the AIA process as "Appreciating What Is."

case story

## Figure 5.1. The AIA Three-Step Process

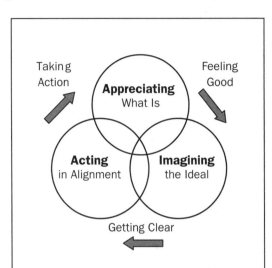

© 2010 www.AppreciativeLiving.com

This first step suggests we look for something to appreciate, the available learning, and the positive possibilities of whatever is showing up in our present experience. We know we are successful with this step when we begin to feel good about the situation, or at least feel better.

In Brenda's case, her mother was a dynamic eighty-five-year-old woman who gave cooking demonstrations regularly and was training for a 5K race just before she passed away. They were very close, talked to each other every day, and Brenda was excited her mother was coming to live with her shortly. When her mother died unexpectedly during a routine surgical operation, Brenda was stunned and angry.

She knew the first step was to "Appreciate What Is," but at first she could not see any good in this situation. She continued trying to find something to appreciate, and eventually she saw a small ray of light. She reflected on the random times her mom would refer to death, and how it was always in a very positive way. Brenda said her mom liked to sing, and when Brenda would tell her she was off-key, her mom would reply it was

OK because she was going to sing like an angel when she got to heaven. This memory made Brenda smile and brought a tiny bit of relief.

Brenda continued looking for something good and remembered that her mom would cite Biblical scriptures and talk about the riches of heaven. Brenda believed her mom thought heaven was a wonderful place, and she felt better thinking about her being in a place she enjoyed. Doing the first step brought Brenda some relief from her intense grief and allowed her to move on to the other steps.

## Gene's First Step

Gene was also able to "Appreciate What Is" about his difficult work situation in a slightly different way. He began by listing three things each day he appreciated about his life in general. Examples he found included his wife and family, nature, and simple pleasures such as laughter and sunsets. The more he appreciated the good things in his life, the better he began to feel.

The second exercise he did was to look for one small way to increase his joy each day. He came up with ideas such as hugging his family, reaching out to others, and being of service. As he engaged in these activities, he really started feeling better, and these improved feelings flowed over into his work experience.

Gene and Brenda were able to feel better in the midst of difficult situations by choosing to find a way to "Appreciate What Is." This is the goal of the first step in the AIA process.

## Imagining the Ideal

The second step in the AIA process is "Imagining the Ideal." The essence of this step is to picture the way you want things to be, which acts like a beacon to guide your actions. On a grand scale, it might be creating a life vision. On a small scale it might be taking a few minutes before a meeting to close your eyes and picture it running smoothly. In either case, you create a mental image of what you want most or what things would look like if they were exactly as you would have them.

*case story*

In Brenda's situation, she visualized her mom being happy on the other side in ways her mom had described while still alive. She found a sense of humor helpful, and regularly pictured her mom singing at the top of her lungs and prancing around up in heaven. Her mom was very proud of how beautiful she was for her age before she died, and Brenda imagined her looking beautiful forever. It made her smile to think of her mom singing happily and beautiful, and it helped release the anger she was feeling over her loss.

In Gene's case, he did a formal, written visualization each week of his ideal, joy-filled life. He included such things as, "My work is meaningful and appreciated," "Life is good," and "My ability to bring laughter, self-confidence, positive attitude, and positive growth to others brings me to a higher level of spiritual development than I had ever imagined."

These weekly visions helped Gene clarify what he really wanted in his life, and became the beacons that guided his actions. For Brenda, the vision served to ease her worries about her mom, and imagine her in an uplifting way. Both were "Imaging the Ideal" in the unique ways that best served their situations.

## Acting in Alignment

The last step in the AIA process is "Acting in Alignment," which means taking action to think or behave in ways that are consistent with what you want most. The action does not have to be physical and can be a change in thinking that comes about from doing an appreciative exercise.

In Brenda's situation, she chose to take action to deal with the guilt she was feeling over her mom's death. She was deeply regretting all the times her mom had asked her to come over or do something but she was too busy. She also felt like she should have done more regarding the surgery and that there was something she missed or should have done to prevent her death.

Brenda realized she has been ruminating on and feeling guilty for all the things she had NOT done for her Mom, so she decided to turn it around and make an appreciative list of all the things she HAD done for her when she was alive. The more she looked, the more she found, and she came to realize she had in fact done an awful lot. After doing the exercise for a period of time, the guilt started melting away and she truly began to feel better.

In Gene's case, he took major action. He realized in his visions how important joy was and that he would never have it with his current employer. So he left the company he was in and started his own business.

Both Brenda and Gene created major transformations by using the three-step process to look at their situations through "appreciative eyes." Gene created a whole new business out of a hopeless job situation, and Brenda was able to move on from intense grief over the loss of her mom and get on with her life.

## Summary

In this case story I presented two examples of how the AIA three-step process can be used to apply the Appreciative Inquiry principles to any situation. While these examples were from personal life, the process works just as well for individuals at the office. Every day is replete with opportunities for individuals to apply the AIA process in their jobs and interactions with others. It is also a powerful approach that can be used in coaching.

Whether dealing with intense grief, job stress, or any other personal difficulty, the steps to handle it appreciatively are the same: Appreciate What Is, Imagine the Ideal, and Act in Alignment. If you follow these steps, a whole new wonderful world will open up right alongside the one you are living; and that's when you'll really be walking the talk.

If you would like to learn more about Appreciative Living, please visit www.AppreciativeLiving.com for articles, books, products, workshops, and training materials. You may also want to visit the AI Commons at http://appreciativeinquiry.case.edu/ where I posted a presentation I gave at the 2009 Global AI conference. It includes an overview of the principles, a chart of the three-step process with sample exercises, and a live coaching session I did with a volunteer.

## Author's Contact Information

Jacqueline Kelm
Appreciative Living, LLC
Charleston, SC
(800) 214-0959; outside the U.S. (843) 881-1106

*case story*

## Appreciative Life Coaching

*By Bob Tschannen-Moran*

What can two people do, separated by an ocean, who have never met but who have the ability to connect using telephone, Skype, and Internet technologies? It turns out they can do a lot when the approach taken focuses on strengths and appreciates possibilities. That is exactly what happened when Tatiana, a professional health coach with aspirations to develop her business, reached out to me in September 2009 for consultation, collaboration, and coaching. From the island tourist destination of Mallorca, Spain, in the Mediterranean Sea, Tatiana dreamt of establishing a successful coaching practice with area residents and health providers. She was not exactly sure what form that might take or how to get from here to there, but she was confident that with a little help she could gain clarity and discover a way forward.

Initially, Tatiana had some work to do on those "voices in her head" that argued against her ability to make this happen. She also had to come to terms with ways in which her own life did not adequately embody the "work-life-kids-marriage balance" that she would be working on with others as a professional health coach. Tatiana dearly wanted to walk the talk and to serve as a role model of well-being, lest she comes across as an expert with a "do as I say, not as I do" message. Those mindset and lifestyle dynamics both required empathy on my part, as I sought to understand and explore her underlying feelings and needs.

Such empathy is an important part of one-one-one coaching. Appreciative Inquiry without empathy is interrogation. That does not mean we pity or sympathize with clients as though they were helpless victims or reflections of our own issues. That rather means that we seek to understand the beauty of what clients are wrestling with, even when that beauty lies hidden under a patina of judgments, evaluations, criticisms, and complaints. The more Tatiana came to understand the richness of her heartfelt yearnings, the more she came to appreciate the life-affirming motivation behind those voices and desires, the more she was able to increase her self-efficacy and expand her view of the possible.

*case story*

The process I like to use for expressing empathy in coaching is called Nonviolent Communication® or NVC (Rosenberg, 2005). NVC encourages practitioners to distinguish between observations and evaluations, thoughts and feelings, needs and strategies, as well as requests and demands (Tschannen-Moran & Tschannen-Moran, 2010). As Tatiana shared her stories with me, I would assist her to play with those distinctions and to discover new ways of looking at her world. It worked. Appreciative empathy paved the way for Appreciative Inquiry.

As in organizational initiatives, one-on-one coaching can also make use of Appreciative Inquiry through the kinds of questions we ask and invitations we make. It is especially helpful to ask a lot of strengths-based questions in the Discovery phase of the process. Such questions connect clients with their capacity. I therefore invite clients to take the Values-In-Action Signature Strengths Questionnaire (www.authentichappiness.sas.upenn.edu) and to write out their answers to the following ten questions. Tatiana answered the questionnaire and then answered all of the following questions in great detail. This laid the foundation for a series of dynamic, strengths-building conversations.

1. *Great Accomplishment:* Write a story about one of your great accomplishments. What happened? When did it happen? Who was involved? What made the accomplishment stand out for you? How did it make your life, and the lives of others, more wonderful? Write the story in detail.

2. *Best Energy:* Write a story about an experience you really enjoyed and had fun with, a time that filled you up with positive energy. What happened? When did it happen? Who was involved? What made the experience stand out for you? How did it impact and spill over into the rest of your life? Write the story in detail.

3. *Real Recognition:* Describe a time when someone expressed sincere gratitude for something you said or did, a time when you made a contribution that was acknowledged by others. What happened? Who was involved? What made the recognition stand out for you? How did you feel? Write the story in detail.

*case story*

4.  *Value Most:* Without being humble, describe what you value most about yourself. When you are most pleased with your life and work, what are you saying, doing, and being? Write out your thoughts in detail.

5.  *Best Environment:* What situations tend to bring out your best? What conditions enable you to shine? Brainstorm every factor that comes to mind.

6.  *Guiding Light:* What do you claim as the guiding value of your life and work? It may not be fully reflected now, but you would like to fully reflect it in the future. Write out your thoughts in detail.

7.  *Three Wishes:* If you could wave a magic wand and make any three wishes come true, what would they be? Dream big and be specific. Write out your wishes in detail.

8.  *Best Legacy:* Imagine that you live many more years and make all the contributions you wish to make. What will be your legacy? How will your obituary read? What will people say at your funeral or memorial service? Write out your thoughts in detail.

9.  *Role Models:* Who are your role models, the people who reflect your own visions and dreams for the way life should be? What do you most admire about them? What are some ways you'd like to challenge yourself to become like them? Write out your thoughts in detail.

10. *Daily Habits:* What daily habits represent your idea of a successful, meaningful, and healthy life? What patterns of behavior are true and right for you? What routines will fall into place when everything is just the way you want it?

As our conversations progressed, Tatiana made the shift from focusing on the shortcomings of her current situation to the opportunities of her emerging future (Scharmer, 2007). Through the use of a future-self exercise during a coaching session and the ongoing creation of a vision board in her home office, a wall-mounted poster on which Tatiana began to portray in words and pictures her desired future state (she would send

case story

me digital pictures of this as it progressed so we could talk about it together), Tatiana had an "aha" experience regarding the question of her "bigger picture and bigger purpose." It is not that she didn't know these things before, but our coaching conversations combined with her work on the vision board to call forth a deeper sense of connection and clarity regarding her identity and vocation. "I think it is better to concentrate on the 'light within,'" she wrote, "and let that shine first of all, rather than all these things that are bogging me down, or not working, or annoying, or hopeless. Then consequent steps will be more intuitive, regardless of what these exactly are." So that is what we did together: we cooked up a clear and compelling vision of the future so as to chart a cogent and captivating path of personal and professional development.

Tatiana described the progression in these terms: "I am looking forward to defining my own long-term aspirations and dreams, both for my work and for myself. I have a kind of 'snapshot' idea but it is not really detailed. This big vision will help me 'lock in' long-term, mid-term, and short-term plans. It will help me to compare that vision to what is happening in my life right now. I guess I have been like a sailboat in the sea, floating here and there. Now it is time to set the destination and steer that way. I most specifically want to work as a professional health coach and I want to work in that field for a long time to come."

To flesh out the details of Tatiana's aspirations, we focused considerable attention on what she had written in response to the question about environments that enable her to shine: "I am at my best in a productive group setting, be it with friends, at work, on a team. I do especially well with people who are near me, who believe in me, or who are very 'connected' themselves. I do well with people who have a high vibration, who are strong, who are complex. I also do well if I have to organize something. Because I have so much energy (always), I am happy being productive. I do well if I can organize my time independently and be flexible (for instance, some days I love to bake and cook all day; other times, I need to just 'throw' dinner on the table!) I do well with variety and in general do not like being told what to do. I do well when I feel accepted and wanted in a situation. I do well when I can balance my time so I get enough time alone, time to think and rest and plan."

*case story*

This insight gave us the opportunity to brainstorm around how Tatiana might find and/or create such an environment. We worked with the concept of designing environments where she could be great just by showing up—not ones that would require her to learn all kinds of new skills or that would force her into an uncomfortable position or manner of working. We strove to envision and then to evoke an environment that would bring out Tatiana's very best and reward her with both meaningful and fruitful work.

As good brainstorming always does, our brainstorming generated a wide variety of new ideas, from the ridiculous to the sublime (Kelley, 2001, pp. 56–62). The wilder the better when it comes to brainstorming. Or, to quote Albert Einstein, "If at first an idea is not absurd then there is no hope for it." We certainly played with many such possibilities, including total upheaval and relocation from the island of Mallorca. In the end, however, we kept coming back to the notion of staying in Mallorca while partnering with larger organizations and group settings. After exploring a number of alternatives, two emerged as leading contenders: a global consulting and training organization with virtual offices and a local hospital and health care organization with physical offices. Although Tatiana did not close the door on the virtual opportunity, she decided to see what she could make of things at the local hospital. Given the hospital's stated interest in serving the expatriate community living in Mallorca, Tatiana could present a ready calling card: she was trilingual (English, Spanish, and German), well networked in the community, and trained as a professional health coach. If ever there were an opportunity to be great just by showing up, this looked to be very promising.

Tatiana began by talking with the hospital director. To prepare for the meeting, we brainstormed ways to reach out and talk with people who were doing similar things in other hospital settings. She wanted to learn how health coaching had been integrated into hospitals and clinics, how clients were referred for coaching, whether coaching was conducted one-on-one or in group settings, how coaches related to the staff team, and how compensation was structured. With my help and the help of colleagues in her coach training program, Tatiana reached a point of confidence and readiness for having the meeting. It turned into a

*case story*

ninety-minute tour of the hospital that went amazingly well, with many happy coincidences including Tatiana meeting several people she already knew. The director and Tatiana ended the tour with a strong, mutual desire to clarify their vision, develop a job description, and move the position forward. The director went so far as to ask Tatiana whether she would consider working exclusively for the hospital. As Tatiana noted, "That was lovely to hear" after all her efforts to put herself out in the world.

It took several months for all this to come together, but once it did Tatiana had a sense of living into her destiny. In addition to one-on-one health coaching with clinic patients, she also started to develop programs for large and small groups using the hospital auditorium as well as a variety of wellness-coaching initiatives for hospital employees. Becoming the resident "Coach Salud" was not a salaried position. Tatiana had loads of internal sales work to do in order to recruit clients and program participants, but the work gave her "a good feeling" and she enjoyed having "a true focus for the first time in years."

None of this might have happened without our appreciative, strengths-based coaching work. Tatiana has indicated that the coaching gave her the extra boost she needed to get going and try her best. After one of our last coaching sessions, Tatiana wrote in an e-mail, "Thanks for the extra time today. I shall have to 'live without you' as I move forward, but I guess I have learned one thing: when in doubt, I can always fill in a questionnaire! Kidding aside, our life coaching sessions have made the difference between night and day for me in many ways. I would not be where I am today with this position were it not for the work we did together."

Such is the potential of Appreciative Inquiry in telephone, Skype, and Internet coaching. It can literally assist people to discover, dream, and design new destinies in life and work.

### Author's Contact Information

Bob Tschannen-Moran
LifeTrek International
coach@lifetekcoaching.com

# CHAPTER 6

# Locate Themes That Appear in the Stories (Discover)

> "Implied in ... scholarly research ... is the intriguing suggestion that human systems are largely *heliotropic* in character, meaning that they exhibit an observable and largely automatic tendency to evolve in the direction of positive anticipatory images of the future. What I will argue is that just as plants of many varieties exhibit a tendency to grow in the direction of sunlight, there is an analogous process going on in all human systems."
>
> David Cooperrider

**AFTER THE INTERVIEWS ARE COMPLETE,** this third core process, *locating the themes that appear in the stories,* encompasses the work of:

- "Mining" the data by looking for themes of what gives life in the organization and

- Expanding the positive dialogue about these themes to people throughout the organization.

This process, heliotropic in nature, encourages the organization to turn toward images of what gives life and, through continuing dialogue, to assure that a future is built on those themes and images.

Of course, since many people will have conducted the interviews—anywhere from two to two thousand in our experience—it is necessary to create a mechanism by which all that data can be absorbed and digested by people in the organization. (Notice that we do *not* say "analyze the data.") The search here is not for the norm, the most mentioned idea, even the best idea. The process of absorbing and digesting data is one that allows people to take it all in and to react to the messages and meaning in ways that move the organization in the direction of the combined positive energy of the members. It is more about creating synergy than about consensus.

The groups working with the interview data can also range from two to two thousand, or even more! Remembering the theory that we get more of what we focus on, it follows the more people involved in sharing the stories, "mining" the data, and identifying the themes of life-giving forces, the more the organization will move in the direction of those themes.

There are many ways of sharing and working with the data, just as there are many choices in the earlier processes about who does the interviewing, who "collates" the data (if that is the decision), and who works with the data to pull out the themes/life-giving forces. Before we get into identifying the choices in data collation and data synthesis (that is, making meaning of the data), let's focus on the idea of themes and what gives the organization life, as well as ways to identify the themes and life-giving factors in the data.

In describing the second core process of AI—*Inquiry into Stories of What Gives Life in the System*—we argued that the very action of asking people to reflect on and tell stories about their exceptional moments in the present or past of their organization and to identify the wishes they have for how things will be different in the future (the wish question) is a powerful intervention in and of itself, which begins to move the system in directions that are positive and life-giving. We argued that it is the combination of positively focused inquiry, positively focused dialogue, and the resultant influence on the collective imagination that propels forward movement. In this third core process of AI, we want to keep those conversations and that dynamic alive and extend them for the same reasons we asked the questions in the first place. However, it's not just a question of talking about good things. Rather, we need to work with the data in a way that continues the inherent value of conversations focused on what gives life while also developing the ground from which we can build shared images, dreams, and visions of a preferred future.

## Identifying Themes

Themes of what gives life are in the information gathered in the generic interviews as well as from the customized protocol interviews. In fact, those themes often come in surprising ways and from surprising places and events!

Themes are important "threads" from the inquiry data. They are short answers to the question: "What do we hear people describing in the interviews as what gives life in this organization?" Locating the themes involves identifying and highlighting those ideas imbedded in the interview data. Identifying the themes continues the "reality-creating conversations" and provides a link between the inquiry we have conducted into the past and the image of the preferred future we will create in the fourth core process. *The themes become the basis for collectively imagining what the organization will be like if the exceptional moments we have uncovered in the interviews became the norm in the organization.*

## Example of the Themes

The following example of themes comes from our work with an international pharmaceutical company. To put the themes in context, this example shows the preceding processes of topic choice, question formulation, and interviewing, as well as the next step after theme selection, which is articulating the dream, a process often referred to as writing "Provocative Propositions." More will be said about that step in the next chapter.

**Topic:** Transfer of learning from the workshop to the workplace. (*Note:* In this example, the topic had been identified by the HR group that wrote the original request for proposal for the evaluation of the simulation training process that had been delivered to nearly five hundred people throughout a major division of their organization.)

**Question:** One of the purposes of the research simulation is to provide opportunities for you to learn about both the research process and about your style of working with a team. The desired outcome is for you to feel that the things you experienced during the workshop are useful in your work in the organization and in your life in general.

In that context, can you tell me some examples (stories) of ways that the things you experienced during the simulation workshop have had a positive impact on your work and/or the quality of your life at work? Tell me a story about that. What happened? Can you tell me another story (example)?

(*Note:* During the start-up session the consultants worked with the internal team—the core group—that guided the whole "valuation" process. We began with an AI training session during which the core group learned about AI theory and experienced the process by doing the generic interviews, agreeing on the topics, and formulating questions that became the official interview protocol for the AI process. The above is one of those questions.)

**Themes:** Transfer of learnings. The major themes that emerged from the examples interviewees gave of applications back in the workplace were as follows:

• Participants overwhelmingly reported a clearer and more detailed understanding of the research system as a whole and of the roles and phases within the research process; application of this knowledge has enabled them to be more efficient and effective in their jobs.

- Many participants reported that they now place a greater value on their personal expertise and are more proactive in making contributions and taking initiative.

- As a result of the experience of teamwork on the program, participants are now using their collective expertise more effectively to make decisions and to progress their research efforts.

- Participants are continuing the process of networking that began on the research simulation and are using their new and broader links within the organization to assist them in developing and working on new ideas more quickly and effectively.

- Many participants have taken the opportunity to examine and further develop their leadership styles; some have also identified and addressed additional development needs for their staffs.

- Participants also report being more purposeful and rigorous in planning their research efforts, more effective in requesting and allocating resources, and more timely and effective in their decision making.

(*Note:* These themes were identified and compiled by the core group and the consultants. First, the answers from the more than one hundred interviews were collated into one document so that all of the answers to the above question were simply listed together under that question. Taking that list, the core group and consultants gleaned the themes listed above. They also compiled the answers to the "wish" questions that applied to the transfer of learning as listed below.)

**Wish Question:** Ideas for how transfer of learnings could be promoted further and for follow-up activities were as follows:

- Build into the program more help with how to apply the learning back on the job; involve managers in preparing participants for the program and in helping them to apply their learnings afterward.

- Make a desk-top tool available.

- Provide other educational forums and follow-up workshops on specific topics.

- Use the model for scenario modeling/challenging assumptions.

(*Note:* The following provocative proposition—an activity that is part of the next core process, *Creating shared images for a preferred future*—was formulated from these themes and used to guide the next stage of work for the HR team.)

**Provocative Proposition Topic I: Transfer of Learnings:** When the simulation program is most effective, the workshop experiences are directly translated to the workplace. With an increased understanding of the research process and the roles of the complementary disciplines, scientists plan more effective research efforts and become more proactive in their interactions with other departments. More timely decisions are made and resources are more focused on critical activities.

By effective teamwork, scientists leverage the skills and expertise of others to plan and progress research efforts more efficiently. With greater confidence in their own abilities to impact drug research, they more actively contribute to scientific discussions and initiate new research activities. Leadership is displayed through proactively developing staff and enabling them to participate in cross-functional initiatives.

**Outcome:** The HR team used this guidance for designing the next simulation training.

Below are some additional examples of the kinds of themes—things that are life-giving—that people identify from the interviews done in their organizations:

1. Themes from interviews with a group of professional sociotechnical systems consultants on the interview query:

"Tell me about a time when are felt most alive as a practitioner?"

- Working with people's core values

- Putting integrity into practice

- Recognizing the "footprints" of our work long after the steps have been taken

- Being real and authentic

- Designing organizations that create more humanity than they consume

2. Themes from interviews with a group of line managers in a social service agency telling stories about their working lives:

- Doing things collectively

- Removing barriers to unity (like the evaluation process), internal collaboration

- Ownership, support, commitment to common good

- Commitment to appreciating each other.

- Getting together, sharing information, and socializing.

- Transitioning from prosperity to austerity can lead to innovation and creativity

3. Themes from interviews with a group of line managers in a national bank:

- Being the best

- Shared ownership

- Cooperation

- Integrity

- Empowering people

There is no prescription for a theme. It is entirely up to the group to decide what gives life in their own system. Often discussions of themes found in the interview data will lead to conversations that uncover other themes the group believes are equally important. The challenge for the AI facilitator is to let the group go where it needs to go with as little constraining structure as is possible to have and still maintain enough order to get the work done. There are no right or wrong answers here; just answers that have meaning to the group itself.

In order to situate the "identifying themes" activity in the overall AI process, we provide two examples. The first shows a set of themes from one of our clients, set, for your understanding, into the context of the process we were using. The second is an example of an exercise you can use to help a group identify themes. These are meant to be *informational*, not instructive, because there are as many ways to get at this process as there are organizations and consultants working with it.

## A Process for Selecting Themes

In a complex system intervention, the work preceding this step has likely been: (1) identifying a core group from the organization; (2) conducting an AI workshop that includes the theory of AI, the generic interview process, and the identification of topics for further study from the interview data; and (3) conducting the interviews. A second workshop with the core group as a minimum and all of the people interviewed as a maximum is a good next step. The second workshop can focus on identifying themes (the subject of this third core process of AI) as well as on tasks that are covered in the next two chapters. For the purpose of illustrating a task statement and process for theme identification, we share with you a process we often use.

### A Theme Identification Exercise

This same process works for topic identification from the generic interviews.

**Instructions:** Choose a work group. Take your interview partner and join two other interview pairs, forming a group of six. (Note: We have used groups of as many as twelve if the group is very large. Interview pairs remain together for this task.) In your group:

- Choose someone to (1) Keep time; (2) Scribe on the chart; (3) Present your final chart

- At your table, each person (briefly) shares one or two of the best stories told by their interview partner. After hearing each other's stories, create a brainstormed list of all the themes that were present in the stories—about high points, what gives life, ideas that "grabbed" you—ideas about what life is like when things are at their best. From your group's "brainstormed" list agree on and select three to five topics for your group, and put them on chart paper. Post the sheets. (*Note:* If you have several topics—i.e., strong leadership, congenial work environment, etc.—each covered by a separate question, you can use this exercise for each separate topic.)

**Themes:** A theme is an idea or concept about what is present in the stories when people are reporting the times of greatest excitement, creativity and reward. For example, in many stories you may hear that when the topic covered by the question is at its best, people report "a feeling of success" or "clarity about purpose," or "fun and excitement." These phrases are "themes." In your brainstormed list, include all of these kinds of phrases that people can identify. Then select three to five themes that the whole group feels are important and that you would all like to have in your ideal work environment and organization.

It is very important at every step of an AI process to be inclusive and expansive. When we deal with data, our default setting is to become reductionist—to place things in priority order or to sort and try to combine ideas. For this exercise, we recommend that you say three to five as an approximate number of themes, but make it clear to participants that you do not want them to be constrained by those numbers. Some number more or less will also be fine. The idea here is to capture those ideas that are most important to people. Once they have some number of themes on the chart and the chart is posted on the wall (fairly close to each other so that they can all be seen easily) it is important not to give in to the inclination to put together similar themes or to combine charts in any way. Leave them exactly as they are. Once the exercise is done, there are ways to note when similar themes have many dots, which serves to emphasize the importance of those similar ideas.

Prepare a chart like the following and post it on the wall:

| Themes | *'s |
|--------|-----|
| 1. |  |
| 2. |  |
| 3. |  |
| 4. |  |
| 5. |  |

Each team answers any clarifying questions about the themes they have listed on the chart. Each person has X number of "dots." Working alone, participants decide, of all the themes on the wall, which are most important to include in their dreams of the future. Another way to decide is to think of those three or four things they want more of in the organization or system. Give them five minutes to decide and place their dots. Use each dot on a separate theme.

(*Note:* We generally give each person three or four of the colored Avery dots. You can also use markers and tell each person that he or she has X number of checks to be used one by a theme. The scattergram is more vivid if you use all one color.)

**Making Sense of the Scattergram:** Ask: What do you notice about the charts? What themes are most important to this group?

(*Note:* At this point the group will often notice similar themes and remark on that. Try to reinforce the idea that every theme on the wall is important to at least one group in the room. The scattergram is to give a visual image of the whole group's energy for certain themes. It is important not to count and put numbers by the dot clusters. Encourage people to see this as a visual of the group's energy. We rarely put any order to the themes, which allows the next step—shared images of a preferred future—to use all of the theme data as the basis for their images.)

Once again, let us reinforce that the AI approach for identifying themes is different from the traditional approach. Within an AI context, something can be a theme (such as what gives life) even if mentioned in only one story. This is different from the traditional approach, governed by scientific ideas about statistical validity, where something has to be mentioned a certain number of times before it can be called a theme.

Our focus in this process is identifying all things that have given life to persons in the system using a very different but inclusive set of criteria. In AI, if just one person in one interview identifies something that resonates, that strikes a chord with others in the system, then it is most likely that it is life-giving for that system. Of course, we also consider something life giving if several people mention it. This is a process for tapping into the intuitive emotional abilities of the group working with the data as they decide what, for them, gives life and energy in the organization. If it resonates with members of the client system, if people say, "YES, I know just what she means!", then it's probably a good bet that this is a theme we should be paying attention to. Bear in mind that this process, like much of AI, is an organic and eminently dynamic process in which if something is missed or misinterpreted at one point it will almost certainly be identified or restated in a clearer way at another point.

## Expanding the Dialogue

Bearing in mind that AI is rooted in the theory that we create our future realities through our current relationships and conversations, the task of pulling themes from the interview data is a marvelous opportunity to engage more people in conversations that focus on those things that give life to the organization. The group chosen to "mine" the data and select the themes can be any configuration the AI consultant and the organization co-create. Typical choices in our experience are:

- The external or internal consultant to the process, and/or

- Members of the interview team, and/or

- Members of the senior guidance group (if there is one), and/or

- All or some significant subset of the folks who were interviewed, and/or

- Various combinations of the above.

In the traditional model of OD consulting, the data is almost always collated and often analyzed by the consultant and fed back into the organization as a report or fed back to a working group for action planning. Remembering the theory that the observer always impacts and changes that which is observed, it follows that in an AI process the consultant would never be the one to analyze the data. Given that clients often are accustomed to and comfortable with certain kinds of processes, it may be a bit of a stretch to talk yourself out of the job of analyzing the data. We *strongly* recommend that you avoid doing that if at all possible since you will, by that act, have theoretically moved yourself and the system out of an AI process. The minimum participation in "mining" the data is the original core group. From there, add as many people as you can talk the client into. Working from the belief that the future is created through dialogue, it makes a great deal of sense to involve as many people as possible in this stage.

If you are successful in having all or some significant subset of the all the folks who were interviewed as part of the group that searches for themes in the data, then you will need to design a process for a large group of people.

Once the themes are identified, the organization is ready to move into the fourth stage of AI—*Creating shared images for a preferred future.*

*case story*

## Appreciative Inquiry at Los Angeles Universal Preschool (LAUP): The LAUP/UDEM Dream Team

*By Terri Egan, Nancy Westrup Villarreal, and Daphne Deporres*

### Client Organizations

For over a decade we have collaborated on field projects teaching AI to students in graduate programs at Pepperdine University and the Universidad de Monterrey. This tells the story of one of these collaborations—a unique project with two clients: Los Angeles Universal Preschool (LAUP) and sixteen students pertaining to the 59th cohort from The Universidad de Monterrey master's in organization development program.

Los Angeles Universal Preschool (LAUP) is a non-profit organization supporting high-quality preschool (pre-k) education for the children of Los Angeles County (LAC). Started in 2004, LAUP was designed to be an independent public benefit corporation, funded by First 5 Los Angeles (F5LA). LAUP is a provider-focused organization that exists to provide continuous quality improvement (CQI) programs to providers throughout Los Angeles County and focuses on expanding preschool capacity and enrollment, and improving the quality of pre-K classroom delivery. Built to be efficient, flexible, and scalable, LAUP is an emergent model for universal pre-k programs state- and nationwide.

Universidad de Monterrey is a private institution located in Mexico created forty years ago. The Master's in Organization Development Program has been in existence for thirty of those years, achieving an outstanding level of prestige in Latin America.

### Client Objectives

This project combined the educational objective of learning about AI and international consulting for the University of Monterrey's master's in organization development students with an employee engagement action research project for LAUP.

LAUP's original objective, as stated by the CEO, was to ascertain the status of employee engagement at LAUP using an appreciative approach.

case story

In a subsequent meeting LAUP staff in the organization effectiveness area requested that the project also focus on the integration of various departments.

## What Was Done

This project took place over two and a half days and touched approximately 90 percent of the organization. The authors co-created the design along with the self-named LAUP/UDEM Dream Team made up of sixteen graduate students from UDEM and fourteen internal LAUP staff facilitators.

The LAUP facilitators were from twelve areas of the organization, selected as those who could champion the change and interact easily with others. The UDEM students were working professionals in the second year of their graduate program in organization development.

**Day 1 a.m.:** The project began with a half-day Appreciative Inquiry workshop conducted by Terri and Nancy at the LAUP site for a group of approx 110 employees. The group represented a mix of levels and positions throughout the organization.

We briefly introduced key concepts of AI illustrated with stories from our own client experiences. The initial interview protocol focused on the topic of a learning community and included the standard generic protocol questions. After the paired interviews, small groups were formed and participants identified themes, created a vision of their shared future, and wrote provocative propositions. This process would become the basis for the topic selection for an all-staff AI meeting the next day.

**Day 1 p.m.:** The LAUP/UDEM Dream Team met to debrief the morning and select the focus of inquiry for the next day's half-day workshop with the entire LAUP staff. The challenging role of being both clients and consultants was underscored for the UDEM students who took the role of observers as Terri and Nancy facilitated a dialogue that included some tension about whether the AI process would result in any specific action.

This was a special learning experience and challenge for the UDEM students because they were simultaneously seeing how to interact

*case story*

with groups in another culture and language as well as another paradigm.

Ultimately, the topics of trust, respect, and communication were identified for the next day. The group broke into LAUP/UDEM pairs to design a process for the next day. Each pair would facilitate a small group of eight to twelve LAUP employees. Each pair created specific interview questions and a design for the Discovery and Dream phases of the process that they would lead for the small group of eight to twelve staff the next day.

The day closed with each pair presenting their discovery protocol and small group design. A key learning point for the afternoon was that, in creating the design for the next day, the LAUP/UDEM Dream Team had moved into the Design phase. This was critical to identify because of earlier concerns that AI in the organization had not moved beyond the Dream phase. The iterative nature of the cycle was reinforced through the intervention.

A quote from one of the UDEM students sums it up the first day as follows:

> "The first day I lived AI, I was able to see the faces of the people when they would discover their perfect dream and had the opportunity to draw it. I enjoyed feeling that energy. That day I learned that positive energy has great strength, but the facilitator must take care of because it can easily collapse."

**Day 2 a.m.:** The morning kicked off with an introduction and skit designed by one of the LAUP/UDEM pairs. The skit, illustrating that one can take an appreciative perspective on any situation, including being stuck in traffic in Los Angeles, drew laughter and set the stage for the day. Soon the meeting room was filled with the buzz of approximately 125 LAUP employees and sixteen UDEM students going through the Discover and Dream cycles.

At the end of the morning each small group presented their images and propositions to the entire room. Individual commitments were generated

*case story*

in the small groups. The checkout was an open invitation to comment on the morning with one word generated by each group.

During this phase it was challenging for the students and facilitators to progress through the process as planned. Some groups moved more quickly, while others lagged behind. This was because some had lived through the process the previous days and others were doing it for the first time. The LAUP/UDEM facilitators found ingenious ways to attend to those who finished early by opening up additional dialogue while the other groups continued working. Nancy and Terri served as observers and coaches throughout the morning.

**Day 2 p.m.:** The LAUP/UDEM Dream Team met to plan the next stage of the process. The challenge was how to best bring the themes, images, and provocative propositions created in the morning forward in the organization.

The team would have two hours in the morning with the senior leaders from LAUP. A two-fold process was designed. First, the leadership team would be introduced to AI through a brief paired interview and theme experience. Second, thought-provoking questions were created for each image and provocative proposition. The day ended with questions about AI and a discussion of how things were going with the intervention. One challenge identified was the persistent distraction of BlackBerries in the culture. The creative solution: A BlackBerry Free Zone for the next morning.

**Day 3 a.m.:** The LAUP/UDEM Dream Team met with the senior leaders. One pair facilitated an icebreaker and paired interviews on the question: "Tell the story about the time you first fell in love with LAUP?" Following the interviews, themes, images, and provocative propositions were created. After a break, the room was set up as a gallery with the previous days' images, propositions, and the accompanying questions set up on the wall. Gallery music was selected, and the senior leaders were led in and given time in silence to review and reflect on what had been created the day before. The UDEM/LAUP facilitators created this design.

The session with the senior leaders closed with a guided imagery and individual commitments elicited from the senior leaders. The CEO asked each of the key groups of stakeholders, the senior leaders, the LAUP facilitators, and the UDEM students to comment on what the process had meant to them.

The LAUP/UDEM Dream Team discussed how to continue the work that they began. Specific plans were proposed including the following.

## Outcomes for LAUP

As a result of the AI experience with UDEM students, LAUP is more educated about AI and consequently more likely to engage in appreciative-type activities. Organizational members express that they can see the value in an appreciative approach. In the past, people did not necessarily understand how the AI philosophy might be applied beyond its use in the LAUP coaching model, where AI serves as a pillar of one of the organization's core competencies.

When exploring the post-AI session landscape for tangible outcomes, participants report that the organization successfully gauged the temperature of how engaged LAUP's employees are. While areas for improvement were readily identified, the fact that employees were so engaged and passionate about the experience suggested they were largely engaged, as well as satisfied. Employee engagement includes the ability to conceptualize a vision for the organization and to be excited about it. Conversely, if employees weren't engaged, it would be difficult to see oneself in the vision. On the whole, employees at LAUP were clearly able to place themselves within a positive vision of the future.

From another perspective, it was surmised that a measure of engagement and satisfaction was required on the part of employees to respond enthusiastically to questions about "LAUP at its best." The themes of respect, trust, and commitment were identified as present in the organization and as areas for improvement.

Employees generally left the session feeling energized and enthusiastic, willing and able to make a contribution to the ideas that came up. However, the question remained, "What are the tangible results?" Participants evidenced energy and commitment, but what about a plan?

Upon review, LAUP has the information needed to move forward. It is clear to the steering committee that the organization needs to follow on and activate the nascent ideas and plans that were conceived during the AI experience. Employees recognize the need for a group to take the lead, with the consciousness that organization-wide ownership of the plans and processes whose inception occurred during the AI process will be necessary for true success. All are aware that nothing is going to magically emerge from the process without commitment to action. The two facilitators who participated in this interview committed to providing this leadership and partnering with others who share their passion. As a result of the conversation it was recognized that momentum needs to be sustained and several "next steps" were articulated:

- Gather the LAUP facilitators

- Capture the data and centralize it (in OE)

- Present data at an all-staff meeting

- Facilitators facilitate discussion about next steps

- Staff re-state, re-visit, renew personal commitments

At the conclusion of the interview with the two staff, a learning surfaced: every time the group discusses the AI process and what came out of it, more ideas are generated. A re-energizing solution-generator kicks into gear triggered by the briefest discussion of the seminal experience. The outcomes of the AI experience can appear to be dormant, but in fact are at the ready, waiting to catalyze further movement.

A final comment: due to the multiple leaders involved in different aspects of the project, a perceived gap between the AI process and follow-on resulted. The interview recounted herein resulted in a recontracting session among a few staff members in the position to provide leadership and support for this effort.

## Outcomes for UDEM

The key objectives for the UDEM students were to learn about AI and have an experience working with a client system in an international context. These quotes (translated from the original Spanish by Nancy) are drawn from the reflection papers UDEM students wrote about the AI experience. They suggest that both objectives were met.

> "I was able to see each part of the process and see future realities without being afraid of what might happen."

> "I now faithfully believe in the effect that AI can have in an organization. People are used to solving problems, and rather than construct using their strengths, so changing that image has high-impact results."

> "The process made me value the necessary silent moments which allow for ideas and concepts to be grasped."

> "I was able to see with clarity what it means to have real consensus and democracy."

> "My issue with a foreign language helped me read non-verbal communications, the unexpressed intentions, and the creativity of being able to express in many ways an idea or concept."

> "I realized that the question that is given to start the process is of vital importance. It can awaken a series of emotions that will lead to improvement of actions or it can be indifferent. In this experience, we learned that, even though the facilitator has a small group, adjustments must always be made and you have to take advantage of the best of each moment, even when you cannot follow the original plan."

## Learnings

Repeatedly, the importance of flexibility and comfort with an emergent process on the part of the facilitator was reinforced in this experience. As one UDEM student charged with observing and facilitating the overall flow of the second day intervention stated:

> "My second learning was that one must feel the group in general, monitor it, and not interact with all the groups in the same manner, because each small group is different. It is not

easy to please all, but it is important to know what the final objective will be so that they all reach it in one way or another."

Staying present in the experience rather than being concerned about the past or the future was also highlighted.

"In this experience, we learned that even though the facilitator has a small group, adjustments must always be made and you have to take advantage of the best of each moment, even though you cannot follow the original plan."

As another student found, powerful questions and topics come from dialogue within the client system:

"I realized that the question that is given to start the process is of vital importance. It can awaken a series of emotions that will lead to improvement of actions or it can be indifferent."

For the three authors, the opportunity to collaborate reconfirmed the fun and power of an ongoing partnership. Specific lessons from the faculty perspective:

- Transfer knowledge and skill to the client as quickly as possible. Nancy, paraphrasing the wisdom of Maria Montessori: "Never do for the students (clients) what they can do for themselves."

- Support from the organization is vital. Access to the organization, logistical support, and the symbolic participation from senior leaders, including the CEO, was graciously provided by LAUP.

- The best AI interventions build capacity within the client system. An internal group of facilitators is a key success factor.

- Tension can sometimes emerge in the context of people discussing what they most long for—process facilitation skills are very helpful when working with AI. Keep the focus on the fact that in every frustration or negative comment is a hidden gem of desire and possibility.

- Teaching and learning is easier under conditions of mutual trust.

*case story*

**Authors' Contact Information**

Terri Egan
Pepperdine University
Graziadio School of Business and Management
terri.egan@pepperdine.edu

Nancy Westrup Villarreal
Universidad de Monterrey
nwestrup@udem.edu.mx

Daphne DePorres
Los Angeles Universal Preschool
ddeporres@laup.net

# CHAPTER 7

# Create Shared Images for a Preferred Future (Dream)

"One of the basic theorems of the theory of image is that it is the image which in fact determines what might be called the current behavior of any organization. The image acts as a field. The behavior consists in gravitating toward the most highly valued part of the field."

Kenneth Boulding, *The Image*

"A vivid imagination compels the whole body to obey it."

Aristotle

"When we dream alone, it is just a dream. When we dream together, it is the beginning of a new reality."

Brazilian Proverb

**THE WORK OF THIS FOURTH CORE PROCESS** is to engage as many organization members as possible in co-creating a shared image of a preferred future. The creation of this future image comes directly from the stories of what has given life as recounted in the interviews of the second core process and the resultant themes identified in the third core process. As the various stories are shared and illuminated, a new historical narrative emerges that gives life to the organization's possible future. The invitation is to imagine an organization in which those special moments of exceptional vitality found in the stories become the norm rather than the exception; when all those themes are present and operating fully in the system. Thus, the fourth core process, is both practical, in that it is grounded in the history of the organization, and generative, in that this core process provides time and space to expand the potential of the organization.

The creation of a shared image of the preferred future often progresses through two stages: (1) the articulation of the dream for the organization and the creation of a visual image expressing that dream and (2) from that image compose a written expression of that most desired future for the organization as a whole.

## Articulating the Dream of an Organization's Future

The first stage of this process, creating the image of the most desired future for the organization, is the time for questions and dialogue about questions, such as the following:

- What is the world calling for our organization to be?

- What are the most enlivening and exciting possibilities for our organization?

- What is the inspiration that is supporting our organization?

Collectively envisioning an organization's future based on its successful past is to weave the web of meaning that endures—continuity, novelty, and transition. To engage in dreaming and envisioning is to invite organization stakeholders to go beyond what they thought was possible. It is a time for them to push the creative edges of possibility and to wonder about their organization's greatest potential. This is the time when the organization's stakeholders engage in possibility conversations about the organization's position, its potential, its calling, and the unique contribution it can make to global well-being.

For many, this is the first time they have been invited to think great thoughts and create great possibilities for their organization. As the various stories of the organization's history are shared and illuminated, a new historical narrative emerges, one that engages those involved in re-creating the organization's positive history which, in turn, gives life to its positive future. Thus, this fourth core process is both practical, in that it is grounded in the organization's history, and generative, in that it seeks to expand the organization's potential.

It is this aspect that makes Appreciative Inquiry different from other visioning or planning methodologies. As images of the future emerge out of grounded examples from its positive past, compelling possibilities emerge precisely because they are based on extraordinary moments from the organization's history. These stories of unique and joyful moments are used like an artist's paint to create a vibrant image of the future.

In more traditional approaches to futuring, there would be an attempt at this point to reconcile differences or find common ground among the dreams of the future. AI, however, is guided not by the reductionist models of the old paradigm but by the constructionist principle and the heliotropic hypothesis. The constructionist principle holds that it is through our conversations that we create the images and frameworks that will guide the actions that create our future. The image of an organization, held in mind and conversation, both drives and limits its activities. To expand, enhance, or change an organization, its image must be reconstructed through conversations among key stakeholders. The heliotropic hypothesis suggests that people and organizations, like plants, will move in the direction of that which is most life-giving.

This first stage of articulating the dream usually focuses on descriptions of the organization's culture, how people are relating to each other, and the overall feel of the organization. The "product" of this stage is a set of expressions or visual images (songs, skits, collages, etc.) that describe the larger "vision" for the organization and a written statement, called a "provocative proposition" or, if that term seems too risky, a "possibility statement," that describes this overall or macro image/vision of the organization.

An example of the image of the macro vision as described in a "provocative proposition" written by an international accounting firm follows:

> "Our company is poised for a positive future because partners at all regions share a basic common vision in relation to the firm's core missions, intent, and direction. It is an exciting, challenging, and meaningful direction that helps give all partners a feeling of significance, purpose, pride, and unity. The firm uses whatever time and resources are needed to bring everyone on board and thus continuously cultivates 'the thrill of having a one firm feeling,' of being a valued member of one outstanding national partnership."

And another example from a large manufacturer of automotive parts states:

> "We have created an organization where everyone experiences themselves as owners of the business—where everyone at all levels feels the organization is theirs to improve, change, and help become what it can potentially become. [Our company] recognizes there is a big difference between owners versus hired hands. Ownership at our company happens in three ways: (1) on an economic level it happens when everyone is a shareholder and shares in the profit; (2) on a psychological level it happens because people are authentically involved; and (3) on a business level it happens when the 'big picture' purpose is shared by all, and all take part at the strategic level of business planning."

## Examples of Ways to Facilitate Creation of Shared Images

### Example for a Guided-Image Exercise

*Note:* Someone—facilitator or volunteer from the group—reads the following directions, or creates his own for the group. Lowering lights is a good idea if you're comfortable with doing that. Pause a bit between sentences to give participants time to imagine.

"Get comfortable, close your eyes if you like, and bring one of the chosen interview topics into your mind. Imagine that that topic has been implemented fully in your everyday life and work. Imagine that it is your first day back at work and you are excited because you know that you'll find a workplace that has more of that topic present. Wander around your workplace and, as you meet people in the course of the day, what pictures emerge that are life-giving and energizing? What are you feeling? What are people doing differently? As you head home from this day, what is life like and how has it changed? What conversations do you have with those at home? What do you tell them about the changes at work? Congratulate yourself for being a part of such a healthy and meaningful change in your work and in your life. Open your eyes and return to this room at your own speed. When ready, share a few words describing your experience."

### Example for a Dream Exercise

*Note:* This is done at tables of six or more. Often the same group made up of interview pairs that forms to identify themes will continue as a work group through the whole process. On the other hand, if one goal of the workshop is for people to meet a wider range of people, then this can be a new group because they will be working with the common data from the scattergram "dot" exercise. Also, this exercise can be done with simple chart paper and markers—lots of colors are nice—or with more imaginative materials for creating pictures and other visuals. It depends somewhat on the budget. When we use lots of materials, we either have

*example*

packets for each table or a resource table with everything on it. We've had several hundred people do this in groups of sixteen plus or minus. And they can do the exercise in thirty minutes. The amazing thing to us is the kind of attention they pay to each other's pictures and visuals even when there are twenty or more presentations! The energy in the room by this time is electric.

- Introduce yourselves to each other: Your name and your work.

- Review the final list of themes from the "dot" exercise and ask for clarity as needed. Select one or several the group agrees as being those it "wants more of" in the organization. Discuss what the final themes that emerged from the "dot" exercise mean to those at your table.

- Create a visual image on the chart paper of this organization when all these themes are present fully and at their best. Be prepared to post your picture and explain it to the larger group.

## Provocative Propositions

We like the adjective "provocative" because a key criterion for these statements is that they elicit an "oh, wow" response from a reader rather than a "ho-hum" response, that is, they stretch, challenge, or interrupt the status quo. In some situations and in some cultures the term "provocative proposition" may not serve well. It is too "provocative" as a title. In those cases, the term "possibility statement" serves well.

David Cooperrider, in an e-mail to the AI listserv, offers the following thoughts on provocative propositions and how that guides the redesign of the organization:

> *"On designing the ideal organization:* What is becoming increasingly clear to me is that if people do great work with [the processes of inquiry and dreaming], then rarely, if ever, do the older command-and-control structures of eras past serve the organization. The new dreams always seem to have outgrown the structures and systems. If we, on an ongoing basis, start

sharing propositions emerging in our work, we might begin seeing patterns and connections, images of post-bureaucratic forms where the future is brilliantly interwoven into the texture of the mosaic of all our inquiries.

"In my experience, which is curious to me, I have never seen people create propositions about creating more hierarchy, more command and control, more inequality, more degradation of the environment, more socially irresponsible business practices, etc. Indeed the propositions, as I've seen them written, have always moved in a direction of more equality, more self-organization, more social consciousness in terms of business practices, and the breakdown of arbitrary barriers between groups and functions. I have wondered ... why?

"By provocative propositions (propositions that stretch beyond the status quo) we mean statements of fundamental belief and aspiration about human organizing—that body of belief of how we want to be related to one another and the ways we want to pursue our dreams. For example, every human organization must deal with questions and beliefs about power, money, and distribution of resources, questions of information freedom, learning, decision-making, etc. Too often we skirt these 'tougher' issues, like the sharing and distribution of resources, or images of ideal power relations—and if and when we do then AI runs the risk of being co-opted and tremendously watered down as an approach to organization re-construction and co-construction.

"So in this stage of AI, we need to deal with the hard issues that are far too frequently not dealt with in OD work. Too often there are taboo areas. When we described AI to Nutrimental Foods in Brazil, for example, we asked the people bringing us in, right off the bat, 'Is there anything sacred about any organizational arrangement or structure that cannot be opened up to all people for dreaming and designing?' The first response was, 'No, everything is open to re-conceptualization.' We said, 'OK, now suppose in the 700-person meeting, people write propositions about sharing the wealth of the company? What if, in the exploration of their fundamental or constitution-like beliefs, the people articulate a vision of co-ownership and fair and equitable distribution of profits?'

"Now perhaps the managers bringing us in would balk? No, they did not.

"In fact they said, without hesitation, 'We are committed to creating the future together, and opening everything to inquiry and the best imagination we have.' Obviously not every leadership group would say this! It is the first project, I am honestly almost ashamed to say, that I have ever gone to this kind of depth with. But the lessons are affecting everything else I'm doing now in my work. I really feel we are at the very beginning of our learning sometimes, and it is great!"

Our experience suggests that once a group has used its collective right brain to image its preferred future using the visual processes described above, the "translation" of that image into a written provocative proposition is much faster and smoother. So we generally connect the writing of the propositions with the group that created the visual. We often use the following handout, including a task statement for the group and an explanation of what a provocative proposition (or a possibility statement) is and how to write one.

## Instructions for Writing Provocative Propositions

As a group, discuss your dream picture and decide how you will put it in writing. You will be creating a possibility statement that describes what the organization would look and feel like when all of the chosen topics are at their best.

(*Note:* The opening statement if you are assigning specific topics or themes to the group would end with...when leadership or technology or the environment, etc., is at its best.)

Write your statement in LARGE print on one or two chart pages.

example

*example*

### *Constructing Possibility Statements (Provocative Propositions)*

A possibility statement is a statement that bridges the best of "what is" with your own speculation or intuition of "what might be." It stretches the status quo, challenges common assumptions or routines, and helps suggest real possibilities that represent desired possibilities for the organization and its people.

By creating possibility statements that make clear the shared visions for the organization's future, a beacon, a set of unique statements that paint a picture of the group's vision of the organization's most desired future, is created. It is this collection of possibility statements that provide the clear direction for all of the organization's activities. Just as a stream always follows the call of the ocean, the organization will move toward its highest and most imaginative visions for the future.

### Criteria for Good Possibility Statements (Positive Images of the Ideal Organization)

1. Is it *provocative?* Does it stretch, challenge, or interrupt the status quo?

2. Is it *grounded?* Are there examples that illustrate the ideal as real possibility?

3. Is it *desired?* If it could be fully actualized would the organization want it? Do you want it as a preferred future?

4. Is it stated in *affirmative* and bold terms?

5. Does it provide *guidance* for the organization's future as a whole?

6. Does it *expand* the zone of possible change and development?

7. Is it a *high involvement* process?

8. Is it used to stimulate intergenerational organizational *learning?*

*Note:* While the groups are writing, comments and coaching are in order. It is often very hard for a group to write in the active voice. Look for "waffle" words such as: aims to, will do, aspire to, etc. If the provocative propositions are dull and ordinary, it is a good idea to ask them to write a few "off the wall" ones to be shared later. Also, consider showing them a few diverse examples, such as the ones below:

*example*

## Guided by the Fire of Our Stories

(Listen)              (Listen)
We hold hope lightly.
(Trust)        (Trust)
We go forward.
(Courage)                (Courage)
Spreading sparks of stories giving strength.
Opening the darkness.

Walking into our facilities you can feel the energy.

- We build upon each other's strengths.

- We respond to the unpredictable with balance and passion.

- We nurture each other with challenge and understanding.

- We step out of defined roles to pursue the extraordinary.

- We seek places never imagined possible.

- We build for the future while living in the present and being grounded in the past.

WE, the people of this organization, consistently find, express, and share

PASSION for our work.
WE are creative!
WE are appreciated!
WE make a difference!
Our PASSION invigorates every cell within us!
WE ARE AN EXCITING PLACE TO BE!

Finally, we refer you to the example of an AI strategic planning process, the ABC Model for Organization Design and Strategic Planning in Chapter 8, to see more fully the application of provocative propositions to the design elements of the organization.

case story

# Advancing the Safety and Quality of Care in the Emergency Department Over Time: A Story with Three Acts

*By Nancy Shendell-Falik, Amy Doran, and Bernard J. Mohr*

## Complexity, Emergence and Appreciative Inquiry — Its Role In Complex Adaptive Systems

Improvement strategies within healthcare tend to be fragmented and linear—with some efforts focusing primarily on technology only, others focusing on patient care, others on cost reduction, and still others focusing on caregiver relationships. And in a fairly stable, structured environment, where the same simple processes and procedures are repeated over and over again, and where *"we can know and predict in great detail what each of the parts will do in response to a given stimulus"* it may be possible to study, analyze, and plan *in great detail* what the many "parts of the system" will do in a variety of circumstances.

But is an emergency department well described this way? Or is it more appropriately characterized as *"a collection of individual agents with freedom to act in ways that are not always totally predictable, and whose actions are interconnected so that one agent's actions changes the context for other agents"*? Our experience at Newark Beth Israel Medical Center (NBIMC) and elsewhere suggests the second description is more accurate—and this may help to explain why, in this setting, the challenge to achieve and sustain measurable outcomes for patients, caregivers, and the institution calls for an "out-of-the-box" approach to performance improvement.

One such approach is Appreciative Inquiry (AI)—which, in its simplest definition, is an umbrella term, describing *a set of collaborative, relational practices that enable accelerated implementation of system innovations in ways that mobilize the human energy and commitment needed... for transformative change in complex adaptive systems.*

Similar to most improvement strategies, the core practice sets that comprise Appreciative Inquiry include:

*case story*

- Data gathering and sense making (the "Discovery phase")

- Visioning/goal setting (the "Dream phase")

- Innovation design (the "Design phase")

- Implementation and measurement (the "Delivery or Destiny" phase)

However, it is AI's distinguishing features that make it more suitable for systems that are more complex: AI places emphasis on:

- *Multi-faceted* ways of knowing and understanding a situation—AI invites wherever possible, the use of story/narrative rather than PowerPoint presentations as vehicles for data gathering and sense making.

- I*nclusion*—even when a representative group functions on behalf of the whole, AI encourages whole system "voice" through a simple, yet powerful activity known as "the appreciative paired interview."

- *Emergent engagement*—recognizing that organizations are more like a constantly changing "river" flowing over constantly changing terrain, AI invites ongoing inquiry into new opportunities and possibilities rather than mechanically "sticking to plan."

- *Simultaneity*—the power of information gathering as an intervention capable of *generating BOTH good data AND also building the relationships and energy* needed for execution—rather than assuming that the latter is something to be created down the road.

- *Scalability and adaptability* for many issues—recognizing that improvement challenges and opportunities come in many sizes and shapes, from one to one relationships to redesign at the scale of the whole, AI invites the use of whatever change activities and organizational forms respond to the need of the moment—be it strategic planning, organizational redesign, team building, or whatever.

*case story*

## Starting Small

Evolving something as complex as an inner city emergency department (serving 250 to 350 patients a day) from good to great, is a journey, not an event. Like a play with many story lines and characters, our own journey has so far included a first and second act, which we want to describe for you. The third act is yet to be written.

Our first act began in early 2005, when Newark Beth Israel Medical Center embarked on a journey to improve the patient handoff process for patients admitted to the telemetry unit from the emergency department. Our strength-based approach engaged the front-line nursing staff in designing and implementing a nurse-to-nurse handoff based on an analysis of times in which the process was deemed exceptional by the staff themselves. This generated a set of significant innovations and a personal level of commitment by the nurses involved, resulting in measurable outcomes and implementation house-wide. The most productive innovations have now been sustained over five years. Greater detail about this first act and the outcomes achieved is available in the *Journal of Nursing Administration, 37(2), 95–104.*

## Taking a Bigger Bite

The success of this handoff project gave us the confidence to explore a broader and more complex initiative in 2008—the redesign of the whole emergency department. Emboldened, we undertook wider and broader participation from the start. Leadership of this "second act" project was by an eighteen-person group of ED nurses and doctors representing front-line staff and leadership along with the vice president of information technology (a key ally as it turned out). Nancy Shendell-Falik (at the time senior VP for patient care services) served as team member and the project sponsor. Amy Doran, assistant vice president, emergency department, and previously a member of our first core group, served as project leader. Bernard Mohr (a professional consultant in strength-based redesign) continued to serve as our thinking partner, coach, and journey guide.

*case story*

We conceived the purpose of our work as *"improving the quality of care, the patient experience, and the quality of life for the caregivers in the emergency department by focusing simultaneously and explicitly on both:*

- The core clinical and operational processes that contribute to patient safety/quality in the emergency department

- The relationships (between and among physicians and nurses) surrounding that work"

Expanded use of Appreciative Inquiry within a healthcare setting has also been part of our intention.

## Using Appreciative Inquiry — Again

With the experience of our first act successfully behind us and an increased comfort with focusing on the positive, we recommitted to the path we had learned. See Figure 7.1 for our design.

*Definition:* From the understanding that "the seeds of our future are planted in the questions we ask to understand the past," Appreciative Inquiry begins with a thoughtful and often evolving exploration of what to focus on, what to study and seek an understanding of. In this project, we considered whether to focus on just the nurse-physician relationship or whether to take on the larger context of the functioning of the emergency department as a whole. Following the AI principle of "wholeness" (the recognition that the emergency department is a "whole" and that all its parts are entangled), we chose the latter. Based both on our own past experience (act one of our story) of redesigning our hand-off processes, a sixteen-person "core group" (representative of the various roles and levels within the emergency department) created a set of inquiry "prompts" which invited stories and narrative descriptions of moments in the emergency department when patient care, safety, and caregiver relationships were at their peak. We also developed our own "map" of the process flow in the emergency department and the activities within each key stage.

*Discovery, Dream, and Design:* In order to engage as many voices as possible in improving the practice environment, sixty of eighty RNs, ten

case story

## Figure 7.1. Appreciative Inquiry 5-D Cycle for ED Redesign

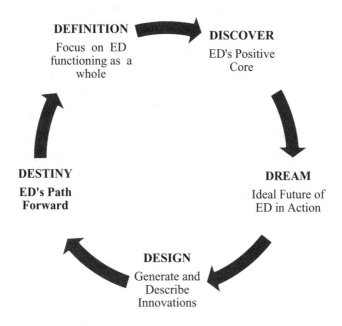

**DEFINITION**
Focus on ED functioning as a whole

**DISCOVER**
ED's Positive Core

**DREAM**
Ideal Future of ED in Action

**DESIGN**
Generate and Describe Innovations

**DESTINY**
**ED's Path Forward**

of eighteen MDs, and thirty of forty ancillary personnel participated in an Appreciative Inquiry Interview. During the interview, staff described best practices and generated improvement possibilities. All participants reported this to be a positive experience toward promoting teamwork— even before any of the suggested changes had been implemented!.

Next came an intensive two-day workshop during which our representative "core group" worked with the "data" from our appreciative interviews to:

**Discover** the emergency department's "positive core," that is:

- Existing behaviors/practices/values to keep or expand

- Signature resources, assets, skills, or other strengths for building our future

- Opportunities for innovation in roles, processes, practices, technologies, etc.

**Dream/envision** (using skits, pictures, etc.) "our ideal future ED in action," that is, How are patients being cared for differently? What do the relationships between nurses, doctors, and others look like? Etc.

**Design** new processes/activities, role shifts, and/or technology and/or procedural changes and or organizational changes. Using an activity called *"Design Propositions"* we generated and described the "innovations" at the intersection of what we most cared about and what we felt would have the greatest payoffs. We ended the workshop by generating and agreeing on the specific initiatives and projects that would bring our innovations into being. We developed our Implementation Roadmap, invited commitments for specific actions/steps and created a process for further involving those members of the emergency department not present at this session in shaping and prototyping the innovations.

**Destiny:** Our path beyond the two-day workshop was influenced by the concept of "rapid prototyping." Many of the innovations (see following section) were implemented with a view to seeing how well they would achieve what we were hoping for and the anticipation that they might require evolution. We also realized that we needed to have an additional "deeper dive" day focused on "patient flow." The innovations we generated from that day are included in the list below.

Some months later, in order to improve continuously, we conducted a one-day "celebration, review, reflection, and next steps" session to make sure that we:

1. Celebrated and Learned from Our Journey So Far about our collective strengths and capacities for clinical and operational Innovation

2. Managed our Remaining Innovations by deciding on their continuing relevance, adjusting and improvising as needed

3. Built Our Capacities for the Future

*case story*

## Our Implemented "Quick Win" Innovations

These included:

- A designated section of the ED (called Expanded Care) was transitioned to a unit for admitted patients who are waiting for a hospital bed with staffing similar to the inpatient units.

- Pyxis was added to Expanded Care to provide medications similar to any other inpatient unit.

- Lower acuity patients are now treated in a designated area called First Care. Two nurse practitioners and a social worker were hired through a grant to expedite care to these patients.

- A voice-activated hands-free system that provides caregiver-to-caregiver communication without having to dial on a keyboard or look for a phone number is utilized to share radiology results with the emergency department physician.

- RFID tags were placed on essential expensive equipment in the emergency department to facilitate locating and tracking.

- Security was relocated from an enclosed booth somewhat removed from activity to the hospitality desk, which is central to the waiting room activity.

- Name and face boards using digital frames were created to identify the close to three hundred people who work within the emergency department.

- Phlebotomists now perform morning blood draws within the emergency department.

- A standing orders/protocols work team was formed to increase the number in use and promote timeliness and efficiency of care.

- An ED redesign web page accessible through the hospital intranet was created in order to provide updates and share progress on this project with all ED staff.

*case story*

Additional and distinct initiatives from the day on "patient flow" included:

- Agreement that there are no hard and fast rules regarding a specific age of adolescent/young adult patients and whether they are placed in the adult or pediatric emergency department. As a team we embraced the provision of safe, quality patient care for the teenage/young adult population in the environment which best meets the patient needs.

- After triage the pediatric charts are handed off to the charge nurse to ensure children are safely managed while waiting to be evaluated by a physician. This can prevent a child from slipping through the cracks while waiting if the child experiences a change in condition.

- Commitment to a bi-directional patient entry, including patients waiting to be called and nurses and physicians actively moving patients in the system when ED flow permits.

- Collaboration between the charge nurse and lead physician to review the charts in the rack to facilitate necessary testing for patients waiting to be seen by a physician. This results in more information being available when the patient is evaluated and can decrease the time to patient disposition and improve patient satisfaction. This addressed the challenge that physicians are reluctant to give orders on patients who are not yet their responsibility.

- Communication by the nurse to the physician that all testing is complete and results are available. This promotes timely treatment and reduce waiting times as patients will not be "forgotten" when the emergency department is extremely busy.

- Projects that the team identified for future implementation included:

  ○ Utilization of a team approach to initially interview patients. This may include the RN, ED technician, physician, and patient access representative. This model would reduce the number of times a patient must share the same information and the team members could collaborate more timely on the plan of care.

○ Implementation of a code mobile alert system based on predetermined wait times for triage and the nurse and doctor rack. This could be a three-tier escalation response that mobilizes internal and external resources.

## Outcomes

The ED staff turnover rate was decreased by 33 percent. This represents an approximate savings of $200,000 annually. Lower turnover also positively impacts patient care and clinical outcomes. Anecdotally, the staff has attributed this to teamwork and a more cohesive work environment. In essence, despite the heavy workload, they report that they enjoy working together. The time from walk-in to EKG has been reduced from thirty-five minutes to twelve minutes: door to balloon time for ST segment elevation myocardial infarction was reduced from sixty-five to fifty-three minutes.

Additional changes, based on New Jersey Peer Group Percentile Ranking, were:

1. *"Communication with Nurses"* increased from 49 percent to 91 percent,

2. *"Responsiveness of Hospital Staff"* increased from 42 percent to 74 percent,

3. *"Communication About Medication"* increased from 31 percent to 95 percent, and

4. *"Recommend This Hospital"* increased from 48 percent to 67 percent.

## Reflections

Our outcomes to date show some significant improvement in the quality of care, the patient experience, and the quality of life for the caregivers in the emergency department. In reflection, we see that by far most of the innovations identified during the process fall into the category of work flow/process improvements—sometimes called the "technical system" in the language of "sociotechnical systems." This leaves a huge body of possibility, sometimes referred to as the "social system," that is, the organizational context within which people work, including but not limited to the design of roles, levels of authority, departmental boundaries, reward systems, management processes for planning and evaluation, and so on.

Although participants in the process were invited to consider changes in the "social system," we now believe that this important arena of innovation does not automatically or easily "come to mind," perhaps because it is seen as an immutable given. With this operating assumption, the choices available in that domain are not easily visible. And yet, we know from decades of research that the organizational environment within which people function is hugely influential in both overall system performance and also the staff's overall day-to-day experience of life at work. Bearing this in mind, we can imagine the possibilities of significantly leveraging the work done so far by undertaking several "next level" interventions, such as:

- Engaging all members of the emergency department in a process of explicitly re-imagining and redesigning the social system

- While at the same time supporting continuous innovation within the technical system by bringing in-house the skills and tools of Appreciative Inquiry for use in an "everyday" way.

## Conclusion

The journey continues. The third act is unfolding. We have learned much in this process, both about the enormous untapped potential that exists within the collective hearts and minds of healthcare staff—a potential that is so much more easily unleashed when the process of improvement starts from a place of "collaboratively creating the future we want," rather than "fixing the problems of the past." We continue to value the importance of continuously monitoring our plans for change and adapting them as new opportunities or challenges arise. And we are critically aware of the need for ongoing sponsorship at one to two levels above the organizational unit (in this case the emergency department) undertaking changes of this nature and would recommend to others considering this sort of journey to ensure that level of sponsorship as early as possible in the process.

## Authors' Contact Information

Nancy Shendell-Falik, RN, MA, CNO, and Senior Vice President
Patient Care Services
Tufts Medical Center

Amy Doran, RN, MSN, APN-BC, Assistant Vice President
Emergency Department
Newark Beth Israel Medical Center
Newark, NJ

Bernard J. Mohr, Ed.M, Partner
Innovation Partners International
bjMohr@innovationpartnersinternational.com

## Appreciative Inquiry with a Search Committee

*By Liz Workman*

Selecting leaders can frequently include judgment about their immediate predecessors. We see this phenomenon when electing a new president, hiring a new CEO, choosing a new PTA president or finding a new minister. Often the selection process is cast in terms of "What we don't want more of."

What does Appreciative Inquiry (AI) look like when viewed through a theological leadership lens ... a lens that asks, "Where is God (or Yahweh or Allah or Buddha or Your Higher Power) in all of this?" How can AI assist in defining and locating a leader?

Leadership positions in religious organizations are often filled in a systematic and prescribed manner. Finding a new priest for an Episcopal church is one of those ... and the application of AI principles can have a significant influence on the process ... and the outcome.

In 2006, the Episcopal Cathedral of St. Andrew's, an eight-hundred-member, downtown church in Jackson, Mississippi, began searching for a new dean (priest in charge). Appreciative Inquiry was an integral part of the process as I worked with its search committee. The twelve-person committee was a carefully selected cross-section of the parish and included an attorney, a clinical psychologist, a youth camp director, a journalist, a physician, an educator, and several businesspeople and retirees.

I asked committee members to focus on the positive aspects as they began imagining their yet-to-be-defined new leader. Operating from that position generated enthusiasm within the committee itself. It helped create a strong sense of mission and a stronger sense of community within this group that was surprising and unexpected by its members.

Early in the process to find a new priest, Episcopal search committees typically consult Church Development Office profiles, a national database of individual Episcopal clergy profiles resulting from detailed questionnaires, noting strengths and specific interests of each priest submitting profile information. Committees use this to help identify priests who may be interested in seeking this position or who may have qualifications resembling the stated needs and desires of the parish. St. Andrew's committee was encouraged to filter this information through the positive lens of AI and concentrate on the positive things St. Andrew's was looking for in a new dean.

Working with search committees in a number of churches, I've seen that the use of this approach to the database is more successful than discarding potential leaders based on what is "wrong" with them. If such a mindset can be addressed and eliminated, the committee will look at the positive. The search takes on a different and more productive direction. Committees begin to form a clearer picture of the desired leader, whether a candidate resulted from the national database or from names submitted by parish members.

AI also came into play as St. Andrew's committee formulated specific questions for all the finalists. The questions addressed topics about which the candidates were pleased or topics that had enriched or encouraged them. Such questions elicit answers significantly different from inquiries such as "What were some of the most difficult times you had?" If such questions are needed, they should be followed with "and what were the things you valued from the learning you received from this difficult time?"

The leadership search process in a religious institution can be deliberate and thorough and sometime lengthy, a challenge for those used to making quick decisions. AI does not lengthen the process. It enriches the process and, more importantly, it enriches the outcome.

At St. Andrew's, the inclusion of the Appreciate Inquiry philosophy in the selection of a new leader helped create energy and strengthen the relationship among the committee members. It led to a unanimous choice from among a number of highly qualified candidates. And it resulted in a smooth and successful transition to its new leader.

**Author's Contact Information**

Liz Workman

Interact

liz@sewanee.edu

# CHAPTER 8

# Innovate Ways to Create That Preferred Future (Deliver)

"Modern management thought was born proclaiming that organizations are the triumph of the human imagination. As made and imagined, organizations are products of human interaction and mind rather than some blind expression of an underlying natural order. Deceptively simple yet so radical in implication, this insight is still shattering many beliefs—one of which is the longstanding conviction that bureaucracy, oligarchy, and other forms of hierarchical domination are inevitable."

David Cooperrider, "Positive Image; Positive Action"

"Appreciative Inquiry is currently revolutionizing the field of organization development…it is a process of search and discovery designed to value, prize and honor. It assumes that organizations are networks of relatedness and that these networks are 'alive.'"

Robert Quinn, M.E., Tracy Distinguished Professor of Management, University of Michigan Business School

THIS FINAL PROCESS ENGAGES (as always) as many members of the organization as possible in bringing to life on a daily and local basis the new images of the future, both the overall visions of the dream stage and the more specific provocative propositions of the redesign stage. It is a time of continuous learning, adjustment, and improvisation. The momentum and potential for innovation is extremely high by this stage of the overall AI process.

For example, one organization transformed its department of *e*valuation studies, to *v*aluation studies, dropping the "e," and with it the accumulated negative connotations that have attached themselves to the word "evaluation." Others have transformed almost every possible function of an organization, changing deficit processes to appreciative ones—focus group methods, surveys, performance appraisal systems, leadership training programs, diversity initiatives, strategic planning, client development, quality management, business process redesign, technology implementation, union management, and employee relations, as well as authority and responsibility structures, roles, and information systems all functioning in an appreciative mode. These changes inevitably create higher levels of excitement, enthusiasm for the work, and commitment from the people involved.

There are many stories about what happens in this "Design" phase of Appreciative Inquiry. One thing is for certain—and no doubt quite clear to you by now—there is no *one* way to carry this forward. There exist many good participative methods for organization design that can be combined with the appreciative perspective of AI. Those combinations lead to generative and creative ways to structure the organization while, at the same time, enabling those in the organization to use the appreciative approach for acclimating to the inevitable shifts and changes. It is not new news to suggest people will acclimate readily to an organizational structure based on the best of what is and reaching toward the best that can be, particularly if those same people were part of the process that created the environment for such change.

So how does organization design or redesign deal with traditional resistance to change? What happens when the old models and processes that have been so reliable in the past no longer work? How can organizations survive in such a rapid pace of change? Employees in organizations have reached a breakpoint![1] It is very likely that the methods, models, and solutions that have worked in the past are now not only useless, but often counterproductive.

What, in the real world, is going on today in the giant organizations of every kind imaginable around the globe that face the challenge of keeping up with the unbelievable rate of change in this 21st Century—a rate of change that is speeding up exponentially? It is, indeed, a new reality and an extremely challenging one for those who cling to the ideas of certainty and predictability. And along with the changes taking place in large organizations, those who work as management consultants or organization development professionals are equally challenged by the expanding rate of change and the shifting nature of "reality"!

On a more hopeful note, in the past decade the rate of innovative solutions to problems that didn't even exist a decade ago, along with creative ways (such as AI) of working in human systems, offers a bit of gold at the end of the rainbow. A classic example is Stavros and Hinrichs' (2009) *The Thin Book of SOAR* (Strengths, Opportunities, Aspirations, and Results), which has spread in the "planning" world of organizations. SOAR replaces SWOT, the traditional planning process of Strengths, Weaknesses, Opportunities, and Threats.

[1]George Land and Beth Jarman, in their book *Breakpoint and Beyond: Mastering the Future Today,* comment (pp. 4–5) that, "The surprising fact is that change itself has changed.... The old rules mandated changes of degree, not of kind.... These great leaps defy traditional wisdom supporting linear and progressive change.... This kind of totally unconventional change process has pushed us to the edge, teetering precariously between two eras. We've reached a Breakpoint! Breakpoint change abruptly and powerfully breaks the critical links that connect anyone or anything with the past. What we are experiencing today is absolutely unprecedented in all of humanity's recorded history.... At Breakpoint, the rule change is so sharp that continuing to use the old rules not only doesn't work, it erects great, sometimes insurmountable barriers to success."

Mainstream and often widely known and used planning processes like Six Sigma and Lean for organizations are beginning to consider adaptations that use Appreciative Inquiry or other generative and positive processes for change in human systems. One set of processes increasingly successful in these times are the ones that deal with "whole system" change. Many of them are very adaptable and are easily aligned with working from a positive, forward-looking perspective. Included among these methods that work very effectively from the appreciative perspective are:

- The Conference Method™ (Axelrod, 1999)

- Participative Design Workshop (Emery, 1993)

- Open Space (Owens, 1992)

- Whole System Design™ (Mohr & Levine, 1998)

- The ABC Model (Watkins & Cooperrider, 2000)

- Future Search (Weisbord, 1994)

- World Café (Brown, Isaacs, & The World Café Community, 2005)

- The Appreciative Inquiry Summit (Whitney & Cooperrider, 2000)

The key to sustaining the momentum is to build an "appreciative eye" into all the organization's systems, procedures, and ways of working. Because AI is of the new paradigm, each time you work with it will be different. It has the power of being totally unique to any group that chooses to take this route to organization transformation and renewal.

This core process is ongoing. In the best case, it is full of continuing dialogue; revisited and updated possibility discussions and statements; additional interviewing sessions especially with new members of the organization; and, a high level of innovation and continued learning. And perhaps the most important learning that comes from this continuous process is about what it means to create an organization that is socially constructed through poetic processes in a positive frame that makes full use of people's anticipatory images and of the realization that inquiry IS change!

## Organization Design Processes

Moving from a powerful image of the preferred future to an organization that lives and breathes the essence of the provocative propositions is a process that takes many forms. The challenge is to invent a process of organization redesign, unique to the organization's culture, that avoids the trap of a mechanistic problem-solving world-view.

Two very different approaches to this challenge are (1) the individual action approach and (2) the whole system design approach. They can be described briefly as follows:

## The Individual Action Approach

In this approach (also known as the *Requests, Offer, and Commitments Approach*), participants are asked to think about the parts of the dream that they want to bring to life. Each participant is given the opportunity to publicly state a simple commitment, make an offer, or articulate a request.

*Simple commitments* describe actions that can be easily taken, typically within one to two weeks and are within the existing authority and resources available to the person making the commitment.

*Offers* are a form of "gift." For example, a participant may "offer" access to a database he or she controls. Or someone may "offer" financial assistance to get a project started. An "offer" may be made in response to a request for collaboration. Offers can come in any shape or form—the more specific the better.

*Requests* are focused on what one person or group needs from another person or group. For example, "The western region call center requests a meeting with the chief information officer to explore upgrading of our e-mail system."

Although particularly appropriate to situations where the focus is on team or small unit development rather than increasing effectiveness in a complex organization, this approach can be effectively combined with the more systemic Whole System Design approach described below.

## The Whole System Design Approach

In this approach, the core group or sponsor team begins by choosing either to (1) select from among the major existing models of organization architecture (for example, the Open Socio-Technical Systems framework, the McKinsey 7S framework; the Weisbord Six-Box framework; the Galbraith Star framework; the Nadler/ Tushman Congruence framework, etc.) or (2) create from scratch its own framework/model. (Later in this chapter is a model created by Watkins and Cooperrider that enables organizations to create a customized process appropriate to their own needs.)

We prefer the second approach because it is more organic and in keeping with the spirit of AI—but either can work.

Once group members have identified within these frameworks the key elements, (information systems, relations with the board of directors, work flows) they then write Provocative Propositions about them as described in the previous chapter. This is somewhat like creating a set of design principles that are then used to guide the more detailed design and implementation of a particular element. The process of requests, offers, and commitments can then be used to move these provocative propositions/Design principles forward.

## A Design Framework: The ABC Model

This organization inquiry model is designed to inquire into the current reality of an organization and to plan its future by focusing on the successes and the life-giving forces that support the work and the people. Once those forces are located and articulated, the organization can move to affirm, expand, and increase those success factors as they imagine the organization's future. This is a departure from the traditional model of organization diagnosis that searches for the problems and shortcomings of the organization for the purpose of "fixing" it.

This appreciative approach is grounded in the theory of Social Constructionism (Gergen, 1991, 1994a, 1994b) that holds organizations as social constructions of those who inhabit and "talk" in them. If organizations are imagined and made by human beings, then they can be remade and re-imagined. The constraints of scientific management theory that images organizations as machines are lifted and the possibility of new approaches and configurations emerges. We create what we imagine!

The model as presented in Figure 8.1 is an example of a global international development organization. The sample items in each

## Figure 8.1. Model for Organization Inquiry

Developed by Jane Magruder Watkins and Davis Cooperrider.

of the three rings and the explanations of those items are meant to be an example. When it is used to facilitate organization design, the organization begins by building the three circles to fit their own organization structure followed by applying the ABC process to the circles they create.

## Assumptions of the Organization Inquiry Model

The Organization Inquiry Model is built on several assumptions. The *first assumption* is that the central organizing principles of organizations are the clarity about the ultimate impact of the work, the core values that are shared, and a common mission of a group of people who work together to meet the mission and goals of the organization. These critical ingredients provide the foundation for the organization. Without clarity and consensus on these ingredients, no amount of organizational excellence related to task and management will insure survival. Conversely, organizations with clarity on the Impact they want to make, shared understanding of their core value and agreement on their mission can survive a great deal of imperfection and ambiguity in their organizational forms. Therefore, the premier task of every organization is to carry on a continuous dialogue making meaning of their work. The definitions of the following terms here are:

| | |
|---|---|
| Impact | The ultimate goal of our work; the conditions that we plan to change; the reason for our existence as an organization |
| Values | The core values that we all share and which form the solid foundation for our work together |
| Mission | The work we will do in the world to achieve our ultimate impact |

The *second assumption* is that organizations are Networks. In this model, what is usually called the "organization," that is, the staff that works in the headquarters office and in the field offices, is called the Team and is seen as the coordinating body for the Network Organization. The organization is envisioned as a network of key stakeholders who gather around the desired Impact, Values, and Mission to accomplish tasks that lead to social transformation. The Network Organization might include the Team; a Board; Donors; Partners; Alliances; and, frequently, Volunteers. Definitions of these terms are described below. However, each organization will have a unique set of actors in this circle. This model describes one possible configuration.

| | |
|---|---|
| Team | The core staff of the headquarters and field offices that work together collaboratively and whose central task is to provide leadership as they coordinate and sustain the work and the relationships of the organization |
| Board | The oversight group whose task is to set policy, provide guidance, and ensure that the organization has the resources it needs to sustain itself |
| Donors | Those who supply the resources and whose tasks encompass providing financial resources and programmatic guidance |
| Partners | Multiple groups of clients/recipients of services who are responsible for collaborating in all planning and implementation of joint programs |
| Volunteers | Groups and individuals who contribute time and skills to the organization |
| Alliances | Other institutions/entities who join in the work of the organization |

The *third assumption* is that in addition to the core of the organization and the leadership network, there are key areas for inquiry on the ways the organization organizes its work. Inquiry into these areas enables groups to discover the life-giving forces, success stories, and generative spirit of their organizations. In this model, example areas for inquiry include Pathway, Governance, Systems, Structure, People, Programs, Sustainability, and Environment. These terms are defined as:

| Pathway | The guiding principles, strategy, plans, and tactics for achieving our mission |
|---|---|
| Governance | How we organize, govern, and manage ourselves; how we make decisions; how we celebrate our achievements; how our governance processes align with our values and our theory of development |
| Systems | The systems and technologies that we use to manage ourselves, to communicate with each other, and to "conference" with the world |
| Structure | The way we organize our work and manage our tasks |
| People | The well-being, fair treatment, and empowerment of our staff team, partners, board members, alliance, and volunteers; the placement of our people in the right positions to make our work flow smoothly; how we value our diversity and celebrate our differences as organizational assets; how we relate to each other; how our rhetoric about valuing people aligns with our organizational behavior |
| Programming | Our development paradigm and the theories that underlie our methods of work; the nature of our work and how it aligns with our vision and values; our programming process |
| Sustainability | How we guarantee the people and resources to assure the health and survival of all or our organizational entities; how we steadily increase our capacity; how we function as a lifelong learning organization committed to continuous improvement |
| Environment | Our understanding of what is going on in the world that impacts our work and our view of the organizational culture and norms that create our work environment |

## How to Use the Organization Inquiry Model

For each of the elements in (1) the core circle; (2) the network organization circle, and (3) the organization of work circle, you will use the ABCs:

A. Appreciative understanding of your organization

B. Benchmarked understanding of other organizations

C. Creation of "provocative propositions" to image your organization's future

## A. Appreciative Understanding of Your Organization

The process begins with your inquiry into your own organization that will provide a clear picture of your organization's strengths, competencies, and life-giving forces. Using this approach, you look for those moments when your organization is at its very best. Using an interview process, members of your staff can interview each other in search of organizational excellence.

Questions might include:

1. Think of a time in your work with this organization when you felt excited, joyful, and at the peak of your form. Tell a story about that time. Describe what you were doing, what others did and how you felt. Tell the story in a way that creates an image for the interviewer.

2. Without being humble, talk about the things that you value about yourself; what are the things that you value about your job in this organization; and what is it that you value about this organization itself; that is, what, for you, gives life to this organization?

3. What do you believe are the core values of this organization? That is, what is the key thing without which this organization would not exist?

## B. Benchmarked Understanding of Other Organizations

Once you have initiated the process in your own organization, you may want to seek out and understand the best practices of other organizations. This is best done as a reciprocal process in which you also share your best practices. Such mutual sharing gives both organizations a way to inform their own practices and to adapt and incorporate some ideas that can inspire innovation and improvement.

Often organizations seek out similar groups to "benchmark," but there can be rich learning and exchange between even the most diverse organizations. Negotiations with potential benchmarking partners should include the parameters of the exchange and agreement on questions to be asked.

Sample questions include:

1. What is the most exciting and successful time you have had working with your organization? Please describe for me what made it so exciting. Are there processes from that event/time that you have incorporated into your work here? Tell me about them.

2. If you had to say the one best thing your company does when it is at its most competent, what would that be? Tell me about it. How does it work?

3  What do you value most about working for this organization?

These questions are intended to be examples only. You will construct questions appropriate to the study that you want to do.

## C. Creation of "Provocative Propositions" to Image Your Organization's Future

Once you have gathered information from your own organization and have benchmarked several other organizations, it is time to make sense of that information in search of an image of the current reality that will serve as a springboard to creating an image of your organization's future. This is an exercise that can be carried out at every level of the organization with any mix of staff and

stakeholders. The process includes sharing the information a
nd stories gathered from the Appreciative Inquiry of your
own organization and the best practices gathered from
other organizations. This sharing is best done as a dialogical process
with any written report aimed at capturing the highlights from the
stories and sharing the high points of the process itself.

A mechanical reporting of facts will not usually lead to exciting
"propositions." Once the verbal or written story of the process is
finished, the group moves to create the most exciting possible future
for the organization that incorporates the best that exists within,
plus new and exciting practices discovered from without. Possibility
propositions are written as though they are already happening, in
the present tense. These become visions for the organization that
guides planning and operations in the future.

This ABC process can be used to study every facet of an
organization. This model suggests that an organization needs to
look, at a minimum, at the two levels described in this framework:

1. The organization itself is conceived of as a network of key
   stakeholders that make up the decision-making and operating
   body for achieving the mission. The Organization Inquiry Model
   suggests an ABC process for each of the six elements: Team,
   Board, Donors, Partners, Volunteer, and Alliances (elements
   should be added or removed according to what is actual in your
   own organization).

2. The second level of inquiry focuses on the various functions and
   guiding principles of the organization, to include Impact, Values,
   Mission, Pathway, Environment, Governance, People,
   Programming, Systems, Sustainability (again, you are encouraged
   to add factors that are relevant to your organization).

Finally, it is essential that some other interactive process be
embedded in the organization as an ongoing dialogue, constantly
appreciating, reframing, and sharing the life of the people and the
meaning of the work that make up the organization. It is this
community meaning-making that creates a flexible, grounded,

generative organization. The ABC model can be used as a framework for the ongoing conversations that will create a true learning organization. As the conversation deepens and expands, the framework itself will be changed and embellished as needed to facilitate the learning about the growth and change that are life-giving forces in all organizations.

## Example of an Application of the ABC Model

The ABC Model was used by an international development agency for their strategic planning process. Following are some of the ways they created the model to fit their own organization. We are including here only a partial reporting of the very complex process that was carried out over a year's time. The important illustration is the way the organization design model was used to consolidate the work into a planning document that was presented to the parent organization in the Philippines. During the several months prior to the workshop, the organization had used an AI interview process with all of the stakeholders that they have listed in the middle circle. And they had asked questions about the business processes that they have in the outer circle. Following the circle diagram we have included some of their outputs so that you can see the innovative use they made of the model.

### Framework: Areas Addressed in the Strategic Planning Process

- Programs
  - Training
  - Collaborative Field Projects
  - Documentation
  - Publications
  - Workshops and Conferences
- Governance
  - IIRR Board
  - Africa Regional Office Advisory Council

*example*

## Figure 8.2. Example of the ABC Inquiry Model

- Structure
  - Management and Operations
  - Communities
  - Organization
  - Relationships
  - Teamwork
- People
  - Human Resources and Personnel Policy
  - Policy and System

- ○ Staff Development
- ○ Equal Employment Opportunity
- Resources
  - ○ Fundraising
  - ○ Facilities
  - ○ Materials
- Environment
  - ○ Image
  - ○ Networking
- Systems
  - ○ Monitoring and Evaluation
  - ○ Management Information Systems (MIS)
  - ○ Resource Management

### *Planning Areas and Team Assignments*

*IIRR: What We Do*

In partnership with disadvantaged communities, IIRR enables people to achieve their full potential.

We with other organizations (CBOs, NGOs, and governments[2]) enable them to help the disadvantaged by building their capacity through:

- Training and mentoring
- Technical assistance

[2]International development organizations are known by several names currently used in the field: In the U.S., private voluntary organizations (PVOs); in international nomenclature, non-governmental organizations (NGOs); in Africa, some are called community development organizations (CDOs); and increasingly in countries newly democratizing, as organizations that build civil society. In this example they are called international development organizations or agencies. In the inquiry model, we use the term global social change organizations (GCSO) (Cooperrider & Pasmore, 1991).

*example*

- Publications and documentation

- Collaborative field projects and action research

### Planning Teams for Strategic Areas

- ○ Team A: Isaac, Lealem, and Mike

- ○ Team B: John, Shashigo, Grace, and Arikew

- ○ Team C: George, Martin, Dorothy, and Estedar

IIRR's priority partners include organizations involved with programs in the areas of:

- Food security

- Rural development

- Environment and natural resources

- Reproductive health and HIV AIDS prevention

- Gender

- Promotion of indigenous knowledge

### Our Strategic Partners

IIRR's diverse group of strategic partners includes:

- Disadvantaged Communities—Those hardest hit by poverty in urban and rural areas with little or no access to basic services.

- Community-Based Organizations (CBOs)—Informal and formal voluntary groups organized around common interests and acknowledged by governments (cooperatives, self-help groups, etc.).

- Nongovernmental Organizations (NGOs)—Non-profit organizations that operate under the legal framework of government. These are formal organizations.

- Governments—Institutions that provide legal and policy frameworks at national and local levels.

- Research and Educational Institutions—Organizations of higher learning involved in research and education (universities, colleges, vocational and technical institutes, and research centers).

- Networks—Groups of organizations and individuals formally or informally coalescing around a common cause (associations, professional societies, consortia).

- Private Sector—Organizations and individuals *outside* of government. These could be for profit (business, consulting firms) or non-profits (NGOs, foundations, and churches).

- Donors—Individuals or organizations that contribute funds and/or other resources. They show concern/interest in IIRR's work and believe in its cause.

- Staff—Paid employees responsible for implementing IIRR's programs and activities. Teamwork is a priority and the teams can utilize volunteers and interns.

- Board—A voluntary group with overall responsibility for policy and fiscal accountability. It helps generate resources and enhances the image of IIRR.

### Governance for IIRR–Africa

IIRR–Africa's management and programs are governed by a global IIRR board and board committees. IIRR's board should be diverse and trustees should enjoy a reputation and status that will enhance the credibility of the organization.

It is recommended that IIRR global board appoint an African Advisory Council. The council will be comprised of Africans or African residents from the countries where IIRR works and who have an understanding of regional issues and challenges.

The council's purpose will be:

- Fundraising

- Enhancing IIRR's image in Africa

- Assisting IIRR–AFRICA in establishing partnerships in the private sector

*example*

The council will be limited to a maximum of five men and women from diverse backgrounds including the private sector, government, and international agencies.

To create a close link between the global board and the council, the council's chair should have an automatic seat on the global board.

### *Program*

In the next five years, IIRR–Africa will provide capacity building support to community-based organizations, small local NGOs, and government through training, mentoring, and collaborative field projects. Priority countries will be Kenya, Ethiopia, Uganda, and Tanzania. Field operational research and process documentation will be key components of the field projects.

IIRR–Africa will also document and disseminate best practices from its own experiences and those of other organizations through workshops, conferences, etc.

Specifically, IIRR–Africa will:

- Develop a comprehensive training policy

- Review curricula and develop training materials

- Conduct fifteen regional courses in project design, PM&E, and development management. Customized courses in these areas as well as in strategic planning, gender, and organizational development will be conducted as necessary.

Six collaborative field projects will be undertaken:

- Gender in Leadership and Decision-Making (Ethiopia)

- Kenya Micro-Fund

- Kenya CBO/NGO Capacity Enhancement and Technology Transfer Project

- Integrated Watershed Management (Ethiopia)

- Watershed Management (Uganda)

example

- Learning Our Way Out (LOWO/Family Planning in Ethiopia)
- Nairobi Urban Gardening Project (status to be determined)

In addition, IIRR–Africa will explore the potential for establishing other projects, for example:

- Partnering with universities and other academic institutions ion training and field projects
- Exploring the possibility of a training program for the youth (needs further discussion)

Ten IIRR–Africa publications are planned:

- Five on best practices
- Five manuals, two on gender and three on training

IIRR–Africa will provide technical support to other organizations willing to document own experiences. Efforts will be made to develop local capacity in documentation.

## Workshops/Conferences

- Eleven workshops, eight of which are related to gender
- Three will be exploratory workshops addressing themes of concern
- Two conferences are planned, one on gender and the other on a theme to be determined

### *People*

In the next five years IIRR–Africa will have a standard personnel policy with clearly defined:

- Salary structure
- Benefit packages
- Performance appraisals
- Staff development
  - Performance appraisal—2000
  - Salary structure and benefit package—2001

*example*

○ Staff development plan—2001

○ Personnel manual revision—2001

### Image and Networking

IIRR–Africa will create an identity and image that reflects the organization's vision/mission/ values to promote our work in Africa.

IIRR–Africa will develop a sound public relations strategy to reflect an excellent and accountable program and to facilitate continuous dialogue with our partners in Africa's development.

We will:

• Formulate a PR policy

• Develop and implement an effective strategy

• Train staff in PR skills

We will establish a fellowship fund to promote participation of women in development.

### Networking

IIRR–Africa will strengthen its networking through publication of a newsletter to share information. We will make use of the Internet, networks, and actively participate in forums that promote our work such as conferences and workshops.

It is ideal when you can get the whole organization involved in an AI process, especially if it is focused on both a strategic planning process and a commitment to redesign their organizational architecture to fit the dreams and ideals that are formulated by the whole system through an AI interview and dialogue process. However, the chance to do such a complete process is relatively rare. But there are many other kinds of innovative uses for AI system-level intervention.

In our practices, we have had the opportunity to design an AI-based (e)valuation process for a large pharmaceutical company, parts of which we have shared in various places in this book.

Another innovation that we have used several times in a large communications company is using AI with survey feedback data. While there was a time when we might have seen AI and survey feedback as incompatible, we are now convinced, as we have said many times in this book, that almost any traditional management or organization development method can be applied in an AI-based process. The survey data is fed back to the employees as successes and opportunities. A large group of representatives from the division involved in the survey comes together to create dreams and designs of what they want to do to increase their successes and meet the challenge of those "opportunities."

In each of these cases—the valuation project and the survey feedback summits—we have gone through lengthy design processes with internal groups to fit AI theory and practice to the organizations' goals for the work. In both cases we were fortunate enough to have excellent internal HR and OD people to work with—in one case the group was already highly skilled in AI while in the other we began with the AI training workshop. In both cases we also had line people who were intimately involved in the work of the divisions helping with the design—and occasionally with the delivery as well. In both cases, we are seeing the impact of AI in many other related projects and activities in those companies. The more comfortable we become with the requirements of the emerging paradigm and with the social constructionist basis for the work, the easier it becomes to trust the organization and the people to know what they want and how to get it. Our work becomes both easier and more fun! And we believe that our best successes are those organizations who have taken on the AI process and made it their own. The old consultant "saw" about working ourselves out of a job can be a reality with AI. And the best part is that there always seem to be new challenges and new clients on the horizon.

In the final chapter of this book, we write about the process that is near and dear to the hearts of those who cling to the hope that there really is a best way to do a job or a task—evaluation.

# Building Momentum for Sustainable Changes in Education: Toronto District School Board

*Sue Derby, Maureen McKenna, Karen Leckie, and Nancy Nightingale*

## Focus of the Appreciative Inquiry

Imagine Student Success: building momentum for sustainable changes in education

## Client

The Toronto District School Board is the fourth-largest school board in North America, with over 550 schools, 270,000 students, and 16,000 teachers. More than eighty languages are spoken in this educational system.

Sue Rowan, then system superintendent of leadership and development for TDSB was eager to explore the idea of "beginning to shift the conversation" in the system using Appreciative Inquiry. She just needed a place to start sowing the seeds of change. The catalyst for moving forward was a mandate from the Province of Ontario Ministry of Education to each school board to identify strategies focused on student success— success that would prepare students not only for college and university, but also for apprenticeships and the workplace.

## Client Objectives

In the spring of 2004 Sue and Maureen began their involvement with what became a watershed initiative known as Imagine Student Success with a simple "conversation for possibility" with Sue Rowan. By September that year, after careful planning with a small core team, Imagine Student Success was born. TDSB embarked on this exciting project with the specific intent to:

- Identify student success from a *student* perspective;

- Broaden understanding of what constitutes student success; and

*case story*

- Support the Student Success Advisory Committee in its overall development of a TDSB vision.

"Imagine being part of a secondary school where every student feels successful; where positive student-teacher relationships flourish; where flexible timetables respond to the many and varied needs of our students; where students and trustees enjoy an ongoing dialogue on the things that matter to them most; where teachers consistently create the learning environments in which students are successful; and the student voice is built into everything we do. This is the dream of Imagine Student Success."

Melanie Parrack, Executive System Superintendent,
Student Success, Toronto District School Board

## What Was Done

After a successful pilot with seven schools, groups of students in grades 7, 8, 9, and 10, representing 115 schools, were trained as "appreciative interviewers." They worked with their Imagine Student Success teacher/ coach to conduct interviews with a selection of other students, parents, school staff, and members of the working community on what success meant to them. The foundational question of the interview was "Tell me a story about a time when you felt successful." Over 2,400 interviews were documented with at least two-thirds of those being interviews with students. Each school interview team "made meaning" of their interviews and came up with a set of common themes. iCohere supported the capture and reporting of stories and themes.

Imagine Student Success phase one was complete when close to one thousand students, teachers, and guests from both the system and the community participated in an Appreciative Inquiry Summit in May 2005. Student participants further refined their definitions of success by interviewing each other and creating images of their desired future for education in TDSB. The Province of Ontario Minister of Education was on hand to hear their hopes and dreams. It was truly an energizing and meaningful day for everyone involved. Within three weeks of the summit,

*case story*

a small group of students were invited to present specific recommendations to the board and to the Ministry about how education can change to ensure student success.

## Outcomes

The board took the student recommendations very seriously and from them crafted five "student success mandates." They also endorsed an advisory group composed of students, teachers, principals, staff, and trustees and appointed a full-time TDSB staff member to lead the initiative. Throughout 2006 five Imagine Student Success committees focused on moving forward on their assigned mandate:

- Student advisory process to trustees and co-curricular activities

- Positive teacher-student relationships

- Pilot programs around flexible timetables

- Professional development for teachers

- Student voice/student surveys

The expansive scope of this initiative propelled the need to build internal capacity around the use of Appreciative Inquiry. As a result the board engaged the authors to conduct customized AI foundations workshops for some staff groups and teachers, assist in developing communication strategies, and conduct think tanks on topics that will ultimately contribute to student success. Having witnessed the possibilities that Appreciative Inquiry presented, a number of managers and educators in TDSB embraced the opportunities to learn more and apply the approach in their various constituencies in the years that followed.

In the short term the impact of Imagine Student Success and AI was felt in several ways:

- Staff, students, and the community could now envision new possibilities for student success.

- Strong positive interpersonal relationships increased through shared imagination.

*case story*

- Stakeholders began to view challenges as exciting, creative opportunities rather than problems.

- Staff, students, and the community were empowered to explore school improvements with optimism and energy.

- The student voice was taken seriously and has expanded.

- Lives have changed.

Following are some mini-stories that illustrate that impact on the system and on the lives of students.

### Karen and Nancy

Karen Leckie, a young teacher who was part of the initial core group, had a dream. That dream was to teach in a school where students would have the freedom and the opportunity to be the best they could be through self-directed learning. In December 2004, after being a pivotal part of the Imagine Student Success pilot, Karen and her principal, Nancy Nightingale, responded to the invitation from the Ministry of Education for proposals on dealing with "Students at Risk." Their proposal was grounded on four key planks:

- The theme of "freedom and independence" from Karen's students' Imagine Student Success interviews;

- Themes from their Imagine A.Y. Jackson parent event;

- Appreciative Inquiry as a foundation for inquiry in the classroom; and

- The Sudbury Valley School Model.

In less than six weeks from proposal submission, Karen and Nancy received funding from the Ministry of Education and began immediately to invite students to participate in a program they called "¡Pod"—a facilitated, self-directed learning program based on AI and featuring democratic decision making, individual time lines, and a student-run code of care committee. Students receive support in reaching particular learning goals. A central component is a vibrant, diverse community of learners who respect the principles of mutual respect and understanding. Students are guided toward meeting the curriculum expectations for the particular credit they are pursuing. Students in ¡Pod can obtain credits in any course currently existing within the Ontario Ministry of Education documents. Students may also obtain interdisciplinary credits that can be used toward the six credits needed for entrance into post-secondary education. The ¡Pod blossomed from five students to more than one hundred students over its first eighteen months—clearly an example of "change at the speed of imagination"! Karen and Nancy were clearly early adaptors of Appreciative Inquiry within TDSB and became serious students and advocates for the application of AI in the system. They both remain passionate contributors to the worldwide AI community.

## Randy

Randy Yeboah was part of the Imagine Student Success initiative and one of the original five ¡Pod students. When Karen and Nancy were invited to showcase ¡Pod as a successful pilot for reaching "at-risk" students, Randy found himself front and centre. He was invited to share his views of this new way of teaching and learning to the Ontario Minister of Education. "Imagine a program that builds on positive relationships: where students, teachers, and administrators are making connections; where teachers have the time to get to know their students on a personal level and develop relationships; where schools function like caring communities," he said. Before Randy prepared and delivered that speech, he attended our four-day AI Foundations workshop. He still loves to recount how he successfully used "stealth AI" throughout! Randy went on to respond to the increasing needs of the community with some other Toronto youths, starting an online dialogue on how they could help young children to avoid guns and gangs. Randy introduced them to Appreciative Inquiry and as a result of inviting them to dream they formed iDREAM—a not-for-profit organization to mentor youth between the ages of six and ten Randy's story continues to be a wonderful example of what happens when we see the possibilities in our youth and shine the light on them. He is now in his last year at York University in Toronto, studying public administration.

*case story*

### Saeid

iPod student Saeid Chavoshi designed a grade twelve course called *Brain Science* and became the first student ever to author his own curriculum within the Ontario curriculum. Being inspired as a result of this achievement, Saeid changed his career path to study cognitive science at Toronto University. In addition to being a full-time student, he operates a not-for-profit organization called www.systemsforchange.ca.

### Alex

Living into his talent for video storytelling, Imagine Student Success core team member and iPod student Alex Kolodkin developed and produced several videos to tell the Imagine Student Success and iPod success stories. Alex will tell you that AI changed his life, and our experience of Alex today is that he embodies the principles in everything he does. Alex is currently a thriving media student at Ryerson University in Toronto.

### Learnings

- Beginning with a core planning team that included staff, teachers, trustees, and particularly students was key to success;

- Student insight into the use of student-centered language was invaluable to the development of the Imagine Student Success interview protocol and approach;

- Pushing forward with one key champion made a big difference in a short time without the need for top-down endorsement from the board;

- Communication in a huge system like TDSB is a real challenge;

- We helped the client develop and implement a communication framework for sustaining the momentum throughout and beyond the initiative; using the many existing communication channels for different audiences in TDSB made a big difference;

- Building internal capacity for AI in a large organizational system such as TDSB is an absolute priority for sustainability and stimulating the ripple effect beyond the primary initiative;

*case story*

- Fanning the ripples of interest within the board through coaching early AI adopters resulted in many AI initiatives: large-scale multi-stakeholder think tanks on topics like autism, school revitalization programs, training administrators and the communications department in AI, changes in the classroom and with administration within schools, and student-led transition programs, to mention a few initiatives;

- Going beyond the scope of the initiative and inviting students twice a year to participate in AI foundations public workshops continues to make a huge difference for everyone involved; and

- Building and nurturing relationships with staff, teachers, and students over a period of years will continue to make a positive difference at TDSB.

The following websites provide additional information for the interested reader:

AI Commons video clips
http://appreciativeinquiry.case.edu/practice/
bibAiStoriesDetail.cfm?coid=8324

Alex Kolodkin's iPod video: www.youtube.com/
watch?v=czV31nFcVMw

Randy's full speech is on
www.tdsb.on.ca/communications/publications/tdsbtodaypdf/
tdsbtodayfeb06.pdf
Transforming High Schools at TDSB through Appreciative Inquiry
www.thesumoexperience.com

www.thesumoexperience.com

**Authors' Contact information**
Sue Derby: sue@thesumoexperience.com
Karen Leckie: karenleckie@gmail.com
Maureen McKenna: mo@thesumoexperience.com
Nancy Nightingale: nrnightingale@yahoo.ca

*case story*

# Introducing Appreciative Inquiry into a Community Network Project in Liverpool, England

*By Tim Slack and Phil Taylor*

## Introduction: Awakening and the Start of a Journey

This story begins in 2006, at the start of a client's journey of discovery and realization. Discovery that a philosophy called Appreciative Inquiry existed and was receiving international recognition. Realization that Appreciative Inquiry not only worked as a methodology in any number of organizational and community settings but that it is a way of life. This case study describes the AI journey from both a client perspective and also how a small AI project was developed and delivered within inner-city Liverpool.

At this time Phil Taylor was an employee of Liverpool City Council and had been for more than thirty years. In that time he had been involved in a range of community consultations, and worked on numerous development and regeneration initiatives. He had also trained extensively as a coach and group facilitator. In 2004 he joined the city council team that was given the task of delivering Liverpool's year as European Capital of Culture for 2008.

## The Client: Liverpool City Council Culture Company

Liverpool City Council established the Liverpool Culture Company in 2000 to coordinate its bid for European Capital of Culture 2008. In June 2003 the UK government announced that Liverpool had beaten off eleven other contenders for the prestigious title. A restructured Culture Company saw the creation of a range of new teams and functions, one of which was the Creative Communities team, which was where Phil's role as cultural infrastructure development manager sat.

As the link person for Liverpool Culture Company with the South Suburbs neighborhood of the city, in the summer of 2006 Phil was invited by the area manager to attend an afternoon seminar that had been arranged to explore how community groups in the area might collaborate or merge

case story

in the future. There were potential tensions between the groups and the dynamic in the room would be interesting to observe.

Phil remembers the day and the following events clearly: "What I remember most of the session was the impact of the group facilitation and the facilitator. I had been involved in many such seminars before, and had known Tim Slack as regeneration manager in Wirral some years previous, and this seemed a departure for him in that I was more used to seeing Tim in more formal settings such as board room situations and council meetings—and wearing 'the suit'! He now seemed much more relaxed and was really engaging the group in the approach he had described at the start of the session. I had never seen the temperature in a room change so much in a few hours.

"I was taken by the way the process Tim was employing moved people from the 'issues' to talking about things that worked and the possibilities. I recall the phrase 'more of what works' being used a few times as well. And, of course, the agreement as the session concluded between the participants to work more closely in future. This left a deep impression on me, and the conversation with Tim after the event made me think about the range of potential situations [in which] I could see this approach working. I was prompted to find out more about Appreciative Inquiry as a result."

(It is worth adding at this point that the parties in the room have since worked together successfully and a government grant totaling £750,000 has recently been announced.)

The opportunity to explore these possibilities soon emerged. As Phil recalls: "Several weeks later I was at a planning meeting with a community group in the Toxteth area of Liverpool. Toxteth is a part of the city which has historically been the home to an African/Caribbean community since the early 19th Century. The Toxteth neighborhood is one of the most disadvantaged communities within the UK. More recently, the area has become the most culturally and racially mixed area in England.

"My experience working with the group had been that whenever we held these meetings they always seemed to stay focused on the problems: same thing led to the same results—nothing appeared to work.

"This time I decided to try and apply what I had observed at the session Tim had facilitated, and to my surprise it worked and worked well. The group focused on the things that had been a source of pride and their achievements, and they also agreed to host a planning meeting for BME and other community groups in the area to look at the potential for joint working. At this point, I decided that Tim at Appreciating People was needed to take the ideas forward, and Appreciating People were commissioned and the brief defined."

## The Brief

Liverpool Culture Company Creative Communities team commissioned Tim's company, Appreciating People, to make contact and work with the BME (British Minority Ethnic) groups within the Toxteth neighborhood over a three-month period using Appreciative Inquiry as an approach to foster collaborative working and a shared future by:

- Encouraging groups to share their resources

- Establishing links of communication

- Forming a network for regular meetings and future planning

These project requirements were in response to concerns raised about groups competing for limited resources as well as project and service duplication.

## What Happened? Approach and Methodology

The main project emerged through an initial pilot meeting in March 2007 to which representatives of all relevant groups and organizations were invited. An invitation by letter to attend a meeting had been the normal approach to bringing together groups, but the meeting was poorly attended and it was felt that this approach had contributed to low attendance. Appreciating People had been asked to facilitate the pilot event, as the client had experienced elements of the AI approach. The format of this meeting was a half-day session using Appreciative Inquiry techniques to facilitate the following aims:

*case story*

- Encourage groups to share their resources

- Establish links of communication

- Form a network for regular meetings and future planning

The AI techniques used at this meeting proved to be a powerful tool for identifying the issues and solutions. Groups were surprised to learn that they all, in fact, have the same goals and issues, and a firm footing for co-operation was established. This included the establishment of a network drawn from the groups that attended the meeting.

Following the meeting, agreement was reached between Appreciating People and the client that further work was required—in particular to change the invitation to a meeting approach to a proactive AI-based project that would combine AI interviews and a mini-AI summit. It was also agreed that original project aims would be retained.

The interview stage consisted of twenty interviews plus significant time identifying the myriad of groups in the area and obtaining an up-to-date database. Over twenty interviews took place either one-to-one or by phone following, principally, the Discover and Dream elements of the 4-D format. At this stage Appreciating People had not added the fifth D (Define) into the process. Subsequently, in future projects this became the norm at the client project planning process. Groups and organizations interviewed ranged from Somali, Chinese, Gambian, Hindu, Arabic, and afro-Caribbean organizations and small community groups.

The interviews were conducted in person or by phone, the purpose being to gather positive stories from organizations and groups and to stress the importance of attending the summit. Interview experience provided significant new information about the local organizations for the client and a sense of positive energy from the organizations that took part.

**Interview Questions**

Q1: Share with me a positive thing you have done for the organization.

Q2: What makes this group/organization a good place to work or be a member of?

Q3: What do you like best about your role in the organization/group?

Q4: Can you describe the work your organization does?

Q5: What part of your work or involvement are you most proud of?

Q6: What has been the best thing your group has undertaken or is doing?

Q7: What makes your organization/group different from similar organizations?

Q8: If you get support from Liverpool City Council/Capital of Culture, what has been the most supportive and positive?

Q9: How would you make it better?

Q10: Share with me three things that would enable your group to be more effective, and what is the most important?

All the interviews provided a wide range of powerful stories with constant amazement to being asked questions around the area of "what works." Some examples include:

"To see the delight on the faces of the Somali women as they watched the Irish dancing."

"I see a future where we all share one voice."

"We need to drop the spears and learn to walk and talk."

## The AI Mini Summit

The Ai summit was held at the end of the interview process, and the information gained from the interviews was displayed on flip charts and banners in the meeting space. Emphasis was placed on showing the stories and achievements. Setting out the room with candles and flowers created a relaxed atmosphere. Facilitating the summit, Appreciating People was helped by client staff that had received initial AI training. The day was full of dialogue and energy sharing, contact details, and experience. From the discussions and dialogue, the groups agreed on a provocative proposition and then identified a number of themes to be addressed.

*case story*

The AI summit positive statement was:

WORKING TOGETHER TO CREATE EFFECTIVE AND SUSTAINABLE ORGANIZATIONS THAT WILL SHARE RESOURCES, SKILLS, AND OPPORTUNITIES

AI summit common themes and areas for sharing skills/resources included:

- Acceptance and celebration of the diversity of arts/culture available in the L8 area

- Development of opportunities for storytelling across the cultures

- Development of newsletters/communication opportunities across the cultures and communities

- Creation of exhibitions to demonstrate cultural diversity

- Opportunities to share and celebrate the different faiths

- Create opportunities for joint funding bids

- Share activities, teachers, spaces, and facilities

- Support the newly established network

As the AI summit process was confined to one day, there had been emphasis on the Discover, Dream, and Design stages from the 4-D process and it was intended that the proposed network take on the Deliver stage.

## Outcomes

Three months after the completion of the project, Appreciating People conducted a number of AI interviews to identify whether the project outcomes were being met and the project's impact.

- The network was in place and operating under its own leadership with no external support. Plans were in place for joint funding of projects, shared events, and combining resources. Network meetings were reported as always being positive.

- Groups and organizations were planning events that included other organizations, which was a change from previous arrangements.

_case story_

- Plans were in place for a newsletter.

- The client, Liverpool City Council Culture Company, had an update contact database and more information about local groups.

- Participants reported that their individual work approach had changed and they were seeing things through an appreciative eye, and that there organizations had a better understanding of their work and future plans.

- The client is now receiving higher-quality funding applications.

- There was a sense of celebration of what was being achieved.

## Postscript: Journey's End and New Beginnings?

Four months after the end of the project, Tim was invited to attend the Muslim Eid celebration at the end of Ramadan at the Al Ghazali Centre in Toxteth. The centre had taken part in the whole project, and as Tim came through the door, he was greeted by one of the staff with the words "Here comes Mr. Appreciating"!!

Two years after the summit, the groups were still meeting on a regular basis and submitting funding applications to undertake project work. Members of the network had also undertaken AI training.

Phil Taylor not only undertook AI training but has since left the employment of the city council and has become an associate partner with Appreciating People as part of his freelance professional practice. It has certainly been a life-changing experience for him that has helped him in all areas of his life and work.

Another impact of the process has been the project's effect on individuals. One participant from the Merseyside Caribbean Association, besides undertaking an AI basic course, has also found new confidence to become involved in city-level work and begin to affect change in her organization.

The Big Conversation was one of the highlights of the Capital of Culture year and a defining moment for AI in the region. After the positive impact Tim and AI had made in Toxteth, Appreciating People continued to work

*case story*

with members of the Culture Company team, as a result in part of Phil's continued involvement and his encouragement of colleagues to learn more and attend a training course.

The creative health and well-being manager, Julie Hanna, delivered a program that sought to evidence the benefits of engaging people in creative activity in health settings and to demonstrate the positive effects of this activity on their health and well-being. While this work is documented globally, there was a feeling that the benefits were not being maximized for a number of reasons, such as lack of a common language.

Julie worked closely with Tim and Appreciating People to create the framework for the Big Conversation, which culminated in a day-long event in December 2008 that saw health and creative professionals come together and develop a shared understanding. The day was a positive, uplifting experience that succeeded where so many other seminars and "think tanks" had failed in bringing people together to develop a strategy and framework for joint working in arts and heath.

Although the Toxteth AI project was a limited piece of work. its effects operated like a pebble in a pond with a growth in interest in Appreciative Inquiry across the public, community, and voluntary sectors in Liverpool.

For further information about Appreciating People and the case studies referred to in this article, go to www.appreciatingpeople.co.uk.

### Authors' Contact Information

Tim Slack
tim@appreciatingpeople.co.uk

Phil Taylor
phil.taylor46@yahoo.co.uk

# CHAPTER 9

# Valuation

"We inhabit a world that is always subjective and shaped by our interactions with it. Our world is impossible to pin down, constantly changing and infinitely more interesting than we ever imagined."

Margaret Wheatley, *Leadership and the New Science*

**THIS CHAPTER COVERS THE MAJOR IMPACT** that the shifting paradigm, particularly the new sciences and social constructionism, have on our concepts and practice of evaluation. It describes AI as an approach to evaluating AI interventions as well as an approach to evaluating any process or situation.

## Classical Evaluation

The encyclopedia defines evaluate as: "To ascertain or fix the value of." Whether it is a performance appraisal for one's job, an evaluation of a project, feedback from a colleague, or criticism from a significant other, the feelings evoked by having one's "value" fixed, ones faults, short-falls, and limitations pointed out, are troubling and unsettling.

In most situations, evaluation carries the burden of "judgment." Even though most traditional evaluations point out successes as well as failures uncovered in an evaluation process, it seems to be human nature to focus on, if not to obsess about, those things that others declare (or that we ourselves fear) do not measure up to some standard assumed to define "perfection." Furthermore, no matter what kind of intervention one makes in an organizational system, the conversation will, at some point, get around to the subject of monitoring and evaluation. Volumes have been written. Methods have been formulated and tested. Millions of dollars have been invested. We yearn to know how our inputs determine outcomes; whether our carefully crafted goals have been achieved; how much return we got for our investment.

We will argue in this chapter that applying the scientific methods of the Newtonian paradigm to human systems is flawed at best, if not actually a useless endeavor. It is one thing to count the number of vaccinations given in an area and relate that to the incidence of the disease in the area covered by the vaccination program. It is quite another to try to determine the impact of any person or group on the performance of a large and complex system.

## Evaluation from an Appreciative Inquiry Perspective

Evaluation from the Appreciative Inquiry perspective works from the assumption that the uncountable number of variables in any human system makes it impossible to determine the one or even several best ways to do any human process. Nor is it possible to replicate what works in one group and assume that it will work the same way in the next. Indeed, working in human systems requires a flexible, open, creative stance that embraces ambiguity and innovation. In any human interaction, each person has an experience unique to that individual and substantially different from the experience of every other person.

Appreciative Inquiry as a perspective for an evaluation process is grounded in several basic beliefs. The first is the *belief that the intervention into any human system is fateful and that the system will move in the direction of the first questions that are asked.* In other words, in an appreciative evaluation, the first questions asked would focus on stories of best practices, most successful moments, greatest learning, successful processes, generative partnerships, and so on. This enables the system to look for its successes and create images of a future built on those positive experiences from the past. Appreciative Inquiry enables organizations to carry out valuations that move organizations toward their highest aspirations and best practices.

Second, the theory that we are all connected, as the new sciences demonstrate, suggests that *there is no such thing as an objective observer.* This implies that every evaluation in a system needs to be understood and planned as a powerful intervention into the system with the power to alter and shape the future of that system.

Finally, an AI valuation process gives the additional *benefit of continuity.* There is no implication that the past is deficient or wrong, simply that we look back for those life-giving forces, those moments of excellence in which we can take pride and use those as guidance to move us into a positive and generative future.

Following is an example of an AI evaluation process.

## An Appreciative Evaluation Example[*]

During 1998, the Research and Development division of SmithKline Beecham Pharmaceuticals undertook an evaluation of a major and innovative simulation-based training program, the SB Discovery Simulation.

This training program had been designed to help scientific leaders and key contributors work effectively within the new drug discovery research paradigm. Over the course of three intensive days, participants worked in research teams utilizing a dynamic computer model of the drug

example

[*]From an article by Bernard J. Mohr, Elizabeth Smith, and Jane Magruder Watkins, 2000.

example

discovery process. The aim was to create a realistic learning environment in which a drug company attempts to maximize its portfolio of research efforts over a ten-year period.

At the time of this evaluation process, 480 people from SmithKline Beecham in the U.S. and the UK had attended the program — a critical mass of the original target population. End-of-course evaluations were conducted for each program. The data collected was largely favorable, with participants reporting an increase in knowledge and understanding in a number of areas. Suggestions for improvements were acted on wherever appropriate, so that the program was continuously refined during the rollout.

The OD group who had led the design and delivery of the Discovery Simulation in conjunction with senior Discovery research scientists were satisfied up to a point that the simulation now worked well and consistently elicited positive responses from those who attended. However, since they had made a major investment in this program, they decided it was important to conduct an in-depth evaluation study to ascertain whether it had made a lasting impact on the organization. If such an impact could be demonstrated, they also wished to determine how to further capitalize on this investment.

To find an outside evaluator, SmithKline Beecham put out a request for proposals to several consulting groups that they knew would offer different approaches, but still with the expectation that they would conduct a reasonably traditional evaluation process in which the consultants would interview people in the company, compile the data, and give the client a report of their findings. The usual report includes the strengths and weaknesses of the simulation and its outcomes and recommendations from the consultants for next steps.

One of the companies that received the invitation to tender was The Synapse Group, Inc., a consulting firm based in Portland, Maine. The Synapse consultants responded with a proposal that turned traditional evaluation thinking on its head. The proposal suggested the use of Appreciative Inquiry to conduct a "valuation process," sometimes called "Embedded Evaluation." They believed that this approach could give SB information about the strengths of the program in ways that would create positive forward momentum by taking the best of what had happened and using it to create a collective image of a desired future as a basis for moving the program in the direction of its best practices.

In alignment with the usual AI process, the consultants and the SB team designed an interview protocol, conducted 104 interviews, created provocative propositions, and created five different reports, each tailor-made for a part of the system. The outcomes were remarkably rich.

## Learning, Innovations, and Reaffirmations from This Case

Some months after the final report had been distributed and its recommendations were well underway to being implemented, the external consultants sat down with the SB Project Manager for the purpose of asking: "In retrospect, what did we learn from this work? What do we consider to be the innovations? What was reaffirmed for us?" Shown below for purpose of illustrating the two worlds (client and consultant) are the lists of "Learnings, Innovations, and Reaffirmations" (Table 9.1) from this case developed independently at first by each party.

As we chatted about our lists, we realized once again the power of partnership—for what constituted innovation for the consultants was a new learning (but not necessarily an innovation) for the client. A case in point was the inclusion of the consultants as part of the interview team. From the consultant perspective this was "innovative" because "normal" in AI practice suggests the importance of limiting the active role of the consultant in interviewing/data collection in order to minimize consultant dependency. The clients "learning" that a partnership between consultant and client generates a synergy not present when the consultants and clients relate to each other in a more traditional manner (the consultant as expert or vendor) was a not a new learning for the consultants. It was a reaffirmation of deeply held beliefs on their parts.

As we shared with each other the things that we had learned, the things we saw as innovations, and the things that we felt were reaffirmed for us, we recognized once more the criticality of our partnership that enabled the consultant and client to build a shared world and a shared language with which to make decisions and conduct the work. Not only did the data reflect a generative and creative picture of the simulation itself, but it also told a powerful story of the pride, loyalty, and commitment that the people of SmithKline Beecham feel for their company. As with all Appreciative Inquiries, it is the innovative, generative, and creative processes that are co-created by client and consultant that becomes a life-giving force for the organization. We realized that we were sharing a reflection about our work together that was, itself, an AI valuation process.

## Table 9.1. Learnings, Innovations, and Reaffirmations

| Client's List | Consultant's List |
|---|---|
| Joint partnership between consultant and client generates a synergy not present when the consultants and clients relate to each other in a more traditional manner (the consultant as expert or vendor). | Joint partnership with the client and ongoing adaptation to the local conditions is key to using innovations successfully. |
| AI does work for evaluation purposes, particularly at Level 3 of Kirkpatrick (identifying behavioral changes). | The scale of a project does not necessarily correlate to the quality of organizational learning. |
| AI is not the antithesis of problem solving. | External consultants may tend to underestimate the client's interest in the theory and constructs underlying the intervention approach. |
| Things that from a traditional evaluation process might be considered impure are OK and helpful within an embedded evaluation/AI process, for example, the use of leading questions, the use of data from the pilot, the use of people who have a vested interest in the outcome as interviewers/data collectors. | By participating as interviewers, the external consultants were able to contribute more to the data compilation and were also able to become more part of the team. We all had similar stakes in the learnings/outcomes. |

## Table 9.1. Continued

| Client's List | Consultant's List |
| --- | --- |
| The "core AI" questions were the ones that produced the richest data. | Before the client can receive innovative assistance, innovation must be present in the worldview of the consultant. And innovations are more likely to come from an outside source who doesn't have a set picture of how things ought to be. |
| The experience of AI interviewing is so positive that it affects the interviewer as well as the interviewee. | HR/OD professionals who have been trained in traditional interviewing styles may find it harder to use the more flexible dialogue protocol approach of AI. |
| Since the data generated are in a qualitative/narrative form, the amount of time for digesting the volume of data is significant (particularly in evaluating applicability/applications). | SB management trusted their internal HR/OD group to conduct the evaluation without a steering committee and the project was completed just fine without a steering committee. |
| The richness of the data allows many more questions to be answered than might be answerable with a more traditional quantitative model of evaluation. | Making assumptions about what clients will or will not be comfortable with can lead to unnecessary constraints on the project. |

## Evaluation as an Integral Part of Any AI Process

In the early 1990s the Global Excellence in Management (GEM) Initiative ran a series of institutes for the leadership of international development agencies. The process included a workshop to help each client system develop a customized interview protocol; time for the clients to conduct the interviews; a six-day residential institute to work with the data and do strategic planning; consultant time over the following year; and a formal evaluation visit twice over the next two years to do an appreciative valuation of their work. The valuation questions included such subjects as the most exciting stories of events following the institute; positive changes in the organization in alignment with their strategic planning process; unexpected positive outcomes for their organization; etc. The valuation interviews were part of a full-day workshop, with the clients and consultants all participating in the dialogue about best and most exciting outcomes. These dialogues became guidance for the ongoing work of the agency. Most of the clients incorporated this practice of appreciative review as a management process for their organization.

This was a major learning for us about the ongoing and iterative nature of AI. A colleague once asked me what to do when an AI process had been very successful over a long period of time but was running out of steam. My cryptic answer was, "Do more AI!" What I was actually referring to was the process of continually valuating with AI questions how the AI process itself is going—questions like: "Share some stories of our most successful and exciting experiences using an AI approach in our company. What things have we liked most? What changes are apparent as a result?" and so on. Once again, the image of the stream comes to mind. It is through the constant shifting and changing of an organization's dialogues that we find the flow toward our imagined future. Using AI as a valuation process on a regular basis assures that the imagined future will be positive.

And so we end this book repeating our mantra: Appreciative Inquiry is a way of seeing and being in the world. It is based on the belief that we can create what we imagine when we open our minds and our social processes to the widest possible dialogue among the largest number of people who are involved and invested in our enterprise. Appreciative Inquiry applied, whether as a planning process or an evaluative process, becomes empowering and life-affirming in any human system.

*case story*

# Valuation of the Effectiveness of AI for the Zambia Police Services Victim Support Unit

*By Mette Jacobsgaard*

The following describes a valuation of the work of the Victims Support Unit (VSU) within the Zambia Police Services. VSU was supported as part of a foreign aid program to support access to justice in Zambia.

## Introduction

A number of journals, associations, and trusts are dedicated to evaluation. Companies, aid donors, and many others have specific guidelines for evaluation. Evaluation is important. Looking at the literature, there does not appear to be a unanimous definition of evaluation. However, those who do try to define what evaluation is suggest some common traits. According to Wikipedia, "Evaluation is systematic determination of merit, worth, and significance of something or someone using criteria against a set of standards." The Evaluation Trust says that "Evaluation is assessing and judging the value of a piece of work, an organization or a service." The Danish International Development Agency (DANIDA) explains, "An evaluation is an examination, as systematic and objective as possible, of the design, implementation and results of projects and their objectives." Value judgments seem to be implied in all cases.

Whereas I do not have a problem with judgments per se, I do question situations where people depend on so-called expert evaluations.

It is not difficult for us to develop criteria for our judgments, but our judgments also involve our values. We have different ways of valuing based on culture, background, access, experience, and education. Evaluation is comparative by nature. Given that evaluations are often carried out by external evaluators, those value judgments are essentially made by the evaluator. They become the judgments of the expert evaluator. At the same time, the whole point of evaluating is to look back to learn in order to move forward and possibly improve on the past. How is it possible that recommendations of an evaluator living one reality can be relevant and even understood by people and projects living another reality? And

*case story*

by the way, by the time the information is filtered it is outdated. This is where Appreciative Inquiry comes in.

Appreciative Inquiry is (e)valuation. Valuation is the determination of the value of something or the act of looking back to see what worked best—what was most valued in the past with a view to increase such value in the future. Appreciative Inquiry not only facilitates self-valuation—it also embeds the valuative process within the organization or project.

## Valuation of Development Aid Projects and Programs

Third-World development is based on assumptions of need. If no need is portrayed, no funds will come forward. This is the basic premise and reality of the world of development aid. "Third World Aid" is in itself a social construct, a reality in which one part of the world has great needs and wants which can be fulfilled by those living in another part of the world, providing the right planning and actions are in place. However, as many evaluations show, efforts generally fall short of the plans, perhaps precisely because we evaluate against the plans and not against the objectives of the project or program—or indeed against the wants and needs of those who should be assisted.

There are several reasons for using Appreciative Inquiry for evaluation. These are:

- The assumption that *everyone* has something to contribute
- The active engagement of the project and those involved with it
- The "empowerment" that comes from respectful self-assessment
- The ownership of the decisions made through the self-assessment.
- AI goes beyond data collection and analysis
- AI goes beyond judgment and taking stock
- AI is participatory
- AI creates ownership of outcome
- AI involves the whole system

*case story*

- AI embeds results

- AI is a process and perspective that can be applied to existing evaluation methods

In most project and program evaluation, there is a need and even a requirement to describe or document what happens in particular with respect to output and impact (written reports are a big part hereof). Using Appreciative Inquiry does not negate this requirement. In fact, in order to secure continued funding, progress has to be documented or related in such a way that the reader feels convinced that the activities/project meets its objectives. Telling, sharing, and documenting stories is the most powerful way of documenting impact and change.

## VSU Zambia

The Victims Support Unit (VSU) was established as a unit within the Zambia Police Service in 1996. VSU was created specifically to address problems of violence affecting women, children, and the elderly. The unit has two main functions: (1) creating awareness amongst the general public through sensitisation and information workshops and (2) counseling victims of crime, crisis negotiation, and intervention to address trauma resulting from victimization.

There are a total of about 350 police stations country-wide in Zambia and about one thousand police posts. The VSU has officers in three hundred of the police stations. Each police station has two or three trained officers, at least one of each gender. The number of cases that the VSU deals with has increased steadily since it opened, from 657 cases in 1997 to 9,282 cases in 2002. The VSU is staffed with specially trained police officers and is a very popular unit within the Police Service, with many officers applying to be part of the unit. The VSU had quickly become widely known and very popular in Zambia. Their success was reported in the local papers, and they saw themselves as "the human face" sympathizing with the public, especially victims of crime.

The VSU has received aid funding from the foreign donor in Lusaka in 2000, 2001, and 2002. The money was spent on training of officers, community workshops, information dissemination, and office equipment.

In 2003 I was asked by the foreign donor to review the achievements of VSU with a view to recommend whether future assistance should be given. Clearly, Zambia Police Service, and the VSU especially, were apprehensive about being evaluated, as the outcome of the review would be decisive in terms of whether future funding would be granted by the donor, which at the time was a major donor in Zambia.

Although there was every reason to believe that funding would continue given the success of the VSU, the fact that an external consultant arrived to evaluate the work put the VSU on the spot and possibly having to defend themselves and their actions. This is a normal reaction in all evaluation cases, and in many cases the client has reason to be worried. Different people, with different values, evaluate change in different ways, and you do not know what you will get when external consultants arrive.

In my initial meetings with the VSU I made it clear that this evaluation would be in their own hands, that they were to evaluate themselves, and that we would focus on their strengths and why it was so important to discover their very best practices in order that they could be learned from and built upon. In the first meeting, we discussed establishing a core group of especially interested officers from the VSU. In the next meeting with those who had volunteered and been selected from the VSU and the Police Service, I asked: "If you were to ask the question; tell me a story about the best experience you have had with the VSU—whose story would you be curious to hear?" It became clear to the officers that they would appreciate the views of stakeholders such as their clients, representatives from social services, the hospital (which dealt with forensic evidence and rape cases), legal aid providers, NGOs, and more. It was agreed that representatives from these stakeholder groups should be included in the evaluation. We agreed to divide the work into three phases:

PHASE I: Core group workshop

Stakeholder workshop

Interview of clients—Lusaka

PHASE II: Planning of field work

Workshop in Western province (three days including client interviews)

Workshop in Southern province (three days including client interviews)

PHASE III: Core group workshop to process all information

Prepare vision for future

Draft project document

In Phase I we started the workshop with the core group by having them interview each other about their best experience of being a member of the VSU and also what their aspirations were for the unit. Based on the themes from the interviews, we discussed the sort of questions they had for further elaboration from the stakeholder group and their clients. We agreed on a protocol of questions for the stakeholder workshop and the clients. We discussed and practiced interviewing and the importance of staying with the generative interview protocol.

The following themes arose from the interviews:

1. When the staff is most excited about being part of the VSU, they have experienced the following:

   • They have had the ability to recognize skills in others

   • There has been a feeling of moving toward a common goal

   • There has been co-ordination

   • They have been able to facilitate

   • Training has been exciting

   • There has been a sense of sharing

   • The situations where VSU has been able to shift the focus (from perpetrators to victims—and there is a better understanding of their role as police service)

_case story_

- They have been able to make a difference
- They have been able to create awareness around gender issues
- They have been able to make decisions
- There has been a feeling of serving society
- They have had clarity of their role
- There have been trust, leadership, and personal commitment
- Cases have been referred
- There has been continuity (in case flow)
- They have experienced internal support
- They have been able to secure convictions
- There has been good corporation

2. The following is felt to be the most important aspects of the VSU:

- The fact that they deal with everyday-life cases
- They are in the forefront of new crimes
- They bridge the gap between the police and the public
- VSU has brought appreciation of the police by the public
- They have a good rating with women and children

3. The following is valued most about one's own position with the VSU:

- The ability to pass on knowledge
- Training
- Personal development
- Specialized training
- It is community centered
- The ability to relate to the most vulnerable

*case story*

4. The following reflects the wishes for the future:

- That they VSU has independent (their own) offices at each station
- More officers should be trained
- Better logistic support (transport and material)
- More investigation equipment
- A database and IT training
- That the VSU is better recognized
- Safe houses for victims
- That the law is more "user friendly"
- Study tours to see how similar units are operating
- The introduction of a debriefing process for officers dealing with victims
- Improved relations with Social Welfare

A discussion was held with respect to what the VSU would like to know from the stakeholders and from their clients. The following were listed:

**Stakeholders**

- How VSU and the stakeholders (NGOs) complement each other
- The wishes of the stakeholders
- Their attitude (toward VSU)
- To know more about working relations (with Social Welfare)
- How they view VSU
- Suggestions (for improvement)
- How much they know about VSU
- Weaknesses (of VSU)
- How VSU can help

It was agreed that the same questionnaire as the one used with the core group could be used with the wider stakeholder group with a few modifications, as follows:

1. When you think back on your experience with VSU, what stands out for you as a time when you felt VSU performed really well? Tell me the story of this situation. Please be specific!

   • Who was there?

   • What did they do?

   • What was it that made the performance so good?

   • How did you contribute to this?

2. What do you feel is most important about VSU?

3. What is it that you value most about your relations with VSU?

4. What is the most important impact that VSU has made on your organization?

5. If you could have three wishes for the VSU for the future, what would they be?

We had a long discussion about how to include and interview the clients who were, after all, victims of crime and violence. Not only were they vulnerable but it was claimed that they may also be suspicious if interviewed by the VSU. At the same time, there was an argument for having the VSU officers conduct the interviews—not of their own clients but VSU officers from other parts of the country interviewing clients of their colleagues. I felt it was important for the VSU officers to hear from the clients directly, to feel the impact of their work. I also reminded the VSU officers that the questions we asked were about best experiences and not about complaints, and the clients would therefore be more likely to feel free to come forward with their experiences.

There was great excitement in the group after the interviews in Lusaka and great expectations and energy to carry the exercise on into two rural provinces, one in the Western and one in the Southern province. As part of the planning, we discussed what aspects of the interview protocol had worked well and whether there was a wish for changes, especially whether there was anything in particular arising from the interviews that the VSU officers were curious to know more about.

At this point we had defined by planning and designing the protocols—discovered in the first workshop and redefined following the first workshop. We had created a new protocol between the two workshops, recorded and described the themes, and used these to redefine and created the protocol to be used in the two up-country workshops. I would like to point to the fact that we did not go through the 4 Ds in the first two workshops. Instead, we circled back around definition and discovery—gathering data.

Only in the two following workshops up-country did we go through all of the 4 Ds.

### The Up-Country Workshops

In the two workshops up-country the VSU had gathered officers from the entire province. Some had to come by boat up rivers and some had long journeys on foot and bicycles. The workshops were held at a central place that had both meeting room and lodging facilities. The logistics involved were substantial.

Apart from the VSU officers, representatives from local NGOs and local government participated. The first day of the workshop was another discovery and recording and discussing the themes. The following day the participants went to the field to interview the clients of VSU, and the day after that they shared the stories they had heard in the field and pulled out even more themes. This way we now had data about VSU and their work from the VSU officers at the provincial level, other stakeholders, as well as the clients of VSU. A substantial amount of data and themes had been collected, which in turn informed the Dream phase and the remainder of the exercise.

### What Stands Out

What stands out for me from this valuation are a number of things best expressed by examples:

*case story*

VSU, like the rest of the Zambia Police Service, lacks transport. Police officers, including the VSU, often have great difficulty getting transport to investigate crime and make arrests, let alone just showing their faces in the communities they serve. There are few resources allocated for cars and motor bikes and, even if the equipment is there, the funds may not be there to buy the fuel to run it. This is a big problem and a complaint that would possibly override everything else had we chosen a problem-focused approach to this review. The resulting recommendation would have been: "Zambia Police Service must allocate funds for fuel." Through our AI process, we heard stories of how successful the VSU had been in reaching their clients—often without delay. This was made possible in those cases where the VSU had worked closely with NGOs operating in their area who were able to give them lifts. Part of the design process therefore focused on how they could collaborate closer with NGOs in general to mutual benefit. The fact that transport is a big problem due to lack of equipment and funds remains. However, the objective of reaching clients can be dealt with without being stuck due to lack of funds.

The power of the stories is not just the story itself—it is the solutions to the problems that almost automatically present themselves.

## The 6th D

There is usually a big requirement for reporting in aid projects. The project needs to report on a regular basis. Using the AI process is an ideal way of gathering data to continuously monitor progress, which in turn will make valuations easier. This can be done by making an inquiry within each of the five Ds generating stories and valuable information about what has worked and how.

- Discovery: Describe what important data the interviews generated— What did we hear?

- Dream: Describe the dreams and how it relates to the objectives of the project.

- Design: Describe the design and explain how it will benefit the project.

_case story_

- Delivery: Describe how the design will be implemented, and finally

- Describe: How you plan to move ahead with the next discovery—Definition.

I have encouraged projects that I have worked with to take time to document and describe each step as they move along with implementation of the project.

### Author's Contact Information

Mette Jacobsgaard
The Manor
Redbourne, Gainsborough
Lincolnshire DN21 4QT
UK
101572.622@compuserve.com

# References and Bibliography

Adams, M.G. (2009). *Change your questions, change your life: 10 powerful tools for life and work.* San Francisco: Berrett-Koehler.

African charter for popular participation in development and transformation. (1990). *U.N. report on international conference on popular participation in the recovery and development process in Africa.* New York: United Nations.

Avital, M., Boland, R.J., & Cooperrider, D.L. (2008). *Designing information and organizations with a positive lens (Volume 2, Advances in appreciative inquiry).* New York: Elsevier/JAI.

Barrett, F.J., & Fry, R.E. (2005). *Appreciative inquiry: A positive approach to building cooperative capacity.* Chagrin Falls, OH: Taos Institute.

Beckhard, R., & Pritchard, W. (1992). *Changing the essence: The art of creating and leading fundamental change in organizations.* San Francisco: Jossey-Bass.

Beecher, H. (1955). The powerful placebo. *Journal of the American Medical Association, 159,* 1602–1606.

Biddle, S. (1976). *Report on the management practices of U.S. private voluntary organizations.* Washington, DC: Office of Private Voluntary Cooperation (PVC), USAID.

Brockman, M. (2009). *What's next? Dispatches on the future of science: Original essays from a new generation of scientists.* New York: Vintage.

Brown, J., Isaacs, I., & the World Café Community. (2005). *The world café: Shaping our futures through conversations that matter*. San Francisco: Berrett-Koehler.

Buckingham, M., & Clifton, D.O. (2001). *Now, discover your strengths*. New York: The Free Press.

Bushe, G., & Coetzer, G. (1995, March). Appreciative inquiry as a team development intervention: A controlled experiment. *Journal of Applied Behavioral Sciences, 31,* 13.

Christakis, N.A., & Fowler, J.H. (2009). *Connected: The surprising power of our social networks and how they shape our lives*. New York: Little, Brown.

Cooperrider, D.L. (1990). Positive image; positive action: The affirmative basis of organizing. In S. Srivastva & D.L. Cooperrider (Eds.), *Appreciative management and leadership* (pp. 91–125). San Francisco: Jossey-Bass.

Cooperrider, D.L. (1995). Introduction to appreciative inquiry. *Organization development* (5th ed.). Upper Saddle River, NJ: Prentice Hall.

Cooperrider, D.L. (1999). Positive image, positive action: The affirmative basis of organizing. In S. Srivastva & D.L. Cooperrider (Eds.), *Appreciative management and leadership: The power of positive thought and action in organizations* (rev. ed.). San Francisco: Jossey-Bass.

Cooperrider, D.L. (2004). *A fusion of strength: A positive revolution in change leadership*. [DVD]. Cleveland, OH: Film Investors Group, Case Western Reserve University.

Cooperrider, D.L., Barrett, F.J., & Srivastva, S. (1995). Social construction and appreciative inquiry: A journey in organizational theory. In D. Hosking, P. Dachler, & K.J. Gergen (Eds.), *Management and organization: Relational alternatives to individualism* (pp. 157–200). Aldershot, UK: Avebury Press.

Cooperrider, D.L., & Srivastva, S. (1987). Appreciative inquiry in organizational life. In W. Pasmore & R. Woodman (Eds.), *Research in organizational change and development* (Vol. 1). Greenwich, CT: JAI Press.

Cooperrider, D.L., & Whitney, D. (2005). *Appreciative inquiry: A positive revolution in change.* San Francisco: Berrett-Koehler.

Cooperrider, D.L., Whitney, D.K., & Stavros, J.M. (2003). *Appreciative inquiry handbook.* San Francisco: Berrett-Koehler.

Cooperrider, D.L, Whitney, D., & Stavros, J. (2008). *Appreciative inquiry handbook: For leaders of change* (2nd ed.). Brunswick, OH: Crown Custom Publishing.

Cousins, N. (1981). *Human options.* New York: Berkeley Books.

Drabek, A.G. (Ed.) (1987). Development alternatives: The challenge for NGOs—An overview of the issues. *World Development, 15*(1), ix–xv.

Drake, S.M. *Creating standards-based integrated curriculum: Aligning curriculum, content, assessment, and instruction* (pp. 151–153). Thousand Oaks, CA: Sage.

Fredrickson, B.L. (2003). Positive emotions and upward spirals in organizational settings. In K.S. Cameron, J.E. Dutton, & R.E. Quinn (Eds.), *Positive organizational scholarship: Foundations of a new discipline.* San Francisco: Berrett-Koehler.

Friedman, T. (2005). *The world is flat: A brief history of the twenty-first century.* New York: Farrar, Stroud and Giroux.

Gergen, K.J. (1991). *The saturated self: Dilemmas of identity in contemporary life.* New York: Basic Books.

Gergen, K.J. (1994a). *Realities and relationships: Soundings in social construction.* Cambridge, MA: Harvard University Press.

Gergen, K.J. (1994b). *Toward transformation in social knowledge* (2nd ed.). Thousand Oaks, CA: Sage.

Gergen, K.J. (1995). *Realities and relationships*. Boston, MA: Harvard University Press.

Gergen, K.J. (1999). *An invitation to social construction*. Thousand Oaks, CA: Sage.

Gergen, K.J. (2009). *Relational being: Beyond self and community*. New York: Oxford University Press.

Gergen, K.J., & Gergen, M. (2004). *Social construction: Entering the dialogue*. Chagrin Falls, OH: Taos Institute.

Grant, D., & Marshak, R.J. (2008). Organizational discourse and new organization development practices. *British Journal of Management, 19*, 7–19.

Handy, C. (1989). *The age of unreason*. London: Arrow Books.

Ingersoll, P., & Ingersoll, J. (1989). Toward partnership in Africa: An in-depth review by African and U.S. non-profit development agency staff. *Consultation report*. Washington, DC: InterAction & FOVAD.

Institute of Medicine. (2006). *Hospital-based emergency care: At the breaking point*. Washington, DC: National Academy Press.

Kelley, T. (2001). *The art of innovation: Lessons in creativity from IDEO, America's leading design firm*. New York: Doubleday.

Kelm, J.B. (2005). *Appreciative living: The principle of appreciative inquiry in personal life*. Wake Forest, NC: Venet Publishers.

Kelm, J. (2008). *The joy of appreciative living*. New York: Penguin.

Kelm, J.B. (2009). *The joy of appreciative living: Your 28-day plan to greater happiness in three incredibly easy steps*. New York: Tarcher.

Lakoff, G., & Johnson, M. (1999). *Philosophy in the flesh: The embodied mind and its challenge to western thought*. New York: Basic Books.

Marshak, R.J. (2005). Contemporary challenges to the philosophy and practice of organization development. In W.W. Burke & D.L. Bradford (Eds.), *Reinventing organization development*. San Francisco: Pfeiffer.

Marshak, R.J. (2009). *Organizational change: Views from the edge.* Bethel, ME: The Lewin Center.

Marshall, I., & Zohar, D. (1997). *Who's afraid of Schrodinger's cat?* New York: William Morrow.

National Transportation Safety Board. (1994). *A review of flight crew-involved major accidents of U.S. air carriers, 1978 through 1990.* Washington, DC: Author.

Oswick, C., Grant, D., Marshak, R.J., & Wolfram-Cox, J. (2010, March). *The Journal of Applied Behavioral Science: Special Issue: Organizational Discourse and Change, 46*(1).

Pareek, U. (2010, January–March). Two forms of OD: Significance of era. *Here and Now, 24*(1). www.isabs.org.

Pasmore, W., & Woodman, R. (Eds.). (1989). *Research in organizational change and development* (Vol. 5). Greenwich, CT: JAI Press.

Pettigrew, A.M., Woodman, R.W., & Cameron, K.S. (2001). Studying organizational change and development: Challenges for future research. *Academy of Management Journal, 44,* 697–713.

Plsek, P.E., & Greenhalgh, T. (2001). The challenge of complexity in healthcare. *British Medical Journal, 323,* 625–628.

Rosenberg, M.B. (2005). *Nonviolent communication: A language of life.* Encinitas, CA: PuddleDancer Press. www.cnvc.org

Scharmer, C.O. (2007). *Theory U: Leading from the future as it emerges.* Cambridge, MA: Society for Organizational Learning.

Senge, P., Scharmer, C.O., Jaworski, J., & Flowers, B.S. (2005). *Presence: An exploration of profound change in people, organizations, and society.* New York: Currency/Doubleday.

Shank, R.C. (1990). *Tell me a story: A new look at real and artificial memory.* New York: Macmillan.

Simonton, O.C., Creighton, J., & Simonton, S.M. (1981). *Getting well again.* New York: Bantam.

Singh, S. (2004). *Big bang: The origin of the universe.* New York: HarperCollins.

Srivastva, S., & Fry, R.E. (1992). Introduction: Continuity and change in organizational life. *Executive and organizational continuity: Managing the paradoxes of stability and change.* San Francisco: Jossey-Bass.

Srivastva, S., Fry, R.E., & Cooperrider, D.L. (Eds.). (1990). *Appreciative management and leadership: The power of positive thought and action in organizations.* San Francisco: Jossey-Bass.

Stacey, R.D. (2002). *Strategic management and organizational dynamics: The challenge of complexity* (4th ed.). Englewood Cliffs, NJ: Prentice Hall.

Stavros, J., & Hinrichs, G. (2009). *The thin book of SOAR: Building strengths-based strategy.* Bend, OR: Thin Book Publishing.

Thatchenkery, T. (2005). *Appreciative sharing of knowledge: Leveraging knowledge management for strategic change.* Chagrin Falls, OH: Taos Institute.

Thatchenkery, T., & Metzger, C. (2006). *Appreciative intelligence: Seeing the mighty oak in the acorn.* San Francisco: Berrett-Koehler.

Tschannen-Moran, B., & Tschannen-Moran, M. (2010). *Evocative coaching: Transforming schools one conversation at a time.* San Francisco: Jossey-Bass.

Watkins, J.M., & Kelly, R. (2009). *Appreciative inquiry theory and practice: The resource book.* Belhaven, NC: Appreciative Inquiry Unlimited.

Watkins, J.M. (2009). The shifting field of OD (Chapter 42). In W.J. Rothwell, J.M. Stavros, R.L. Sullivan, & A. Sullivan (Eds.), *Practicing OD: A guide for leading change.* San Francisco: Pfeiffer.

Watkins, J.M., & Mohr, B.J. (2000). *Appreciative inquiry: Change at the speed of imagination* (1st ed.). San Francisco: Jossey-Bass/Pfeiffer.

Wheatley, M. (1994). *Leadership and the new science: Learning about organizations from an orderly universe.* San Francisco: Berrett-Koehler.

White, L., Tursky, B., & Schwartz, G. (Eds.). (1985). *Placebos: Theory, research, and mechanisms.* New York: Guilford.

Whitney, D., & Cooperrider, D.L. (2000). The appreciative inquiry summit: An emerging methodology for whole system positive change. *Journal of Organization Development Network, 32,* 13–26.

# About the Authors

**Jane Magruder Watkins** has worked in the field of organization development for more than forty years. She has worked in and consulted to organizations in the business, government, and not-for-profit sectors in over sixty-five countries around the globe. Since the mid-1980s, she has worked with David Cooperrider, who articulated the concept of Appreciative Inquiry as a theory and philosophy that has shifted the practice of OD from a deficit-focused process to AI's appreciative perspective. This shift enables organizations to focus on their strengths and hopes for the future while valuing and learning from the best of the past. At the 4th Global Conference on Appreciative Inquiry in Katmandu, Nepal, in the fall of 2009, Jane was awarded the first "Lifetime Achievement Award" for spreading AI around the globe.

Because the emerging global environment and the accelerating pace of change is calling for new and innovative processes and approaches to change, Jane sees Appreciative Inquiry as a bridge that enables organizations, communities, individuals, and couples to embrace the emerging paradigm, re-creating themselves and their realities by imagining and living into their own unique visions of their desired future. As the rate of change in human systems has accelerated, the AI approach of focusing on what is working and what is desired has spread around the globe. As an early innovator in the use of Appreciative Inquiry, Jane has experimented with its application in all aspects of organizational life in multiple settings and cultures and in all aspects of personal growth and human development.

Jane has held director-level positions in two international development agencies, served on the director's staff of the Action Agency, and has owned her own business. While she has consulted in organizations from the corporate and government sectors, her passion and focus since the 1960s has been on issues of justice and equality, with particular focus on race and gender issues in all organizations and cultures around the globe.

Since 1997, Jane has been co-owner with her husband and partner, Ralph Kelly, of the consulting firm Appreciative Inquiry Unlimited. She served as chair of the board of the NTL Institute for Applied Behavioral Science (the organization that pioneered the field of organization development and change) and is an Emeritus member of NTL, currently serving as Steward of the Appreciative Inquiry Community of Practice. She established an Appreciative Inquiry Certificate Program with a partnership between NTL and the Weatherhead School at Case Western Reserve University that is offered in the United States, with expanding programs in the UK and Europe, South Africa and India. She is a founding partner of AI Consulting.

Jane teaches Appreciative Inquiry in Pepperdine University's MSOD and Ed.D. programs and with the OSR master's program at the University of Seattle. She also teaches AI through NTL and in client organizations. She has published several articles about AI and is lead author of *Appreciative Inquiry: Change at the Speed of Imagination*. Jane has an MA in English literature; an MS in organizational development and two years of post graduate research and study at Cambridge University, UK.

You may reach Jane at jane@appreciativeinquiryunlimitedd.com and (757) 259-9942.

**Bernard J. Mohr** is the author of multiple books, articles, chapters, and journal issues dealing with collaborative organization innovation and design. Over the past four decades he has served as thinking partner, coach, and facilitator to clients in healthcare, manufacturing, retail, pharmaceuticals, education, and government in the United States, Central America, the Caribbean, Western Europe, Canada, and the Middle East.

In 2005, after twenty-five years as CEO of a professional services firm, Bernard co-founded Innovation Partners International. On the belief that organizations are the primary social institutions of our time, Bernard and his partners collaborate with clients in creating sustainable change at the intersection of innovation, human benefit, technical feasibility, and financial viability.

As one of one of the original pioneers in the field of Appreciative Inquiry, Bernard co-created the NTL Institute Certificate in Appreciative Inquiry and has served as dean of those programs. He is also co-inventor of the Innovation Summit and a primary contributor to the emerging field of generative design. In addition to the first edition of this book, he also co-authored:

- *Essentials of Appreciative Inquiry: A Roadmap for Creating Positive Futures* (Pegasus Communications)

- *The Appreciative Inquiry Summit: A Practitioner's Guide for Leading Large-Group Change* (Berrett-Koehler)

He has taught collaborative organizational innovation and design at the Universities of Ottawa, Concordia, Dayton, and Cornell, as well as the Canadian Centre for Management Development and the Danish Center for Management.

Bernard is an advisory board member of the Taos Institute, Plexus Institute associate, and senior fellow of NTL Institute for Applied Behavioral Science. He holds a BA (cum laude) in organizational psychology (University of Waterloo), an Ed.M. in organizational learning (University of Toronto), and a diploma in organization design (Columbia University).

Send an email to Bernard at bjMohr@InnovationPartners.com or call (207) 874–0118.

**Ralph Kelly**, principle and managing partner of Appreciative Inquiry Unlimited, is a well-known teacher and practitioner of the

Appreciative Inquiry approach to organization change. He is a very experienced organization development consultant who has been in the field since the late 1960s and has been an innovator in Appreciative Inquiry for over a decade. He teaches with his wife and partner in Appreciative Inquiry Unlimited, Jane Magruder Watkins, and offers training for consultants who want to be masters in the use and application of Appreciative Inquiry and for organizational leaders who want to apply AI in their management and leadership roles.

He regularly teaches the philosophy and concepts of Appreciative Inquiry in the Taos Institute; the NTL Institute; the Wilgespruit Fellowship Center in Roodepoort, South Africa; Pepperdine University's MSOD program in Monterrey, Mexico, and San Jose, Costa Rica; Seattle University's master's program, Organizational Systems Renewal; The Roffey Park Business School in the UK; and in client organizations.

His interest in training people for outstanding performance began with his work as personal services division manager in Allstate Insurance Company, where he managed and provided training for excellence in customer relations and service throughout a four-state regional office with more than 200,000 policyholders.

From the late-1960s and for thirty years he focused on his role as priest in the Episcopal Church U.S.A., where he became a part of that church's commitment to interpersonal, cross-cultural training for organizational excellence. He was a founder of the Program and Consultation Skills Service (PACS) in the southern United States. He did this work with individuals, in conferences, and with congregations. He founded and pioneered multi-racial camping programs for people with mental and physical disabilities and used his training and consultation skills to launch a medical service project with
Episcopal churches in Latin America. For the past fourteen years, he has taught AI and has done organization development from the AI perspective in multi-denominational settings in the United States and abroad.

His work in the corporate sector includes, among others: GTE, Smith-Kline Beecham, Air Canada, and Zain Telecommunications in Bahrain, Jordan, and Lebanon.

In the not-for-profit sector, Ralph's clients have included: The Academy for Education Development, Catholic Relief Services in the U.S.A. and Kenya; University of Hawaii Conflict Resolution Faculty; International Institute for Rural Reconstruction in the Philippines, Kenya, and Ethiopia; The Asian Development Bank in the Philippines; University of Wisconsin Medical School; the American University of Kuwait; Tompkins-Cortland Community College; La Guardia Community College, Williamsburg/James City County (VA) Schools; the Wilgespruit Fellowship Center in Johannesburg, South Africa; and HOPA Mountain.

He holds a master's degree in theology from the University of the South and bachelor's degree in psychology from Millsaps College.

You may contact Ralph at ralph@appreciativeinquiryunlimited.com or (757) 259-9942.

Page references followed by *fig* indicate an illustrated figure; followed by *t* indicate a table; followed by *e* indicate an exhibit.

# What will you find on pfeiffer.com?

- The best in workplace performance solutions for training and HR professionals

- Downloadable training tools, exercises, and content

- Web-exclusive offers

- Training tips, articles, and news

- Seamless on-line ordering

- Author guidelines, information on becoming a Pfeiffer Partner, and much more

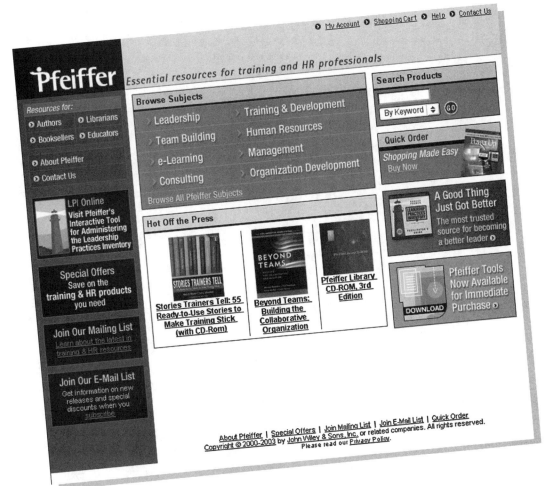

Discover more at www.pfeiffer.com